The Good Carbs Cookbook

About the authors

Alan Barclay PhD is a consultant dietitian and busier than a honey bee in a field of flowers. He has published more than 30 scientific papers in peer-reviewed journals, worked for Diabetes Australia (NSW) and is currently science editor of *GI News*, the University of Sydney's Human Nutrition Unit's health newsletter. His recent books include, co-author *The Ultimate Guide to Sugars and Sweeteners* (The Experiment) and *Reversing Diabetes* (Murdoch Books). He's a discerning and delightful diner and is learning to be a chef.

Kate McGhie is a chef, home cooks' inspiration and champion of Australia's rural producers. She has been writing and talking about food longer than a rare vintage red wine is cellared and her popular column in Melbourne's *Herald Sun* reaches a million readers every week. Her previous books were both award winners: *Cook* (Hardie Grant) and *Apple Blossom Pie: Memories of an Australian Country Kitchen* (Murdoch Books). Kate's recipe for life? Curiosity, enthusiasm and optimism. Her favourite meal? The next one.

Philippa Sandall is a writer, publisher, mentor and founding editor of *GI News*, which she has built to more than 100,000 subscribers worldwide. The essential ABC's of her life include activity, books and cats, the latter she finds endlessly fascinating. So much so she derives great fun working on her ships' cat website: www.seafurrers.com. Her most recent books include *Sticks, Seeds, Pods and Leaves* (with Elizabeth and Ian Hemphill), and co-author, *The Ultimate Guide to Sugars and Sweeteners* (The Experiment). She's a soft touch for members of the fraternity of felines.

Vibrant, smart energy recipes for every day

The Good Carbs Cookbook.

Dr Alan Barclay, Kate McGhie & Philippa Sandall

MURDOCH BOOKS

SYDNEY · LONDON

Foreword
By Jennie Brand-Miller

In some quarters, carbohydrates get an undeserved bad rap. But books like the *The Good Carbs Cookbook* are ahead of the curve, taking advantage of new knowledge of why carbs belong in a healthy diet. If you are a student of human evolution, you will learn that dietary carbohydrates have played an instrumental role throughout our 3-million-year journey from a small upright walking ape (Lucy, *Australopithecus afarensis*) to the tall, smooth-skinned creature with a very large brain who can perform high-level maths as well as prolonged strenuous marathons (*Homo sapiens sapiens*). How do we know that carbohydrates were important? Well, it's written in our genes as well as our physiology.

The academic study of the diet of Paleolithic humans is currently a lively topic of research that integrates information from anthropology, archaeology and nutritional sciences, as well as genetics and physiology. In 2015, a small multidisciplinary group of scientists proposed that our brain, reproductive and other tissues, such as the oxygen-carrying red cells in the blood, could *not* have evolved the way they did without a rich source of glucose molecules in the diet (*Quarterly Review of Biology.* 2015; vol. 90, no. 3, pp. 251–68.).

The most telling evidence includes the fact that we have evolved multiple copies of the salivary amylase gene, AMY1, which kicks off the digestion of the starch in cooked foods. AMY1 has no other function. Amylase cannot act on raw starch, only starch that has been broken down by heat and water. And the product of starch digestion by amylase is millions of glucose molecules. To perform the act of cooking, humans must have mastered the use of fire, and some scientists such as Richard Wrangham, professor of anthropology at Harvard, have gone so far as to say 'cooking made us human'.

Today, we know that humans vary in AMY1 copy number from two to as many as sixteen copies. This raises some interesting questions – why were multiple copies an advantage? Did it mean these people digested more starch per meal? Did it make starch taste better – sweeter perhaps? Did it mean more calories were absorbed?

Or did the additional glucose derived from starch digestion provide a specific advantage such as the ability to outrun prey or the likelihood of successful offspring? Our studies at the University of Sydney indicate that those with a higher copy number show a higher blood glucose response after consuming any starchy food. It raises the intriguing possibility that a higher blood glucose level at early stages of human evolution was a distinct advantage.

Specific tissues prefer glucose as their major fuel source. Glucose fuels our energy-demanding large brain and fetal growth as well as strenuously exercising muscles. Having multiple copies of AMY1 allows us to digest starch faster and release glucose into the blood more rapidly and, in theory, permits greater feats of human endurance. Glucose powers the growth of a healthy human fetus born with substantially more body fat than any other primate. Low maternal glucose levels means a small baby with little body fat who fails to thrive outside the womb.

Humans have adapted to dietary shifts in the past. For example, we know for certain that mutations in genes causing lactase persistence (which means we can digest the sugar in milk – lactose) became widespread over the past 5000 years. But the key point about the increase in AMY1 copy number is that the genetic signature suggests it may have begun as long as 1 million years ago. That's a long time in the course of human evolution. The advent of cooking of starchy foods meant a concentrated source of pre-formed glucose became available for the first time. In theory, therefore, we are programmed to utilise and enjoy starchy foods.

The challenge is to ensure we consume the high-quality carbs that are digested at a rate our bodies can accommodate, preventing burnout of our insulin-producing machinery. Alan Barclay, Kate McGhie and Philippa Sandall are to be commended for giving us no excuse – easy, practical and most of all nutritious and delicious recipes that give us not just good carbs but a micronutrient and phytonutrient mix that is second to none. So next time you hear that carbohydrates should be limited, think again.

Professor Jennie Brand-Miller (AM, PHD, FAIFST, FNSA, MAICD) is an internationally recognised authority on carbohydrates and the glycemic index with over 250 scientific publications. She holds a Personal Chair in Human Nutrition in the Boden Institute of Obesity, Nutrition, Exercise and Eating Disorders in the Charles Perkins Centre at the University of Sydney.

Contents

Introduction

The Good Carbs Cookbook is for everyone who enjoys deliciously wholesome food and loves to cook. It's packed with recipes using the foods from our fields, farms and gardens that celebrate natural goodness and enrich our experiences of cooking, sharing meals with family and friends, and enjoying life. We have also put some fun facts on the table to get a lively conversation going.

We want to share our enthusiasm for what we call good carbs – the plant foods the natural world has provided for us: fruits, vegetables, beans, peas, lentils, seeds, nuts and grains. These foods and the traditional staples we make from them, such as noodles, pasta and good-quality grainy breads, fill the shelves of our produce stores and markets, and inspire us to head for the kitchen and expand our healthy-eating choices with delicious food every day.

GOOD CARB CHOICES

In times past, the only carb foods to hand for our Paleo forebears were good carbs – fruits, berries, shoots, seeds, beans, roots and tubers. And they ate what they could gather or they went hungry. Their naturally roving eye, however, was always on the lookout for new and tasty experiences to fill a rumbling tummy – greener grass, fatter game, riper fruit, choicer berries, nuts, seeds, tubers, and buzzing bees suggesting honeycomb was not too far away.

Our world of supersized supermarkets with groaning aisles is very different. We still have that roving eye, but it's almost overwhelmed by a surfeit of choice when it comes to food, much of it highly refined, with ingredient lists that often sound like they really belong in a pharmacy. So we end up with dietary dilemmas and endless advice (often contradictory) on the 'good things to eat' and the 'bad to avoid'.

But sorting the good from the not-so-good (in terms of wellbeing and waistline) is not rocket science – Michael Pollan sums it up in a nutshell: 'Eat foods made from ingredients you can picture in their raw state or growing in nature.'

Putting that into practice, picture what you're about to put in your shopping trolley growing on a farm, or in a garden, or grazing in a field in the not too distant past. Imagine fruits and nuts on trees, berries on bushes, veggies including beans and peas growing in gardens, cows in cowsheds being milked, and fields of grains being harvested to be milled and made into traditional, minimally processed staples such as breads, porridge, pasta, noodles, couscous, burghul (bulgur), kasha and more.

If it's a challenge to work out what you are holding in your hands (say, a large tin of 'protein powder') is actually made of, let alone visualise its ingredients in their raw state or growing in nature, back on the shelf it goes.

There's no need, however, to take the picture principle to the level of obsessive five-star purity. Occasional treats are very much a part of life. And we, like everyone else, find it incredibly easy to picture cacao beans dangling on a branch when we look at a bar of dark chocolate, despite the foil and double wrapping.

Making better choices about the food we eat – where it has come from, how it's grown and how animals are farmed – matters. It's not only good for our health, it's vital for the health of our planet. Our food should not only be sustaining, but sustainable.

We appreciate that we are very fortunate to live in times when it's possible to be fussy about food sources and choices in this way, which was not generally an option for our forebears and is certainly not for many people in some parts of the world today.

10 THINGS WE LOVE ABOUT GOOD WHOLESOME CARB FOODS

1. We love the way they power the brain.
2. We love the way they fuel the muscles.
3. We love the energy they give.
4. We love the good stuff (vitamins and minerals) that comes with them.
5. We love their keep-it-regular fibre habit.
6. We love preparing meals for family and friends with them.
7. We love the traditional foods they put on the plate.
8. We love the variety and pleasure they bring to the table.
9. We love the way they feed the world.
10. We love their lighter footprint on the planet.

GOOD CARB COOKING

Our regular meals, like the recipes we have created for this book, are mostly plant based and built around seasonal fruit and vegetables, beans, grains and traditional staples. As for other ingredients, we like our dairy foods from contented cows, our eggs from really free-ranging, happy hens, our meats from animals that have been well cared for and lived a good life in fields not feedlots or factory farms, and our seafood from sustainable sources.

Don't be afraid to get creative with our recipes. A recipe (with, perhaps, the exception of baking) is a starting point, not necessarily a formula. Think of them as being similar to those touristy road maps leading to lovely destinations from which detours can be taken. If you are missing an ingredient, improvise using what you have in your fridge or on your pantry shelf. You may stumble on something unexpected and glorious.

STOCKING THE GOODS

Good food starts with good ingredients. And that means good shopping. Supermarkets are convenient, and most ingredients for the recipes here can be sourced there, but also look in delis, fruit and veg shops, butchers, fishmongers and fresh produce markets.

- Herbs are always freshly picked or purchased. We use spoon measures for small quantities (up to 3 tablespoons chopped, which is about ¼ cup) and after that we move up to handfuls, as we tend to just step out into our gardens and grab one. (1 handful parsley or mint leaves, for example, is about ½ cup loosely packed. Our recipes use lots of fresh herbs, especially parsley. Unless we specify curly leaf, it's flat-leaf (Italian) parsley.

- Salad greens are also freshly picked or purchased and generally specified in handfuls or cups, which are loosely packed unless otherwise stated.

- Garlic cloves are medium and plump. If you have super-large garlic, use a little less than the recipe specifies. And if they are very small, use a bit more.

- Milk is regular, full-fat cow's milk. If you use reduced-fat milk because that's what you have on hand or you prefer to substitute a plant-based 'milk', be aware that the end result of the dish may be somewhat different.

- Yoghurt is full-fat natural pot-set yoghurt (preferably Middle Eastern), which never curdles when heated and has that tart edge to it. Using yoghurt in recipes can be tricky when it has added thickeners and fillers, as some tend to split when heated.

- Eggs are free range and medium (59 g/2 oz) unless otherwise stated.

- Chicken is free range, meat is grass fed, fish and seafood are from sustainable sources.

- Oil is mostly regular olive oil. We specify in the ingredients list when extra virgin olive oil will be the better choice. Some recipes call for vegetable oil. In this case, use what you have on hand. A few of our favourites are cold-pressed grapeseed oil, which has a neutral flavour; walnut oil for dressings and accenting winter veggies; avocado oil to add fullness to dishes or whisked with orange juice for a bright dressing, and cold-pressed rapeseed oil with its buttery and slightly grassy flavour.

- Butter is unsalted unless specified.

- Salt is sea salt flakes (kosher salt) as it blends faster and better than granular salt.

- Pepper is freshly ground white pepper in cooking unless otherwise specified.

GOOD MEASURING

Few home cooks in Australia, for example, bother with precise weighing and measuring unless they are baking. For family meals, they pull out their trusty measuring cups and spoons, and that's all you need for most of these recipes. For those who prefer to weigh things, we have also included the equivalent metric measures. Note that we say 'equivalent'. Measures are rounded up and down following the standard procedure. All measures are level.

- **Spoons:** We used the 20 ml Australian tablespoon (4 teaspoons) in our recipes. Tablespoons in the US and UK are 15 ml tablespoons (3 teaspoons). So if using those, just add an extra teaspoon of the ingredient for each tablespoon specified in savoury dishes.

- **Cups:** We used the 250 ml (9 fl oz) Australian measuring cup in our recipes. Cups in the US and UK are a little smaller, about 235 ml.

Most of the measuring sets we buy today have US or UK measurements. As long as you are consistent with scales or the cup and spoon you are measuring with, then the outcome will be successful.

Too many people become overly concerned about measuring, placing too much emphasis on precise quantities. For the most accurate method of measuring you have to weigh every single ingredient – just as professional cooks do. This becomes more critical in large-scale cooking.

The best measuring equipment in the kitchen will always be your nose, eyes, hands and fingers … and remember, practice makes perfect. The more you cook the more relaxed and confident you'll become, making it easier to judge weights, amounts and sizes for things you use regularly, such as herbs and salad greens or potatoes and tomatoes so you won't need to measure and weigh them each and every time you cook.

WHAT'S IN THE GOODS?

We wrote this to be a family-friendly cookbook packed with simple and delicious recipes to get you racing to the kitchen and creating mealtime memories with family and friends. Our overall intention is to equip you with the basics about good carbs and their chums, good fats and lean protein.

We have kept an eye on portion size and kilojoules (calories), and serves of each dish are suitable for a typical adult. Of course, serving sizes are averages, and none of us have standardised families – men and teenage boys generally eat more than women and children.

The foods we have used in *The Good Carbs Cookbook* are grown under naturally varying conditions, and are not highly processed into pharmaceutical-like uniformity. The nutritional information provided is therefore based on averages, not dissimilar to those numbers found on the nutrition information panels on packaged foods, and your foods' composition will vary from time to time. So use the numbers as a good guide, but not as an exact prescription.

We are very aware that some people need to keep an eye on carb quantities to manage their blood glucose levels. We are also conscious that others need to count the kilojoules (calories) to help achieve and maintain a healthy (or healthier) weight. To help with this, you'll find the nutritional analysis for each recipe at the back of the book (see pages 244–49).

If you want the nitty gritty on how we derived the data, we analysed the recipes using FoodWorks, which incorporates the AUSNUT and NUTTAB databases. Where necessary, we supplemented this with data from the US Department of Agriculture (http://ndb.nal.usda.gov/ndb/search).

Simplify your life so you can enjoy it. Ditch diet fads, feel good about the food you produce, buy, cook and eat, and enjoy the pleasure it brings each day with family and friends.

Vegetables

We certainly have an appetite for vegetables and can't imagine meals without them. Often they make the meal. It wasn't always so. Like many kids facing a dinner plate of meat and two or three cooked (typically boiled) veg, we also struggled with the usual suspects – cabbage and cauliflower – along with (in our case) beans, pumpkin, carrots and peas.

It's hard to imagine a dinner time when the spotlight wasn't on 'eat your vegetables'. But it wasn't all that long ago, in fact a bit over 100 years. The discovery of vitamins and minerals in the early years of the twentieth century was the wakeup call, and 'Dr Vitamin' (aka Elmer Verner McCollum, 1879–1967) was the key player in making sure vegetables made up a bigger part of the dinner plate. He claimed they were 'protective foods' because 'they were so constituted to make good the deficiencies of whatever else we liked to eat'.

But, it's not just the leafy ones that matter. It's all of them, because, as Harvard's Professor Walter Willett says, 'so far, no one has found a magic bullet that works against heart disease, cancer and a host of other chronic diseases as well as fruits and vegetables seem to do'.

Today, we are spoiled for choice when it comes to vegetables. The produce aisles are overflowing. This is perhaps because 'vegetable' is a culinary, not a botanical term. We can take our pick from fruits such as avocado, cucumber, marrow, tomato, capsicum (peppers) and green beans; bulbs such as onion and globe artichoke; stalks such as celery and asparagus; flower stalks and buds such as broccoli and cauliflower; roots and tubers such as carrot, potato and sweet potato; as well as the proverbial leafy greens, including spinach, lettuce and cabbage.

And there's more. We have an array of edible dried seeds from the legume family: beans, peas and lentils. In this book, we have given legumes a chapter of their own because they are also rich sources of protein and play a key role in vegetarian and vegan diets.

We aren't going to tell you to eat your veggies, but we hope that with our recipes you'll find them hard to resist and pile your plate high.

HOW MUCH VEG?

Dietary guidelines around the world recommend we have around five serves, or 2–3 cups, of vegetables (including legumes) a day depending on our age and life stage. Here's what the serving size they are talking about looks like:

- ½ cup cooked green or orange vegetables (broccoli, spinach, diced or mashed carrots or pumpkin)
- 1 cup leafy salad vegetables
- 1 medium tomato
- ½ cup sweetcorn kernels
- ½ medium potato or sweet potato
- ½ cup cooked dried or tinned beans, peas or lentils.

Note: For people with diabetes, serve sizes of starchy veg and legumes are based on equivalent carbohydrate amounts to help them manage their blood glucose levels. They are:
- 1 medium potato or ½ small sweet potato
- ½ cup cooked dried or tinned beans or lentils, or 1⅓ cups cooked garden peas.

COOKING: THE GAME CHANGER

Ever tried to munch a raw potato and ended up with a sore stomach? Starchy roots and tubers tend to be difficult for us to digest raw because their energy reserves (the starch) are stored in hard, compact granules that our digestive system can't process without help. Cooking provides that help. During cooking, water (either in the food itself, or in more recent times, from the pot) and heat expand these compact

granules. Some of the granules burst and release individual starch molecules, allowing the starch-digesting enzymes in our mouths and the small intestine to get on with the job, because they now have a greater surface area to attack. (On page 236, we explain more about the ins and outs of carbohydrate digestion.)

'There is no way that taking a pill can replace eating fruits and vegetables … In theory, one could cram all the good things that plants make – essential elements, fibre, vitamins, antioxidants, plant hormones, and so on – into a pill. But it would have to be a very large pill, and no one can honestly say what should go into such a pill. Or in what proportions. Health issues aside, the biggest drawback is that a pill would always taste like a pill. It can't give you the earthy smell and taste of a fresh ear of corn, the sweetness of a juicy tomato still warm from the afternoon sun, the crunch of an apple, the festive green of a snap pea or broccoli floret, or the smooth nutty taste of an avocado.'

PROF. WALTER WILLETT
Eat, Drink and Be Healthy

In her foreword, Prof. Jennie Brand-Miller reminds us not only of the importance of carbs in human evolution but how cooking starchy foods such as tubers was central to the dietary change that triggered and sustained the growth of the human brain. In fact, says primatologist Prof. Richard Wrangham, author of *Catching Fire: How Cooking Made Us Human*, 'it's hard to imagine the leap to *Homo erectus* without cooking's nutritional benefits'. He believes we have been cooking for a long time. About 1.8 million years ago our teeth and our gut became small, a change that can only be explained, he says, by our ancestors getting softer foods and more nutrition, and 'this could only have happened because they were cooking. It's what made our human diet "human" and is the most logical explanation for our advances in brain and body size over our ape ancestors.'

It appears that our ancestors were roasting. And not just the meat the men hauled back to camp. The roots and tubers the women and children gathered over the day were thrown on the fire to soften up, too. They probably also discovered that roasting does a lot more than cook food. It transforms it.

There's nothing like roast veg. Dry oven heat caramelises any natural sugars on the surface, evaporating some of the water and concentrating the flavour.

THE ART OF ROASTING VEG

Here are our five tips for roast veg, crisp on the outside, hot and steamy on the inside and with a deep, delicious sweetness:

- Cut starchy vegetables (potatoes and sweet potato) into chunks or long flat pieces about the same size to ensure even cooking. Roast for about 15 minutes before adding the quicker-roasting veggies, such as carrots and parsnips, which can be left whole (if small) or sliced lengthways.
- Make sure your vegetables are dry before roasting – this will make them crisp.
- Lightly brush the vegetables with a thin layer of oil, which will help them brown faster and more evenly.
- Arrange vegetables in a single layer in a sturdy roasting pan. They need good airflow while they roast, so don't cram them together as overcrowding can result in soggy veg.
- Lightly season with salt and freshly ground pepper along with whatever other flavourings you fancy (unpeeled garlic cloves, thyme, rosemary, orange zest, ground cumin or fennel seeds).

GROWING

The vegetable garden is the perfect place to learn how to taste and not merely eat food. For Kate, who comes from a farming background, a veggie patch has always been a part of life wherever she has lived. She remembers a childhood when wise old hands would tug a baby carrot from the soil, pluck a sun-warm tomato, or snap off a crisp green bean and give them to her so she could experience the beauty and energy of the earth.

Anyone with a vegetable plot or herb pot will agree that there is nothing quite like the satisfaction of making things grow: pride in achievement; delight in that ripe tomato or bunch of basil, and pleasure in popping out to pick what you need for the evening meal. You can also save on trips to the produce store, enjoy the outdoors and discover the joys of composting, worm farming and dealing with pests and diseases in an environmentally friendly way. People with green fingers make it look easy, but growing your own produce has its challenges. If you are a newcomer, ask for tips, start small, do your homework and plant vegetables and herbs that practically grow themselves.

BURIED TREASURE

The fleshy underground parts of a plant (roots and modified plant stems) are where carbohydrate energy a plant needs to grow is stored. We tend to label them root veggies or starchy carbs. But not all are roots and only a few, such as potatoes, sweet potatoes taro and yams, are really starchy.

	UNDERGROUND EDIBLES	POPULAR 'ROOT' VEGGIES
TRUE ROOTS	**Taproots** – the main root	Beetroot (beets), carrots, celeriac, parsnips, radishes, turnips
	Tuberous roots – lateral or secondary 'storage' roots	Sweet potatoes
MODIFIED PLANT STEMS	**Rhizomes** – fleshy, spreading underground stems	Arrowroot, galangal, ginger, licorice, turmeric, wasabi
	Corms – short, swollen underground or underwater stems	Taro, water chestnuts
	Tubers – swollen underground storage 'stems' that can vary considerably in size	Jerusalem artichokes, potatoes, yams

BEETROOT

Don't put out the white napkins when beetroot (beets) are on the menu. It's a serious stainer. Beetroot's vibrant colours come from its betalain pigments – betacyanin in red–purple beetroots, betaxanthin in golden and orange beetroot. Originally, they were prized for their leaves but the Romans dug deeper and discovered the roots were good. They probably weren't the purple–red ones we know today as these didn't make a regular appearance until the 1500s when gardeners and plant breeders had come up with varieties to add colour and flavour to soups, stews, gratins and salads. Roasting is the best way to cook beetroot, as it intensifies their sweet flavour. A foil-wrapped tennis-ball-sized beetroot will take about 40 minutes to cook in the oven, while baby beets are done in 20 minutes; they're best cooked with their skins on: simply wash the beetroot (taking care not to break the skin), wrap in foil leaving the roots intact and at least 2.5 cm (1 in) of stalk on top, then roast in a preheated oven 180°C (350°F). Once cooked, the skin will just slip off.

WHAT TO LOOK FOR

Choose firm, smooth beeroot and avoid soft, shrivelled or flabby ones, as these are signs they are tough and fibrous. Ready-to-eat vacuum-packed baby beets are a handy alternative when time is short. If buying whole or sliced beets in jars or tins, check out the amount of sodium on the nutrition information panel.

HOW TO STORE THEM

Cut off most of the green tops so they do not pull moisture away from the root, leaving about 2.5 cm (1 in) of the stem attached. Pop the unwashed beets in a plastic bag, wrapping it tightly around them and squeezing out as much air out as possible. They keep in the fridge for up to 3 weeks like this.

WHAT'S IN THEM?

A medium raw beetroot (about 90 g/3¼ oz) has about 165 kilojoules (40 calories), 2 g protein, no fat, 7 g carbs (7 g sugars, 0 g starches), 3 g fibre, 45 mg sodium, 240 mg potassium and a moderate GI (64) when cooked/tinned; the GL is low (4).

WHAT ELSE?

Don't waste the slightly bitter-tasting leaves. If they're young and fresh, chop and wilt them in a little olive oil or a dab of butter, or toss them into a salad mix. Rosy young beetroot tops have an earthy quality and won't turn grassy (as spinach does) when cooked in stock, although the stock will be a delightful pink.

HERO RECIPES

Shredded beetroot, carrot and nashi slaw with cumin and lime dressing (page 32)
Beetroot with orange-sherry dressing and soft herbs (page 35)
Pan-roasted sweet potato and beetroot with grapefruit glaze (page 72)

CAPSICUMS

Speedy underestimates the rate at which the Old World embraced the New World's zesty chilli. 'Try these hot peppers,' said Columbus proudly introducing them to Europe in 1493 – after all, pepper (pimento or black pepper) was what he was looking for. Within 200 years they were widely cultivated throughout Europe, Asia and Africa as the tongue-tingling spice we know today. At the same time, a mild, sweet variety was also evolving. And what a veg. Red, orange, yellow, green, purple: the crisp, juicy flesh of capsicums (sweet peppers) sets the taste bar high. It's no wonder they've made themselves at home in kitchens around the world, stuffed, or sliced into salads or stir-fries, or roasted and often peeled.

WHAT TO LOOK FOR

Enjoy fresh capsicums in season when they are at their very best. They should have firm, bright skins and no soft spots or wrinkles.

HOW TO STORE THEM

Don't buy more than you need, as they're best fresh. If you pick up a plastic-wrapped tray for a bargain price, unwrap them when you get home, as they need to breathe a bit. They will keep their crunch and sweetness in the crisper drawer in the fridge for a few days.

WHAT'S IN THEM?

A medium raw capsicum (about 90 g/3¼ oz) has about 80 kilojoules (19 calories), 1.5 g protein, 0 g fat, 3 g carbs (3 g sugars, 0 g starches), 1 g fibre, 2 mg sodium, 135 mg potassium and a low (estimated) GI and GL.

WHAT ELSE?

Red, orange and yellow capsicums are not only sweeter than regular green ones, but they keep their colour better when cooked. If a recipe calls for strips of peeled roasted peppers and you are short on time, there are numerous good brands of jarred 'fire-roasted' capsicums preserved in olive oil, or buy them from your favourite deli.

HERO RECIPE

Eggs coddled in a spicy capsicum and tomato sauce (page 38)

CARROTS

The carrots our forebears tugged from the soil may have been more appetising than other roots on offer, but they weren't like the orange, juicy and sweet carrots we enjoy today. Those carrots only appeared around the 1500s. They were certainly seen as a healthy addition to the diet. 'They do nouryshe with better iuyce than the other rootes,' wrote Sir Thomas Elyot in 1536 in his popular *Castell of Health* that went through an impressive 17 printings. While our new-age carrots boast eye-catching hues, it's their sweetness that makes them popular raw and cooked. They make a gorgeous, crunchy snack or side dish; are added to salads, soups, stir-fries and bakes; and are an essential ingredient in mirepoix and sofritos to flavour stocks, soups, stews and sauces. A roast dinner just wouldn't be the same without them.

WHAT TO LOOK FOR

Whether they're orange, red, yellow or purple, look for firm, bright skins that glow and have no signs of splitting. Generally, small to medium carrots will be better choices, often sweeter and juicier than large ones, which can be woody and fibrous. If buying bunches of baby carrots, avoid any with particularly wilted green tops.

HOW TO STORE THEM

Carrots like to be kept cool and moist or they will dry out. Pop them in a plastic bag in the fridge and use them up within a few days.

WHAT'S IN THEM?

A medium-sized raw carrot (about 130 g/4½ oz) has about 170 kilojoules (41 calories), 1 g protein, no fat, 6 g carbs (6 g sugars, 0 g starches), 5 g fibre, 49 mg sodium, 348 mg potassium, and a low GI (39); the GL is low (2).

WHAT ELSE?

Does colour make a difference? Prof. Philipp Simon, who has studied carrots of all colours for over 35 years and tasted hundreds of thousands of them, says that 'Pigments don't appear to affect the flavour, but overcooking gives them an unpleasant "violet" taste.'

HERO RECIPES

Carrot and red lentil soup with lemon (page 41)
Potato and silverbeet with a carrot, nut and oat crust (page 42)

CAULIFLOWER

This three-in-one veg gives you an edible head of creamy florets and crunchy white stems encased by tender green leaves. Forget the substitute-for-potatoes-or-rice scenario and make the most of this affordable and versatile member of the cabbage family. Stir-fried, steamed, boiled or raw, cauliflower happily takes on bold flavours of sharp cheeses, biting mustards, spicy curries, Asian sauces and tangy pickles. It makes excellent soups from the simple and soothing to the sublime and delicate. Roasting cauliflower concentrates its sweetness, and puts it in a class of its own as side dish, salad or finger food with dips.

WHAT TO LOOK FOR

No plastic. Unwrapped is the way to go. Choose heads (or half heads) with tight, firm, creamy-white florets, and steer clear of any with black, slimy spots, which are signs of mould. Check the stems too and make sure there are no cracks or splits. Frozen florets will be fresher than those pre-packed plastic trays of florets that are often past their best-before date.

HOW TO STORE THEM

A head of cauli will keep in the fridge for a few days in a plastic bag.

WHAT'S IN THEM?

Half a cup of cooked cauliflower florets (about 90 g/3¼ oz) has around 90 kilojoules (22 calories), 2 g protein, no fat, 2 g carbs (2 g sugars, 0 g starches), 2 g fibre, 13 mg sodium and 284 mg potassium. Because cauliflower is so low in carbohydrate, it is not possible to measure its GI.

WHAT ELSE?

The milky head is the one we are most familiar with, but these days you'll find orange, green (broccoflower) and purple caulis that hold their colour when cooked, making for a rather spectacular dish.

HERO RECIPES

Cauliflower and leek soup (page 43)
The original roasted whole cauliflower (page 45)

CELERIAC

Knobbly celeriac or celery root may not be one of the best-looking vegetables around, but it pays to get under its skin. When peeling them, have a bowl of water with a few drops of vinegar or lemon juice to hand, to help to prevent discolouration, as the flesh darkens once cut. Once peeled, you can grate, shred or finely slice and serve it with a tart dressing. The classic dish is the French céléri rémoulade (julienned strips of celeriac in a Dijon-mustard-flavoured mayonnaise), but its fresh, mild celery flavour makes it a very adaptable vegetable in soups, stews and gratins.

WHAT TO LOOK FOR

Enjoy celeriac in autumn and winter when it's in season. When it comes to choosing one, size matters. Look for medium-size roots that are heavy for their size and have no soft spots. Pass on the overly large ones. They may look like best value, but they can be spongy in the middle. With small ones, you could be cutting most of it away – that's a lot of effort for a little result. Look for a less knobbly celeriac with relatively smooth skin, which will help avoid waste when it comes to peeling.

HOW TO STORE THEM

Wrap in paper towel to keep moisture at bay and place in a plastic bag in the fridge for up to 2 weeks.

WHAT'S IN THEM?

A cup of grated celeriac (about 155 g/5½ oz) has about 250 kilojoules (60 calories), 2.5 g protein, no fat, 4 g carbs (4 g sugars, 0 g starches), 8 g fibre, 33 mg sodium, 686 mg potassium and a low GI and GL (estimated).

WHAT ELSE?

Although this vegetable has been around for a long time, it's a relative newcomer to mainstream produce stores. Give it a go. It's delicious.

HERO RECIPES

Celeriac slaw with capers, walnuts and lemon (page 46)
Roasted celeriac and carrots with mirin and apple juice glaze (page 49)

EGGPLANT

There's so much to like about glossy, deep-tasting eggplant (aubergine). The meaty flesh becomes silky in texture when pan-fried, oven-roasted, stuffed, mashed or puréed. We identify eggplant so closely with Middle Eastern and Mediterranean classics – Turkey's stuffed specialty imam bayildi, smoky baba ghanoush and all-time favourites ratatouille, moussaka, caponata and melanzane parmigiana – that it's easy to forget Asia was originally its home, where they are added to stir-fries, stews and hotpots and whipped up into spicy pickles. Cut them just before cooking to avoid discolouration, and whichever way you cook them, they will need oil to develop that creamy texture. If you plan to fry them, remember that eggplant will soak it up like a sponge and a light salting prior to frying helps reduce that. Charring them over a gas flame or oven roasting brings out eggplant's delightful smoky flavour.

WHAT TO LOOK FOR

Once a specialty item, eggplant is now mainstream and comes in an astonishing array of colours, shapes, sizes and textures. Look for firm eggplants with shiny skins; the gloss is lost once they are past their prime.

HOW TO STORE THEM

Handle them with care – eggplant skin is thin and can be easily damaged. Never refrigerate an eggplant, as this contributes to its bitterness. Buy them as you need them and be mindful that they will keep in the fruit bowl for only a day or two.

WHAT'S IN THEM?

A small raw eggplant (about 320 g/11¼ oz) has about 295 kilojoules (71 calories), 3.5 g protein, 1 g fat, 8 g carbs (8 g sugars, 0 g starches), 8 g fibre, 16 mg sodium, 540 mg potassium and a low GI and GL (estimated).

WHAT ELSE?

Commonly, it is thought that salting eggplant draws out the bitterness, but it actually draws out moisture (eggplant is over 90 per cent water), thus giving you a firmer-textured slice or round that is ideal for fritters and slow baking. Modern varieties no longer require pre-salting to get rid of any bitterness. (Bitter eggplant stays bitter even if salted.)

HERO RECIPES

Roasted ratatouille with hummus (page 40)
Eggplant with chopped green capsicum and pomegranate sauce (page 50)

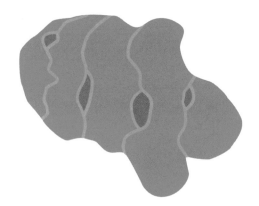

JERUSALEM ARTICHOKES

They have nothing to do with Jerusalem or globe artichokes. They are sunchokes (and a member of the same family as sunflowers), and their sweetly succulent tubers were cultivated by Native Americans long before any European foot plonked itself down in the New World. They have their devotees, but many people dodge them because their windy reputation is extremely well deserved. Jerusalem artichokes are rich in a soluble fibre called inulin that our gut bacteria have to work at with gusto (and share their enthusiasm). They are so rich in inulin, they are one of the main commercial sources. If you have tended to steer clear, be bold and check out their earthy, slightly smoky flavour in soups and stews, as a side dish or in salads, but always cooked and never raw. As for the origin of their name, it's a mystery.

WHAT TO LOOK FOR

This is a veg for the cooler months and is at its best during autumn and winter. Look for firm tubers free from blemishes and soft spots.

HOW TO STORE THEM

Store in a plastic bag in the fridge for up to a week.

WHAT'S IN THEM?

A medium, boiled Jerusalem artichoke (about 120 g /4¼ oz) has about 315 kilojoules (75 calories), 3 g protein, no fat, 14 g carbs (3.5 g sugars, 10.5 g starches), 4 g fibre, 6 mg sodium and 604 mg potassium. The GI and GL are unknown as they have not been tested.

WHAT ELSE?

To help take the wind out of their sails, combine them with another veg or serve small portions to let your digestive system get acclimatised.

HERO RECIPE

Salad of red leaves with fennel and Jerusalem artichokes (page 53)

ONIONS

Onions are indispensable. We use them on a daily basis in sauces, soups, salads, stews, stir-fries and roasts just as our forebears did for thousands of years. They are one of the earliest cultivated vegetables. And while we may tug this underground bulb from the soil, it is not a root veggie. Peel an onion and you are peeling away its fleshy leaves packed with nutrients and the sugars that release their sweetness with long, slow cooking. Slicing raw onions can certainly be a tear jerker and there's no easy solution. Over the years, cooks have devised many ways to prevent this, from freezing the onions to wearing goggles or holding their breath, but they are rarely completely effective. The best way to avoid teary eyes is to avoid bending over the onion while cutting it, and using a razor-sharp knife (with great care).

WHAT TO LOOK FOR

Choose firm brown, white or red onions with no soft spots or blemishes.

HOW TO STORE THEM

Dry onions have a long life and are best stored with plenty of ventilation. If you keep them for a long time they tend to sprout, but you can still use the sprout and what's left of the onion.

Spring onions (green onions/scallions) can be stored in a container filled with 2–5 cm (¾–2 in) water, covered with a plastic bag, and kept it in the fridge for about a week. Alternately, wrap them in damp paper towel and refrigerate for a week.

WHAT'S IN THEM?

One medium raw onion (about 90 g/3¼ oz) has about 130 kilojoules (31 calories), 1.5 g protein, 0 g fat, 5.5 g carbs (4 g sugars, 1.5 g starches), 1.5 g fibre, 12 mg sodium, 124 mg potassium, and a low GI and GL (estimated).

WHAT ELSE?

The distinctive flavour comes from sulphur compounds, part of a chemical armoury protecting onions from attack in the ground, and providing a savoury depth in our cooking pots.

HERO RECIPES

Trio of onions and herb salad with ricotta on toasted grain bread (page 54)
Chicken stock (page 55)
Lemon chicken with golden onions and green olives (page 56)

PARSNIPS

In their heyday, parsnips were a starchy staple to fill the tummy, but they also gave our meals a touch of sweetness. They were served up as vegetables from the Middle Ages through to the eighteenth century, but they would also appear in jams, puddings and tarts. Parsnip wine had numerous fans too, as did parsnip beer. We love their distinctive, nutty flavour and perfume, but it doesn't appeal to everyone. While you are very unlikely to find parsnips on the menu in France, the Italians discovered their charm and included them in ragù di manzo e pastinaca (beef and parsnip braise cooked in wine) and cremoso pastinaca sformato (a bit like a parsnip soufflé cooked in a shallow dish). They also found parsnips to make fine fare for pigs destined for prosciutto crudo.

WHAT TO LOOK FOR

Buy loose parsnips rather than prepacked, and pick out the young and fleshy ones with smooth, creamy, blemish-free skin. Larger parsnips tend to have rather woody, fibrous cores that can make for tough eating.

HOW TO STORE THEM

Like other root veg, store in a cool, dark place but not the fridge. They're best eaten as soon as possible after you buy them, as they tend to dry out and become wrinkly rather quickly. It's a good idea to only buy as many as you can eat within a day or two at most.

WHAT'S IN THEM?

A large raw parsnip (about 160 g/5¾ oz) has about 365 kilojoules (87 calories), 3 g protein, no fat, 16 g carbs (8 g sugars, 8 g starches), 4 g fibre, 30 mg sodium, 672 mg potassium, and a low GI (52) when cooked; the GL is low (8).

WHAT ELSE?

Try them raw. You can grate the perfect parsnip like a carrot and make a salad with dried fruits (dates are delicious). You'll find they're less parsnip-pungent this way, but not as juicy as carrots.

HERO RECIPES

Lamb shanks with winter vegetables and parsley-mint gremolata (page 58)
Parsnip, celeriac and potato mini bakes (page 59)

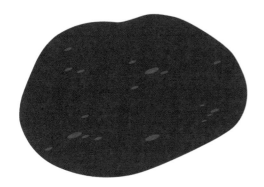

POTATOES

Every day more than a billion people will eat potatoes one way or another. It's up there with rice, wheat and corn as a feed-the-world crop. So it's hard to imagine them ever being the new kid on the block. But they were slow to cross the Atlantic arriving from the Americas some years after tomatoes and sweet potatoes. Then, for a number of reasons including deep suspicion of their family ties (to the deadly nightshade family), it took us another hundred years or so to give them a regular spot on the dinner plate. A versatile veg, they are baked, boiled, steamed, grated, fried, stuffed, mashed and added to soups, salads and stews. They're the perfect 'waste not, want not' ingredient, as any leftovers can be 'upcycled' in the next meal. If you have eggs and leftover potatoes and other vegetables lurking in the fridge, you have the makings of potato cakes or pancakes, a frittata or a crispy bubble and squeak.

WHAT TO LOOK FOR

The trick with potatoes is to buy them loose; this will help you avoid the ones going green. Pick out potatoes that are firm and a uniform colour with no wrinkles or blemishes. It's a good idea to only buy as many as you can eat within a few days.

HOW TO STORE THEM

Pop them in a paper bag, or a dark-coloured perforated plastic bag or a hessian bag and store in a cool and dark spot. They don't mind a bit of humidity – after all they are made up of about 80 per cent water. Storing them in the fridge is a no-no.

WHAT'S IN THEM?

A medium raw potato (about 150 g/5½ oz) has about 435 kilojoules (104 calories), 4 g protein, no fat, 20 g carbs (1 g sugars, 19 g starches), 3 g fibre, 5 mg sodium, 675 mg potassium, and a high GI (77) when cooked; the GL is moderate (15). While some varieties of potato such as Carisma and nicola have lower GI values, on average most potatoes are high GI.

WHAT ELSE?

Light is the problem for this underground tuber whose natural environment is dark. When exposed to light, potatoes can accumulate chlorophyll, which turns the skin green. While the green may be unsightly, it's the glycoalkaloids (mainly solanine) that can develop along with chrolophyll that makes potatoes taste bitter. If you eat a lot of green potatoes they can be potentially toxic. Of course everyone knows that you peel or cut off the green bits.

HERO RECIPES

Simple fish stew with potatoes (page 60)
Potato patties with yoghurt and green herb sauce (page 61)
Potato salad with green beans, peas and buttermilk-herb dressing (page 63)
Potato and pea curry (page 64)

PUMPKIN

What's not to like about rambling pumpkins (squash) with their softly hairy stems and elegant tendrils reaching for the sun? Boil and steam them for a quick side dish or soup, or roast when you want concentrated flavour and creamy sweetness. Toss some seeds on the compost and bingo, you'll find yourself with a pumpkin patch. Perhaps one of the earliest cultivated crops – remains of *Curcubita moschata* have been found in Mexico dating back some 7000 years to about 5000 BC. Pumpkins are also one of the biggest in the squash family. Swiss grower Beni Meier holds the Guinness World Record for heaviest pumpkin, which weighed in at 1054 kilograms (2323 pounds).

WHAT TO LOOK FOR

Look for pumpkins that feel heavy and hard, and are free from bruises, splits and soft spots. If there is still a stem attached, make sure it is dry.

HOW TO STORE THEM

Whole pumpkins will keep for a long time if stored in a well-ventilated area. If you buy a segment wrapped in plastic, it has a much shorter life, as the cut surface can go mouldy. Pre-packed, peeled and chopped pumpkin is convenient but needs to be kept in the fridge and used as soon as possible after buying.

WHAT'S IN THEM?

A cup of raw diced pumpkin (about 120 g/4¼ oz) has about 200 kilojoules (48 calories), 2.5 g protein, 0.5 g fat, 8 g carbs (5 g sugars, 3 g starches), 1.5 g fibre, 1 mg sodium, 414 mg potassium, and a moderate GI (66) when cooked; the GL is low (5).

WHAT ELSE?

While size may matter to some, flavour matters more to most of us. At the top of the tasty list are sweet, minimal waste butternut pumpkins; easy-peel, versatile jap or kent; and thin-skinned jarrahdale pumpkins with a flavour and smoothness that's hard to beat.

HERO RECIPES

Trio of pumpkins roasted with chestnuts and hot mint sauce (page 65)
Roasted pumpkin soup with harissa (page 66)

SWEETCORN

It's hard to beat the juicy burst of sweet corn kernels straight from the cob. Peel back the husk of a fresh ear of corn and we are munching through the neat kernel rows of a very big grass seed head that was cultivated in the Americas for thousands of years before Christopher Columbus arrived on the scene. Although 'officially' a grain, the particular variety of corn we tuck into is very much eaten immature, as a vegetable. Boil, steam, microwave, bake or barbecue and serve them piping hot with just a dot of butter and sprinkle of salt. Alternatively, add the kernels to soups, stews and stir-fries; fritters and frittatas; chowders and crepes; salsas and salads; muffins, breads and corn cakes, or toss whole baby corn into stir-fries.

WHAT TO LOOK FOR

Buy cobs with green husks and dry silk or tassels intact for the sweetest flavour and if you can get a peek at the kernels, they should be plump, not shrivelled. As the natural sugars in the kernels start converting to starch once the husk is removed, resist buying pre-packed shucked ears. Frozen cobs and kernels make a handy year-round substitute.

HOW TO STORE THEM

If you want it sweet and tender, then eat fresh corn the day you buy it. However, it does keep well in the fridge in a plastic bag for a few days. Don't peel away the husk until you are ready to cook.

WHAT'S IN THEM?

A medium cob of raw sweetcorn (100 g/3½ oz), which is equivalent to ½ cup (90 g/3¼ oz) sweetcorn kernels, has about 430 kilojoules (103 calories), 4 g protein, 1 g fat, 16 g carbs (1 g sugars, 15 g starches), 4.5 g fibre, 530 mg potassium, 3 mg sodium and a low GI (48) when cooked; the GL is low (8).

WHAT ELSE?

Corn is also used to make numerous gluten-free wholegrain products with an absolutely distinctive flavour that's like no other grain.

Polenta is essentially a dish, not an ingredient. It is made mostly from medium-ground dried corn. Grits are coarsely ground cornmeal. Instant polenta has been par-cooked to speed up the cooking time and lacks the rich corn flavour.

Corn grits, which you will mostly come across in the US, are chopped up dried kernels you can use in soups or stews or serve as a side dish.

Hominy grits are corn grits that have been treated with an alkaline solution (nixtamalised).

HERO RECIPES

Chopped salad of sweetcorn, soya beans and quinoa with lemon-basil dressing (page 68)
Chicken and corn soup with toasted tortilla and avocado (page 69)
Roasted corn with chilli and lime peanut butter (page 71)

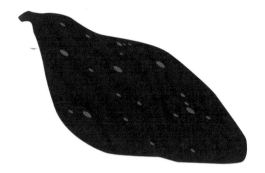

SWEET POTATO

They were cultivating sweet potatoes in Central and South America for about 7000–8000 years before Columbus arrived. He thought they looked like yams and tasted like chestnuts, and shipped them back to Spain along with chillies and chocolate. Like ducks to water, sweet potatoes took to local conditions and thrived in the Mediterranean climate. This was just the beginning of their global conquest – sweet potatoes are now grown in more developing countries than any other root crop. Their big advantage over regular potatoes is that their skin does not develop green patches (see page 27). They are easy to prepare – peel or scrub and roast, boil, steam, mash, add to stir-fries or use in place of pumpkin (squash) in desserts. Sweet potatoes are not as sweet as pumpkins, and are much starchier, so they will thicken a dish more if substituted.

WHAT TO LOOK FOR

Look for sweet potatoes with firm skin that are free from blemishes, cracks and soft spots. Choosing ones that are similar in size makes it easier to achieve even cooking. We like the small to medium ones with plump middles and tapered ends.

HOW TO STORE THEM

They are good keepers, like potatoes, and should be stored in a cool, dark spot. Don't store them in the fridge because this will encourage softening and sprouting.

WHAT'S IN THEM?

A small raw orange-fleshed sweet potato (about 200 g/7 oz) has about 585 kilojoules (140 calories), 4 g protein, no fat, 28 g carbs (11 g sugars, 17 g starches), 6 g fibre, 20 mg sodium, 490 mg potassium and a moderate GI (61) when cooked; the GL is medium (17). Note that purple skinned sweet potatoes with white flesh have a high GI (75).

WHAT ELSE?

Sweet potatoes come in a variety of colours, shapes and sizes. It's the orange-fleshed sweet potato that we like to roast and use in recipes for its colour and flavour.

HERO RECIPES

Pan-roasted sweet potato and beetroot with grapefruit glaze (page 72)
Sweet potato, quinoa, spinach and red lentil burgers with tahini-mint yoghurt (page 74)

TOMATOES

As you gaze on the countless varieties of tomatoes in the produce store wondering which to buy, it's hard to believe this acidic fruit got off to a slow start. It was a long slog from feared to revered and feted at festivals. Now we can't get enough of them – fresh, roasted, dried, tinned, juiced, and made into soups, sauces, salsas, pickles and preserves. They are also one of the most popular vegetables with home gardeners, despite certain inherent challenges. It seems obvious to recommend buying them in season, but we can't overstate the importance. Ripeness is all. And in salads and sauces the quality of the tomatoes is the key to the success of the dish.

WHAT TO LOOK FOR

Choose ripe, red tomatoes that still have a bit of green stem attached. Out of season, make the most of tinned tomatoes – whole, diced or crushed – and opt for a good-quality brand.

HOW TO STORE THEM

If they are slightly underripe, leave them on the windowsill or kitchen bench. Otherwise, store them, stem down, out of direct sunlight and use within a day or so. Don't store them in the fridge. Tomatoes are a sunshine fruit: the cold breaks down their cell walls and causes them to go mushy.

WHAT'S IN THEM?

A medium fresh tomato (about 170 g/6 oz) has about 110 kilojoules (26 calories), 2 g protein, no fat, 3 g carbs (3 g sugars, 0 g starches), 2 g fibre, 10 mg sodium, 334 mg potassium and a low GI (33); the GL is low (1).

WHAT ELSE?

Just as well we love tomatoes because they give us the red pigment lycopene, which may reduce the risk of prostate cancer in men but is also said to help us keep our cholesterol numbers in the right zone and protect our skin from UV damage. And don't fret about cooking tomatoes or using them tinned, because lycopene is more available when puréed and cooked with oil. There are so many tomato products – from tomato paste (concentrated purée) to passata (puréed tomatoes) and other tomato-based sauces – that are useful to have on hand.

HERO RECIPES

Fresh tomato sauce for pasta (page 75)
Tomato and fig salad with burrata and date-mint dressing (page 77)
Green tomatoes with a chopped olive and herb sauce (page 78)
Salmon curry with lychees and tomatoes (page 81)

SHREDDED BEETROOT, CARROT AND NASHI SLAW WITH CUMIN AND LIME DRESSING

This slaw is all about the crunch factor. Summer parades frivolous soft leaves and ripe tomato salads, but come winter it's time to enjoy the deep flavour, vivid colour and crunch of raw beetroot and carrot. Toss in the juicy white flesh of nashi and lightly splash with a subtly spiced dressing, and you have a salad to start or end a meal. It's particularly good with grilled meat and oily fish.

PREPARATION TIME: 20 minutes | **SERVES:** 6

CUMIN AND LIME DRESSING
⅓ cup (80 ml/2½ fl oz) vegetable oil
finely grated zest of 1 plump lime
¼ cup (60 ml/2 fl oz) lime juice
1 teaspoon ground cumin
sea salt flakes

2 medium carrots, scrubbed
2 medium beetroot (beets), peeled
2 nashi
½ teaspoon chilli powder
1 tablespoon lightly toasted sesame
    seeds
3 tablespoons finely chopped raw
    almonds (or walnuts)

Make the dressing by whisking the oil, lime zest and juice, and cumin in a small bowl. Season with salt to taste.

Shred the carrots and beetroot using a mandoline, a blade attachment on the food processor or vegetable turning slicer, and put in a bowl. Without peeling the nashi, halve, remove the core and cut into thin matchstick strips. Add to the bowl with the chilli powder, sesame seeds and almonds. Pour over the dressing and lightly toss.

TIP Black sesame seeds look striking in this salad.

BEETROOT WITH ORANGE-SHERRY DRESSING AND SOFT HERBS

This is a pretty salad, wonderfully easy to pull together and gorgeous to eat. However, grappling with fresh beetroot can leave you and your kitchen looking a little bit like a butcher's shop. Instead of boiling beetroot, wrap them in foil and they will steam-bake to perfect tenderness. This method saves on a lot of cleaning up time.

PREPARATION TIME: 20 minutes | **COOKING TIME:** 15 minutes | **SERVES:** 6

Rinse the beetroot and cut the leaves off, leaving about a 3.5 cm (1½ in) stalk. Put the beetroot in a large pot, cover with water and bring to the boil. Reduce the heat and simmer for about 15 minutes, or until the beetroot are tender. Drain in a colander and, when cool enough to handle, gently rub the surfaces to remove the skins and stalks. Sit the beetroot on thick paper towel to absorb some of the moisture and pat dry.

Put the shallot, vinegar, orange zest and juice, chives and almonds in a bowl and whisk lightly to blend. Add the chervil with salt and pepper to taste, and gently toss. Slice the beetroot, arrange on a platter and spoon the orange-herb dressing over. The salad is tastier if served at room temperature.

1.5 kg (3 lb 6 oz) medium beetroot (beets)
1 large shallot, finely chopped
¼ cup (60 ml/2 fl oz) sherry vinegar
finely grated zest and juice of 1 large orange
3 tablespoons chopped chives
3 tablespoons chopped raw almonds
small bunch chervil, roughly chopped
sea salt flakes and freshly ground pepper

TIPS Try different varieties and colours of beetroot for a spectacular effect.

Chervil is a very soft aromatic herb closely related to parsley. Fresh parsley leaves are the closest substitute for chervil in appearance and taste.

FERMENTED BEETROOT, CARROT AND CAULIFLOWER

The vegetables must be of the highest quality for fermenting. Other than the ratio of salt to water for the brine, there's no one-size-fits-all recipe and it's easy to create your own. However, to achieve perfect results there are tips aplenty, so please do read 'fermenting vegetables', opposite, before you start.

PREPARATION TIME: 40 minutes | **MAKES:** 3 × 2 cup (500 ml/17 fl oz) jars

3 garlic cloves, peeled and bruised

2 medium beetroot (beets), peeled and cut into thin sticks

2 cups (500 g/1 lb 2 oz) small cauliflower florets

2 large carrots, peeled and cut into thin sticks

1–3 tablespoons fine sea salt

5 cups (1.25 litres/44 fl oz) filtered water

VARIATIONS Broccoli florets chopped in a similar size to the cauliflower or small trimmed and halved brussels sprouts can make lovely 'green' additions. The quantity of each vegetable can vary, but a roughly equal amount of each works well. The garlic is an optional add-in. Try injecting your own flavour notes with different spices and herbs – peppercorns, dill fronds, chilli, fresh ginger, bay leaves, fresh horseradish, caraway seeds, juniper berries, mustard seeds.

Put the garlic in the sterilised jars (see opposite). Cover with alternating layers of the beetroot, cauliflower and carrots, leaving about 2.5 cm (1 in) at the top.

To make the brine, stir the salt in the water to dissolve, and pour the brine slowly over the vegetables all the way to the top of the jar to eliminate trapped air. Use a wooden skewer to poke the vegetables to release any trapped air bubbles in the jar. Add more brine if necessary, making sure all the vegetables are completely covered in the brine (any contact with the air can cause the vegetables to spoil).

Weigh the vegetables down with a small glass jar partially filled with water, a water-filled zip-lock bag or clean saucer with a weight on top. Stand the jars in a baking dish to catch any brine that spills over. Screw the lids on the jars loosely to allow the fermentation gases to be released.

Let the jars sit at room temperature (no higher than 22°C/72°F) for at least 48 hours before tasting. The longer they sit, the stronger the taste. Taste it every day, and if you like the texture and complex flavour, it is ready.

Once the vegetables have reached the desired taste, remove the weights, screw the lids on tightly, label, and store the jars in the fridge. As long as the vegetables remain submerged in the brine, they'll keep for months.

FERMENTING VEGETABLES

Choose super-fresh, preferably certified-as-organic vegetables because of the naturally occurring bacteria on them. Chemical sprays or pesticides can inhibit the good bacteria during the fermentation process. Wash your vegetables thoroughly under cold running water before preparing them, and keep the size and shape consistent within each batch to ensure even fermentation. Slice hard veggies (such as beetroot) thinly and cut softer veggies (zucchini) thickly to help preserve their shape.

- Coarsely grated veggies will require a quick ferment time and works best for hard or crunchy vegetables.
- Whole vegetables will generally require a longer fermentation time than grated or thinly sliced. Radishes, green beans, baby brussels sprouts and pickling (short) cucumbers look beautiful fermented whole.

The most important point to remember is that fermentation is an anaerobic process: it will only occur without air. The vegetables must be kept under the brine at all times.

SALT Only ever use a fine sea salt. Never use iodised table salt as it contains anti-caking agents that will cause the ferment to cloud. The iodine will also interfere with the fermentation process. The salt draws out moisture and allows the natural bacteria on the vegetables to do the fermenting; prevents the growth of other bacteria and mould, helping prolong the life of the vegetables and keeps them crisp.

How much salt you use is a matter of personal preference. Start by salting lightly, as it's easier to add more if required. Keep in mind, the more salt, the slower the fermentation. And the less salt, the quicker the process. However, too much salt can halt the fermentation process and not enough salt may not keep the veggies crisp and can produce surface moulds. As a guide use 1–3 tablespoons salt per 5 cups (1.25 litres/44 fl oz) water.

WATER To avoid all contaminants and to keep the cultures in your ferment healthy, preferably use distilled water.

CONTAINER Wide-mouthed Mason jars or glass jars with a rubber seal band and clip-lock lid make perfect containers. Do not use non-stick coated containers or metals such as copper, aluminium or cast iron, which react with the acids in fermented food, affecting flavour and colour. These metals can also leach into the food.

THE PROCESS Fermentation is a continual process, and flavours, textures and aromas will change and develop over time.

Bubbling – after about a day or so you may see slight foaming, which is not uncommon for veggies that have higher sugar contents, such as carrots and beets. It's harmless and should disappear after a few days. The bubbles in the jars are gases formed by the fermentation process and are a good sign that fermentation is established. Some veggies get off to a slow start and don't bubble as much.

Aroma – if the container is opened after a few days of fermenting, it should have a strong, sour, vinegary but pleasant aroma. If it smells unpleasant it may be a stage in the fermentation process. Leave for another 3–5 days and if the aroma doesn't improve, discard it. As long as the ferment smells and tastes pleasant, the culture is doing well.

Flavour – taste the vegetables daily until they reach the flavour and texture you prefer. Always use a clean spoon to take out what you're eating and never eat out of the jar, as you will contaminate the entire batch with bacteria from your mouth.

STORAGE Keep it cool in a cellar, cool pantry or in the fridge where the fermentation will continue very slowly, allowing better flavours to develop.

EGGS CODDLED IN A SPICY CAPSICUM AND TOMATO SAUCE

The perfect dish for brunch or a busy weeknight meal. Make it as mild or as spicy as you like by adjusting the paprika. Generally Spanish paprika is less intense than its Hungarian counterpart. Use smoked paprika if you want a deep woodsy flavour.

PREPARATION TIME: 20 minutes | **COOKING TIME:** 30 minutes | **SERVES:** 6

¼ cup (60 ml/2 fl oz) olive oil
1 large onion, halved and thinly sliced
1 large red capsicum (pepper), deseeded and thinly sliced
3 garlic cloves, thinly sliced
1 teaspoon ground cumin
1 teaspoon sweet paprika
½ teaspoon cayenne pepper
⅔ cup (400 g/14 oz) tin chopped tomatoes with juice
1⅓ cups (200 g/7 oz) fresh cherry tomatoes
sea salt flakes and freshly ground pepper
⅔ cup (100 g/3½ oz) crumbled feta (optional)
6 eggs
2 tablespoons chopped coriander (cilantro)
6 corn or wholegrain tortillas

Heat the oil in a large frying pan over medium–low heat. Add the onion and capsicum, and cook gently for up to 15 minutes, until very soft. Add the garlic and cook for 2 minutes. Stir in the cumin, paprika and cayenne pepper, and cook for a further 1 minute. Tip in both the tinned and fresh tomatoes and then add salt to taste. You may need a little pepper to balance the heat of the paprika and cayenne. Simmer gently for about 8 minutes, until the fresh tomatoes have started to collapse. Stir in the feta, if using.

Make six holes in the mixture with the back of a large spoon and gently crack an egg into each of the holes. Season the eggs with a little salt and pepper, put the lid on the pan and leave to cook over moderately slow heat for exactly 5 minutes. The egg whites should be just set with a hint of a wobble and the yolks should be runny in the middle. (Remember, they will keep cooking once you take them off the heat.) Scatter with fresh coriander and serve with warm tortillas.

TIP In some sauce- or stew-like recipes, tinned tomatoes are a better choice because they are densely packed and have a high concentration of flavour that is not affected by heat.

ROASTED RATATOUILLE WITH HUMMUS

All along the entire Mediterranean coast there are many variations of this popular traditional French Provençal vegetable dish. Like a curious traveller, this version takes a taste of several countries along the way.

PREPARATION TIME: 15 minutes | **COOKING TIME:** 18 minutes | **SERVES:** 6

4 long thin eggplants (aubergines)
2 medium onions
2 large zucchini (courgettes)
3 small red capsicums (peppers), halved and deseeded
½ cup (125 ml/4 fl oz) olive oil
3 garlic cloves, crushed
12 large cherry tomatoes
sea salt flakes and freshly ground pepper
2 tablespoons finely chopped oregano leaves
1 cup (220 g/8 oz) store-bought or homemade hummus
6 wholegrain pita bread or corn tortillas

Preheat the oven to 190°C/375°F (fan 170°C/325°F).

Prepare the vegetables by cutting them roughly into evenly sized small chunks.

Put the oil and garlic in a roasting pan, add the eggplants, onions, zucchini and capsicums, toss them together well. Roast for about 18 minutes or until the vegetables are tender and slightly charred. Add the tomatoes and roast for a few more minutes, until they start to blister and pop. At this stage, all the vegetables should be well browned. Add salt and pepper to taste and then sprinkle over the oregano. Give the pan a few good shakes to mix all the ingredients together.

Place a mound of hummus on each pita bread (or tortilla), spread out with a spoon and top with a generous serve of vegetables. Serve warm or cold.

TIP For a slightly different flavour and a lively colour, use a yellow, green and red capsicum.

CARROT AND RED LENTIL SOUP WITH LEMON

A soothing comforting soup, with a hint of sweetness from the carrots, an earthy depth from the lentils and a subtle warming spicy note of cumin. A squeeze of lemon before serving gives it a lively kick. This soup can be frozen, without the lemon juice and parsley, for up to a month.

PREPARATION TIME: 20 minutes | **COOKING TIME:** 45 minutes | **SERVES:** 6

Put the oil, onions, carrots and celery in a large pot over medium heat and gently cook with the lid on for 10 minutes, until the vegetables are soft. Add the garlic, ginger, if using, cumin, and season with salt and pepper. Cook gently until the mixture is aromatic and then add the lentils and the stock. Bring to the boil, reduce the heat and then simmer for about 30 minutes. Preferably using a blender, purée the mixture to your desired consistency – smooth or chunky. Just before serving, add a sprinkle of parsley and a generous squeeze of lemon juice to each bowl of soup.

TIPS Leave the ginger out if you prefer, but it does give the soup a tangy freshness and warm mellow sweetness.

The splash of lemon juice added just before serving brightens the soup, helping to balance the flavour.

¼ cup (60 ml/2 fl oz) olive oil
2 medium onions, chopped
5 large carrots, scraped and chopped
2 medium celery stalks, diced
3 garlic cloves, crushed
2 teaspoons finely grated ginger (optional)
2 teaspoons ground cumin
sea salt flakes and freshly ground pepper
1½ cups (315 g/11 oz) red lentils, rinsed
9 cups (2.25 litres/76 fl oz) chicken stock
2 tablespoons finely chopped parsley
1 small lemon, for squeezing

POTATO AND SILVERBEET WITH A CARROT, NUT AND OAT CRUST

This is an excellent dish to accompany grilled meat or fish, or a stand-alone meal for meat-free eaters. Impressive, too, if cooked in individual ramekins. Sliced zucchini can be added to the vegetable mix and grated parsnip would add a slightly nutty flavour to the crust.

PREPARATION TIME: 20 minutes | **COOKING TIME:** 1 hour | **SERVES:** 6

2 tablespoons olive oil

¼ cup (45 g/1½ oz) finely diced short-cut bacon (optional)

4 shallots, thinly sliced

8 thyme sprigs

½ cup (125 ml/4 fl oz) chicken stock

3 silverbeet (Swiss chard) stalks

10 small potatoes, scrubbed

sea salt flakes and freshly ground pepper

3 large carrots, scraped and coarsely grated

½ cup (50 g/1¾ oz) chopped almonds or pecans

⅔ cup (65 g/2¼ oz) traditional rolled oats

1 tablespoon butter, melted

1 teaspoon black mustard seeds

Preheat the oven to 180°C/350°F (fan 160°C/315°F).

Heat 1 tablespoon of the oil in a pan over medium–high heat. Add the bacon, if using, shallots and thyme, and cook, stirring occasionally, for 5 minutes or until the shallots are soft and golden. Add the stock, bring to the simmer, then remove from the heat.

Trim off the thick coarse ends of the silverbeet stalks and discard. Finely shred the leaves and tender part of the stalk and scatter over the base of a sturdy ovenproof baking dish – about 6 cups (1.5 litres/52 fl oz) capacity. Slice the potatoes very thinly crossways retaining the shape of the whole potato, and arrange in a single layer in the baking dish, on top of the silverbeet, so they fit in snugly.

Pour over the bacon mixture and season with salt and pepper. Put the grated carrots in a bowl with the nuts, oats, melted butter, mustard seeds and remaining oil. Toss well and spoon over the potatoes. Cover the dish with foil and bake for 30 minutes. Remove the foil and continue cooking for about 20 minutes, or until the carrot crumble is crisp and browned.

TIP Don't be tempted to substitute anything for the oats. Rolled oats will give a nice chewy texture, whereas steel-cut (unrolled) oats take longer than the other ingredients to cook and will impart a raw oat taste. Instant oats are pre-cooked and will break up when baked.

CAULIFLOWER AND LEEK SOUP

How best to describe this soup? From Louis P. De Gouy, *The Soup Book*, 1949: 'Soup is cuisine's kindest course. It breathes reassurance; it steams consolation; after a weary day it promotes sociability ... there is nothing like a bowl of hot soup, its wisp of aromatic steam making the nostrils quiver with anticipation.' Nothing else need be said.

PREPARATION TIME: 15 minutes | **COOKING TIME:** 25 minutes | **SERVES:** 6

Cut the cauliflower in half, remove the thick core and discard only the very toughest pieces of stalk. Finely chop the rest of the core (there is much flavour there). Separate the cauliflower into florets and chop the big pieces.

Melt the butter with the oil in a sturdy pot and add the leek. Cook over a gentle heat, covered, for 5 minutes, or until softened but not coloured, and then add the potato, cauliflower and stock. Simmer for 15 minutes or until the cauliflower is very tender and the potato begins to break up. Remove the soup from the heat and pour in the milk. Pour the soup into a blender (or use a hand-held blender) and process until smooth. Return the soup to the pot, add salt and pepper to taste, and stir in the lemon juice. Heat just to boiling point. Ladle the soup into bowls and garnish with cashews and chives.

1 large cauliflower
1 tablespoon butter
1 tablespoon olive oil
1 large leek, pale part only, washed and chopped
1 large potato, peeled and chopped
6 cups (1.5 litres/52 fl oz) chicken stock
1 cup (250 ml/9 fl oz) milk
sea salt flakes and freshly ground pepper
juice of ½ lemon
3 tablespoons chopped cashews
1 tablespoon chopped chives

TIP Leeks burn easily, so the trick is to cook them slowly over gentle heat with the lid on the pan to encourage them to steam in the oil and butter as they cook.

THE ORIGINAL ROASTED WHOLE CAULIFLOWER

Sometimes simple is best. Cauliflower is so accommodating to many other flavours and textures (think pine nuts, currants, capers) but properly roasted it is sensational with just a drizzle of Sunday-best olive oil and, if liked, a squeeze of sharp lemon. A whole head of cauliflower roasted builds up a nice contrast between a deeply browned, almost crisp exterior, and tender, meaty interior.

PREPARATION TIME: 5 minutes | **COOKING TIME:** 45 minutes | **SERVES:** 6

Preheat the oven to 220°C/425°F (fan 200°C/400°F). Line a roasting pan with baking paper or grease with olive oil.

Trim the base of the cauliflower so it stands upright and then put it in a large pot. Fill the pot three-quarters with water and add 1 teaspoon salt. Cover the pot, bring to the boil and then immediately reduce the heat to a lively simmer and cook for 8 minutes. Drain well to allow the steam to evaporate and help dry the cauliflower.

When the cauliflower is cool enough to handle, rub all over with the oil, making sure it gets in between the florets. Sprinkle very lightly with salt flakes. Roast in the prepared roasting pan for about 35 minutes, depending on size, until golden brown and cooked. To test, pierce the cauliflower with a thin-bladed knife and if there is no resistance it is done.

1 medium cauliflower
sea salt flakes
¼ cup (60 ml/2 fl oz) olive oil

TIP The best cauliflower for roasting whole should have snowy white, tightly packed florets nestling in bright green leaves. Blanching before roasting gets rid of strong odours, keeps the florets tender after roasting and shortens the roasting time. Instead of blanching the cauliflower in water, you can steam it.

CELERIAC SLAW WITH CAPERS, WALNUTS AND LEMON

Used raw in this refreshing winter salad, celeriac has a lovely fine-textured, delicately crisp flesh with mellow citrusy, resinous notes. A masterful combination when mingled with bursts of briny capers and the crunch of walnuts. For a sharper dressing, leave out the sugar and perk it up with a good Spanish sherry.

PREPARATION TIME: 20 minutes | **SERVES:** 6

1 celeriac (celery root), peeled
1 lemon, halved
sea salt flakes and freshly ground pepper
⅓ cup (80 ml/2½ fl oz) extra virgin olive oil
2 teaspoons sugar
1 tablespoon red wine vinegar
4 tablespoons capers, rinsed
¾ cup (90 g/3¼ oz) chopped walnuts
1 handful parsley, chopped

Shred the celeriac into strips as long and as thin as possible (ideally, use a mandoline or the shred attachment of a food processor). Put the celeriac in a bowl and squeeze half the lemon over to prevent the celeriac discolouring. Add salt and pepper to taste – remember the capers will provide some of the briny tang.

Juice the remaining lemon and whisk in a large bowl with the oil, sugar and vinegar. Taste and adjust by adding more vinegar, or lemon juice. Add the capers, walnuts and parsley, then toss well. This slaw will stay crisp at room temperature for an hour or so.

ROASTED CELERIAC AND CARROTS WITH MIRIN AND APPLE JUICE GLAZE

When roasted, these hero veggies become as tender as butter, boasting crisp caramelised edges. This is a particularly felicitous combination of roasted veggies enlivened with a zing of ginger and refreshing mint, but any root vegetable can be teamed with celeriac – parsnip, swede (rutabaga), turnip or beetroot (beet).

PREPARATION TIME: 20 minutes | **COOKING TIME:** 30 minutes | **SERVES:** 6

Preheat the oven to 180°C/350°F (fan 160°C/315°F).

Cut the celeriac and carrots into even-sized chunks and put in a large baking dish. Drizzle over the oil, sprinkle lightly with salt and pepper, and toss the vegetables together. Roast for about 25 minutes, or until tender and starting to brown.

In a bowl, whisk together the mirin, apple juice, garlic and ginger, and then pour this over the vegetables. Toss lightly to coat and then continue to roast for a further 10 minutes, or until the vegetables are well glazed. You may have to give them a gentle push around the pan to glaze evenly. Sprinkle with the mint just before serving.

1 medium celeriac (celery root), peeled
5 medium carrots, scraped
2 tablespoons olive oil
sea salt flakes and freshly ground pepper
½ cup (125 ml/4 fl oz) mirin
½ cup (125 ml/4 fl oz) apple juice
1 garlic clove, crushed
2 teaspoons finely grated ginger
few mint leaves

TIP As there are several qualities of mirin, ranging from the authentic fermented mildly sweet rice wine to artificial mirin, choose a mid-range quality. It will be impossible to produce the lovely glaze using low-end, artificial mirin. If you are stuck, sake sweetened with sugar is an acceptable substitute.

EGGPLANT

EGGPLANT WITH CHOPPED GREEN CAPSICUM AND POMEGRANATE SAUCE

Combining sweet but tart pomegranate with veggies and nuts is as old as time itself. Depending on the variety, pomegranate seeds vary in colour.

PREPARATION TIME: 20 minutes | **COOKING TIME:** 10 minutes | **SERVES:** 6

2 eggplants (aubergines)
about ⅔ cup (170 ml/5½ fl oz) olive oil
¼ cup (60 ml/2 fl oz) pomegranate
    syrup
2 tablespoons cold water
1 garlic clove, crushed
2 tablespoons coarsely chopped
    walnuts
½ teaspoon finely chopped oregano
sea salt flakes
1 small green capsicum (pepper),
    deseeded and finely chopped
4 tablespoons pomegranate seeds

Trim the eggplants and cut them crossways into 6 mm (¼ in) thick slices. Heat about one-third of the oil in a large non-stick frying pan over medium–high heat. When hot, add a few eggplant slices at a time and fry, turning once, until golden on each side. Remove and drain on paper towels. Add more oil to the pan (you may need a little more oil as the eggplant will absorb it quickly) and continue to fry the slices in batches.

Put the pomegranate syrup in a small pan with the water and heat until warm. Add the garlic, walnuts, oregano and add salt to taste. Transfer to a blender or food processor and blitz to make a rough-textured sauce. Arrange the eggplant slices on a serving dish, sprinkle with the chopped capsicum and spoon over the sauce. Garnish with the pomegranate seeds and serve.

TIPS Pomegranates vary in sweetness and tartness. To release the seeds, cut the pomegranate in half and then, holding it away from you over a bowl of cold water, give it a good strong thwack. The seeds, well most, will pop out from the internal white pulpy membranes. Flick the few obstinate ones with a small knife or finger. The seeds sink and any inedible pulp floats.

Keep in mind that pomegranate juices stain – impressively so. To remove stains from your hands rub with a slice of raw potato or with a mixture of lemon juice and table salt.

SALAD OF RED LEAVES WITH FENNEL AND JERUSALEM ARTICHOKES

Knobbly Jerusalem artichokes have a nutty flavour and can be cooked in the same way as potatoes and parsnips. They are also excellent roasted with a spritz of lemon, before merging with Mediterranean flavours. The tonic bitterness of radicchio is extremely agreeable as a contrast to rich (or fatty) and strong flavours.

PREPARATION TIME: 15 minutes | **COOKING TIME:** 15 minutes | **SERVES:** 6

Preheat the oven to 180°C/350°F (fan 160°C/315°F).

Cut the artichokes into quarters lengthwise, toss with enough oil to lightly coat them and then season with salt and pepper to taste. Put them in a roasting pan, squeeze the lemon juice over and tuck the lemon shells and thyme sprigs among the artichokes. Roast for about 15–20 minutes, or until they feel slightly soft and are sticky on the bottom. Take the artichokes out of the oven and let them cool in the pan. Thinly slice the fennel lengthways and put in a large bowl. Tip in the artichokes, radicchio, olives and watercress.

In a bowl, whisk together the ingredients for the dressing. Pour the dressing over the salad and gently turn the salad to mix.

TIP An easy way to prepare Jerusalem artichokes is to use a spoon to gently scrape off the skin, which helps gets in and out of the crevices.

8 medium Jerusalem artichokes, scraped
olive oil, to drizzle
sea salt flakes and freshly ground pepper
1 plump juicy lemon, halved
4–6 thyme sprigs
1 medium fennel bulb, trimmed
300 g (10½ oz) radicchio, rinsed and roughly chopped
12 large pitted black olives
1 handful baby watercress

DRESSING
¼ cup (60 ml/2 fl oz) balsamic vinegar
1 teaspoon Dijon mustard
¼ cup (60 ml/2 fl oz) olive oil

TRIO OF ONIONS AND HERB SALAD WITH RICOTTA ON TOASTED GRAIN BREAD

More of a bruschetta-style open sandwich, this has a lively taste where the mixed onions play off each other without overpowering the delicate ricotta and freshness of the herbs. Cottage cheese could be used instead of ricotta.

PREPARATION TIME: 20 minutes | **SERVES:** 6

1 medium red onion, thinly sliced

1 shallot, finely chopped

1 tablespoon finely snipped chives

2 teaspoons salted capers, rinsed and drained

sea salt flakes and freshly ground pepper

1 handful mint leaves, roughly chopped

3 handfuls parsley, roughly chopped

1 handful basil leaves, roughly chopped

¼ cup (60 ml/2 fl oz) olive oil

1 tablespoon finely grated orange zest

2 tablespoons fresh orange juice

6 slices toasted grain bread

100 g (3½ oz) fresh ricotta

Roughly chop the sliced onion and put in a bowl with the shallot, chives and capers. Add salt and pepper to taste, keeping in mind that the capers will add saltiness. Leave to sit for 10 minutes so the onions release some juice and the flavours meld. Add the mint, parsley and basil to the bowl with the onions. Pour in the oil and add the orange zest and juice. Toss lightly and pile on the toasted bread. Dot all over with ricotta and serve.

TIP Brine-cured capers tend to be slightly firmer, with a subtle 'floral-grassy' flavour, whereas the salt-cured (which must be rinsed several times in water to remove the salt) are tender, with hints of 'meaty, fermented' flavours.

CHICKEN STOCK

This is a delicate all-purpose stock suitable for soups, braises, vegetables and sauces. Chicken stock is the essence of cooking – it flavours without colouring. The flavour is extracted from the bones, vegetables and herbs using a gentle heat. You can use any chicken but a stewing bird will have more flavour. Always start a stock with cold water and never boil; a contented simmer is all that is required. Try to continually skim impurities right from the beginning of cooking to give a clear stock. For a stronger chicken flavour add more bones and reduce the finished stock by one-third.

PREPARATION TIME: 10 minutes | **COOKING TIME:** 1½ hours | **MAKES:** 10 cups (2.5 litres/85 fl oz)

It is important to thoroughly rinse the bones, remove any visible blood and discard any internal organs as they will cloud the stock. Put the chicken bones in a large stockpot with the water. Slowly bring to a simmer over medium heat, skimming off any impurities and fat. Add the carrot, leek, onion and bay leaf. Bring the stock back to a gentle simmer and continue to cook for 1 hour, skimming continually. (To skim, move the stockpot partially off the heat so that only one side of the stock continues to simmer actively. The foam will accumulate towards the calm side of the pot, becoming easier to remove.)

Remove the pot from the heat and allow to stand for 10 minutes – this will settle any particles left in the stock. Slowly pour the stock through a strainer lined with muslin. If you pour too quickly, you will disturb the impurities and spoil the stock – you can use a ladle. Allow the stock to cool as quickly as you can, then remove any surface fat. Cover and refrigerate for 4 days or freeze for up to 4 months.

1 kg (2 lb 4 oz) chicken bones
12 cups (3 litres/101 fl oz) cold water
1 large carrot, scraped and chopped
1 small leek, rinsed well, white part only, chopped
1 small onion, chopped
1 bay leaf

LEMON CHICKEN WITH GOLDEN ONIONS AND GREEN OLIVES

With a nod to an unctuous Moroccan tagine, the spice mix is mild and the turmeric produces a gorgeous golden colour in the onions when the chicken is cooked. Ground ginger withstands higher cooking temperatures than fresh ginger, without changing its flavour.

PREPARATION TIME: 25 minutes | **COOKING TIME:** 1 hour | **SERVES:** 6

3 garlic cloves, crushed
1 teaspoon ground cumin
½ teaspoon ground chilli
2 teaspoons ground turmeric
½ teaspoon freshly ground pepper
1 handful coriander (cilantro) leaves
    and stems, chopped, plus extra,
    finely chopped, to garnish
1 handful parsley, chopped
¼ cup (60 ml/2 fl oz) lemon juice
½ cup (125 ml/4 fl oz) olive oil
4 skinless bone-in chicken thighs
4 skinless bone-in chicken drumsticks
5 medium onions, thinly sliced
sea salt flakes
2 teaspoons ground ginger
1 lemon, thinly sliced
1 cup (250 ml/9 fl oz) water
1 cup (180 g/6½ oz) pitted green olives

Combine the garlic, cumin, chilli, turmeric, pepper, coriander, parsley, lemon juice and 2 tablespoons of the oil in a large bowl. Add the chicken and toss until evenly coated in the spice paste. Cover the bowl with plastic wrap and marinate in the refrigerator for 4 hours.

Heat 2 tablespoons of the remaining oil in a large sturdy heatproof pan over medium–high heat. Working in batches, add the chicken pieces and fry for about 10 minutes, turning once until golden brown on both sides. Transfer the chicken to a plate and cover loosely with foil to keep warm.

Put the onions in the pan with the remaining oil and add salt and pepper to taste. Cook for about 10 minutes, stirring occasionally, until the onions soften. Return the chicken to the pan with the ginger, lemon and water. Bring to a lively simmer and then reduce the heat to medium–low and cook, covered, for about 40 minutes, or until the chicken is cooked through. Test by piercing the meat near the bone with a fine skewer and if the juices run clear, the chicken is cooked. Remove from the heat and scatter with the olives and extra coriander. Lovely served with couscous or brown rice.

TIP A firm white fish can replace chicken in this dish. Leave the skin on, cut it into serving portions and marinate for 1 hour. Cook for 5 minutes on each side before adding to the softened, golden onions and then continue to cook for a further 15 minutes.

LAMB SHANKS WITH WINTER VEGETABLES AND PARSLEY-MINT GREMOLATA

The meaty leg of lamb may get all the love, but the muscular shank has a deeper, richer flavour that long, slow cooking teases out for fork-tender succulent mouthfuls. These lamb shanks take well to bright-tasting garnishes like gremolata casually strewn over before serving. It's hard to imagine that once upon a time, butchers threw in a shank with a roast – for free – to use to make soup, or as a treat for the dog.

PREPARATION TIME: 25 minutes | **COOKING TIME:** 2 hours | **SERVES:** 4

2 tablespoons olive oil
4 lamb shanks
4 large shallots, thinly sliced
sea salt flakes and freshly ground
    pepper
4 large parsnips, peeled and cut into
    large chunks
4 Jerusalem artichokes, scraped and
    sliced
4 cups (1 litre/35 fl oz) chicken stock
1 tablespoon chopped rosemary leaves

PARSLEY-MINT GREMOLATA
1 handful parsley, chopped
1 handful mint leaves, chopped
finely grated zest of 3 lemons
4 garlic cloves, crushed

Preheat the oven to 180°C/350°F (fan 160°C/315°F).

Heat the oil in a sturdy, ovenproof pan over medium heat, and, when hot, add the lamb shanks. Turn and cook for about 5 minutes, or until well browned all over. Add the shallots, and salt and pepper to taste, then cook until the shallots are soft and golden. Add the parsnips, artichokes, stock and rosemary. Give the pan a few good stirs and then cover with foil. Put in the oven and cook for about 1½ hours or until the lamb is tender. Remove the foil, increase the oven temperature to 200°C/400°F (fan 180°C/350°F) and cook the lamb for a further 10 minutes.

Use a spatula to remove the meat and vegetables to a platter. Cover the platter loosely with a tent of foil to keep warm. Skim the fat from the cooking liquid. Place the pan directly over medium heat on the stovetop and simmer the cooking liquid until it thickens slightly to form a thin gravy.

To make the gremolata, mix the parsley, mint, lemon zest and garlic in a small bowl using a fork. Serve the shanks and veggies with some of the gravy spooned over, then scatter over the gremolata.

PARSNIP, CELERIAC AND POTATO MINI BAKES

Looks matter. Perhaps this is why bulbous, knobby celeriac is considered a ne'er-do-well, a bit of a rough-around-the-edges veggie and too often overlooked. But looks can be deceiving. Lurking under the skin, celeriac has a powerful flavour of celery meets walnuts with sweet notes of aniseed. And it refuses to be bullied by other strong flavours and spices.

PREPARATION TIME: 20 minutes | **COOKING TIME:** 35 minutes | **SERVES:** 6

Preheat the oven to 180°C/350°F (fan 160°C/315°F). Lightly grease a medium 6-cup muffin pan with oil. Cut 12 × 8 cm (3¼ in) strips of baking paper and criss-cross two strips in each muffin cup.

Peel the potato, parsnip and celeriac. Cut the celeriac in half and then slice all the vegetables as thinly as possible (ideally, use a food processor with a slicing blade).

Place the vegetable slices in a bowl, and add salt and pepper to taste. Pour the melted butter and milk over the top, then toss gently to thoroughly coat the vegetables. Layer the mixture into the muffin cups, pressing down lightly with your hand until each is full. Pour any remaining milk mixture over the tops and bake for about 35 minutes, or until the vegetables are golden and cooked. Remove from the oven and allow to rest for 10 minutes before running a knife around the edges. Lift out using the paper strips.

1 tablespoon olive oil
1 large potato
1 large parsnip
1 small celeriac (celery root)
sea salt flakes and freshly ground pepper
2 tablespoons butter, melted
½ cup (125 ml/4 fl oz) milk

TIP Once the celeriac is peeled, the crisp, snow-white flesh can be kept pristine with a splash of lemon juice. Unlike other root veggies, celeriac makes a sloppy mash so it's best to mix it with its weight of potato to produce a satiny mash.

SIMPLE FISH STEW WITH POTATOES

Stew is such an encouraging word in a recipe title. It suggests no fuss and that regardless of how inexact the preparation, the end result will be deliciously appreciated. This is a really simple stew based on the grand seafood dish bouillabaisse (a comparatively expensive and fiddly concoction), topped up with potatoes. Poor man's bouillabaisse it may be, but it's decidedly luxurious in taste.

PREPARATION TIME: 20 minutes | **COOKING TIME:** 25 minutes | **SERVES:** 6

1 kg (2 lb 4 oz) fillets mixed firm-fleshed fish (such as warehou, mahi mahi)

2 medium onions, chopped

1 leek, white part only, chopped and rinsed

4 garlic cloves, finely chopped

2 large tomatoes, chopped

500 g (1 lb 2 oz) waxy potatoes, peeled and cut into chunks

3 long strips of orange zest

2 sprigs each of thyme, parsley and dill

1 bay leaf

about 6 cups (1.5 litres/52 fl oz) water

1 kg (2 lb 4 oz) mixed shellfish (raw prawns/shrimp, scrubbed mussels, clams, crab)

sea salt flakes and freshly ground pepper

3 tablespoons chopped parsley leaves

Cut the fish into large chunks, checking carefully for any fine bones and removing them. Put the onions, leek, garlic, tomatoes and potatoes in a large sturdy pot. Lay the fish on top with the strips of orange zest, the thyme, parsley, dill and bay leaf. Pour the water over, or enough to cover, and cook gently for 10 minutes. Add the shellfish making sure none of the mussels or clams have broken shells. Cook over a gentle heat, covered, for 5–8 minutes or until the mussels open. (Don't worry if a few are stubborn and don't open.) Use a slotted spoon to transfer the fish, shellfish and potatoes to a warm plate, and cover with foil to keep warm.

Bring the fish liquor in the pot to a rapid boil and cook until reduced by about one-third. Pour the liquor through a fine-mesh sieve, add salt and pepper to taste, and divide between serving bowls. Add the fish, shellfish and potatoes evenly to each bowl and serve sprinkled with parsley.

TIP Use your preferred combination of seafood and shellfish. You can opt for all fish and no shellfish, and you don't need to use expensive fish. Choose firm, white-fleshed sustainable fish at the best market prices.

POTATO PATTIES WITH YOGHURT AND GREEN HERB SAUCE

Serve these patties as a snack, starter or alongside grills. Although they have the appearance of small birds' nests made in a hurry, it's the taste that counts.

PREPARATION TIME: 25 minutes | **COOKING TIME:** 12 minutes | **MAKES:** 6

Coarsely grate the potatoes and carrot separately in a food processor. Squeeze any moisture from the shredded potatoes and put into a bowl with the carrot. Add salt and pepper to taste (remember, the feta will add a salty tang). Add the feta, spring onions and eggs and stir.

Heat a shallow layer of oil in a non-stick frying pan. Scoop a large spoonful of the potato mixture (it will make 6 large patties but you can make them smaller), shape into a patty and put into the hot pan. Continue with the rest of the mixture without overcrowding the pan, and avoid turning the patties too soon – you want them to form a nice crust on the underside. Carefully turn each one, and if they collapse a little, push them back into shape. When both sides are golden, lift the patties out and drain on kitchen paper.

Combine the yoghurt and herbs in a small bowl, adding a little salt if necessary. Serve the patties with a dollop of the herbed yoghurt.

250 g (9 oz) potatoes, scrubbed
1 medium carrot, scraped
sea salt flakes and freshly ground pepper
⅔ cup (100 g/3½ oz) crumbled feta
2 spring onions (green onions/scallions), finely chopped
2 eggs, beaten
¼ cup (60 ml/2 fl oz) olive oil
½ cup (130 g/4½ oz) natural yoghurt
1 tablespoon chopped mint leaves
1 tablespoon chopped parsley

TIP Choose a floury potato such as desiree to keep the moisture under control in the mixture.

POTATO SALAD WITH GREEN BEANS, PEAS AND BUTTERMILK-HERB DRESSING

The secret of any good potato salad is to use a firm, waxy potato such as kipfler or pink fir apple, as they keep their shape much better than floury types. The latter also fall apart when tossing and end up as mush because they absorb too much dressing. Adding a splash of vinegar to the boiling water helps hydrate and tenderise potatoes without them falling apart.

PREPARATION TIME: 25 minutes | **COOKING TIME:** 20 minutes | **SERVES:** 6

Put the potatoes in a large pot, cover with cold water and bring to the boil. Simmer for about 12 minutes, or until tender to the point of a thin-bladed knife. Remove with a slotted spoon leaving the water in the pot. Cool slightly, peel off the skins, if liked, and then cut into chunks and put in a bowl.

Bring the pot of water used to cook the potatoes to a simmer and drop in the green beans. Cook for about 3 minutes, then add the peas and simmer for a further 2 minutes, or until the vegetables are just tender. Drain, refresh under cold water and drain again well. Tumble the vegetables into a bowl with the potatoes.

Combine the buttermilk, sour cream, herbs, shallot, vinegar, mustard, if using, spring onion, lemon zest and radishes. Add salt and pepper to taste. Pour the dressing over the potatoes while they are still warm, and toss gently to coat. Serve at room temperature.

> **TIP** To peel or not to peel? For a more rustic appearance, leave the skins on the potatoes. However, make sure there's enough cut surface area to absorb the dressing.

6 large potatoes, scrubbed
300 g (10½ oz) green beans, cut into 3 cm (1¼ in) lengths
⅔ cup (100 g/3½ oz) garden peas
⅔ cup (170 ml/5½ fl oz) buttermilk
⅓ cup (85 g/3 oz) extra light sour cream
1 tablespoon chopped parsley
1 tablespoon chopped chives
1 tablespoon chopped mint leaves
1 tablespoon finely chopped shallot
1 tablespoon white vinegar
1 teaspoon wholegrain mustard (optional)
1 spring onion (green onion/scallion), white part only, thinly sliced
½ teaspoon finely grated lemon zest
4 medium radishes, very thinly sliced
sea salt flakes and freshly ground pepper

POTATO AND PEA CURRY

This is the type of dish where you don't have to plan ahead, as most, if not all, of the ingredients are everyday staples. As they cook, the potatoes absorb the curry flavours and help to slightly thicken the sauce.

PREPARATION TIME: 20 minutes | **COOKING TIME:** 30 minutes | **SERVES:** 6

500 g (1 lb 2 oz) potatoes, peeled
2 tablespoons vegetable oil
2 medium onions, sliced
1 small red chilli, deseeded and finely sliced
1 teaspoon finely grated fresh ginger
1 teaspoon cumin seeds
1 tablespoon mild curry powder
1½ cups (375 ml/13 fl oz) chicken stock
1 cup (155 g/5½ oz) garden peas
sea salt flakes
½ cup (130 g/4½ oz) natural yoghurt
3 tablespoons roughly chopped coriander (cilantro)

Cut the potatoes into large chunks and cook in a large pan of lightly salted water for about 4 minutes, or just until tender.

Heat the oil in a large, deep pan over medium heat and add the onions, chilli, ginger, cumin seeds and curry powder. Cook for about 10 minutes, or until the onions are golden and the mixture is fragrant.

Add the potatoes with the stock, stir a couple of times and then gently simmer for about 10 minutes, or until the potatoes are just tender (if they are overcooked, they will be mushy). Add the peas and cook for a further 5 minutes.

Whisk the yoghurt in a small bowl. Scoop out about ¼ cup of the curry sauce and stir it into the yoghurt well, then pour back into the pan with the coriander (this stage prevents curdling). Stir once to blend, remove the pan from the heat and serve with grilled meat, fish or poultry.

TIP A handful of raw cashews will fill the crunch gap.

Frozen peas can be used and added without thawing.

TRIO OF PUMPKINS ROASTED WITH CHESTNUTS AND HOT MINT SAUCE

Each of these pumpkins (squash) has its own distinctive texture and flavour. Butternut pumpkin has dense, dry, sweet-tasting flesh. Kent has a nutty flavour and yellowish-orange flesh that is soft and drier than most other varieties. And jarrahdale has full-flavoured sweet flesh. If you don't have all varieties then just use one, and don't let it be an excuse for missing out on this wonderful dish with the last-minute mint sauce drizzled over.

PREPARATION TIME: 25 minutes | **COOKING TIME:** 25 minutes | **SERVES:** 6

Preheat the oven to 200°C/400°F (fan 180°C/350°F).

With a small sharp knife, carefully make a deep vertical slit into the middle of the hollow side of each chestnut. Place them in a roasting pan and cook in the oven for 15–20 minutes, or until the slit has opened and the chestnut inside is a caramel-gold colour. Wrap them loosely in a clean tea towel to cool and then lightly squash the chestnuts with your fingers to remove the shell.

Peel the pumpkins, remove any seeds and cut into thin wedges. Place in the roasting pan, season with salt and pepper, and toss with the oil, honey and chestnuts. Reduce the oven temperature to 180°C/350°F (fan 160°C/315°F) and roast for 20 minutes, or until the pumpkin is caramelised and tender.

To make the mint sauce, heat the oil in a small pan over medium heat and add the garlic. Fry for a couple of minutes or until the garlic is golden brown. Add half the mint with the cumin seeds and fry for a further minute. Carefully add the vinegar (it may spatter when it comes into contact with the hot oil) and simmer for just 20 seconds, then remove the pan from the heat. Stir in the remaining mint, and salt and pepper to taste. Lightly toss the roasted pumpkins and chestnuts and serve with the hot mint sauce spooned over.

18 fresh chestnuts
300 g (10½ oz) butternut pumpkin (squash)
300 g (10½ oz) kent pumpkin
300 g (10½ oz) jarrahdale pumpkin
sea salt flakes and freshly ground pepper
¼ cup (60 ml/2 fl oz) olive oil
¼ cup (60 ml/2 fl oz) honey

MINT SAUCE
¼ cup (60 ml/2 fl oz) olive oil
2 garlic cloves, finely chopped
1 handful mint leaves, finely chopped
1 teaspoon cumin seeds
2 tablespoons red wine vinegar

ROASTED PUMPKIN SOUP WITH HARISSA

We know how impossibly sweet pumpkin becomes when roasted. We also know that harissa is a fiery chilli spice paste indispensable in North African cooking. Introduce one to the other with mild-mannered restorative chicken stock and you have a soup, whose recipe you will, understandably, refuse to share.

PREPARATION TIME: 15 minutes | **COOKING TIME:** 40 minutes | **SERVES:** 6

1 kg (2 lb 4 oz) butternut pumpkin (squash)
4 large roma (plum) tomatoes, halved
1 medium onion, peeled and thickly sliced
4–5 garlic cloves, peeled
4 rosemary sprigs
⅓ cup (80 ml/2½ fl oz) olive oil
6 cups (1.5 litres/52 fl oz) vegetable or chicken stock
1 tablespoon harissa paste
sea salt flakes and freshly ground pepper
2 tablespoons extra light sour cream

Preheat the oven to 200°C/400°F (fan 180°C/350°F). Line a baking tray with baking paper.

Peel the pumpkin, roughly cut into chunks and arrange on the baking tray with the tomatoes, onion, garlic cloves and rosemary sprigs. Drizzle with the oil and roast for 30–35 minutes, or until the pumpkin is tender and just starting to blister.

Remove the rosemary sprigs and then tip everything into a blender or food processor, and add the stock and harissa paste (if you prefer a more mouth-puckering taste, add more harissa, but only a little at a time). The mixture may be too much for the blender, so you may need to work in batches. Blitz until smooth and add salt and pepper to taste. Pour the soup into a pot and bring to a gentle simmer, adding more stock if you want a thinner consistency. Swirl in the sour cream and serve.

TIP The sour cream can be left out or replaced with natural yoghurt.

CHOPPED SALAD OF SWEETCORN, SOYA BEANS AND QUINOA WITH LEMON-BASIL DRESSING

Salad eaters can be divided into two groups: chopped devotees who claim in every bite you can get a little bit of everything, and tossed salad traditionalists who sniffily suggest chopped is the lazy approach to salad, turning all those small chunks into a homogenous gloop. In this combo, no gloop – the chopped salad eaters win out.

PREPARATION TIME: 25 minutes | **COOKING TIME:** 15 minutes | **SERVES:** 8

1 cup (250ml/9 fl oz) water

⅓ cup (65 g/2¼ oz) quinoa, rinsed

1 cup (200 g/7 oz) sweetcorn kernels

1 cup (170 g/6 oz) tinned black beans, drained and rinsed

1 cup (170 g/6 oz) tinned red kidney beans, drained and rinsed

1½ cups (250 g/9 oz) shelled fresh soya beans (edamame)

1 red capsicum (pepper), deseeded and chopped

1 large handful coriander (cilantro) leaves, chopped

6 spring onions (green onions/ scallions), sliced

4 garlic cloves, crushed

½ cup (125 ml/4 fl oz) lemon juice

¼ cup (60 ml/2 fl oz) salt-reduced soy sauce

2 tablespoons Dijon mustard

1 handful basil leaves, roughly chopped

2 tablespoons olive oil

Put the water and quinoa in a pot and bring to the boil over medium–high heat. Reduce the heat to low, cover and simmer for about 15 minutes, or until the quinoa is tender. Drain thoroughly.

Put the quinoa, corn, well-drained black and red beans, soya beans, capsicum, coriander and spring onions in a large bowl. Whisk together the garlic, lemon juice, soy sauce, mustard and oil in a bowl. Pour over the salad and toss lightly. Cover and chill for an hour before serving. This is also lovely served with grilled fish, chicken or burgers.

TIP Tinned beans can have a tremendous amount of salt and must be well rinsed in cold water before using. Although rinsing helps, it won't eliminate the salt cooked into the beans. If possible, buy the salt-reduced variety.

CHICKEN AND CORN SOUP WITH TOASTED TORTILLA AND AVOCADO

Much of the depth of flavour in this soup comes from the first step of gently cooking the veggies in oil. Once there's a slight sizzle, put the lid on the pan to keep the aromatic moisture in while the veggies soften.

PREPARATION TIME: 25 minutes | **COOKING TIME:** 25 minutes | **SERVES:** 8

Heat the oil in a large pot, and when hot add the onion, garlic, corn, zucchini and carrot. Cook gently for about 8 minutes or until the vegetables soften and then add the stock, chickpeas and salt to taste. Cover and simmer for 15 minutes.

Shred the chicken and stir it through the hot soup with the chilli and half of the coriander. Lightly toast the tortillas and cut them into fine strips.

Ladle the soup into serving bowls, garnish with a few avocado slices, tortilla strips and the remaining coriander. Serve with lime wedges for squeezing over the soup.

TIP Poach the chicken the day before you want to make this and use the stock for the soup.

2 tablespoons olive oil

1 medium onion, finely chopped

2 garlic cloves, crushed

2 medium corncobs, husks removed and kernels scraped

1 medium zucchini (courgette), finely diced

1 medium carrot, finely diced

10 cups (2.5 litres/85 fl oz) chicken stock

2½ cups (400 g/14 oz) tin chickpeas, drained and rinsed

sea salt flakes

2 medium (about 320 g/11¼ oz) boneless, skinless chicken breasts, poached

1 small red chilli, finely chopped

2 handfuls coriander (cilantro) leaves, coarsely chopped

3 large tortillas

1 ripe avocado, destoned and sliced

1 small lime, cut into thin wedges

ROASTED CORN WITH CHILLI AND LIME PEANUT BUTTER

Although a simple pleasure, devouring corn on the cob is often best done when alone – it's not one of those things to invite spectators with all those delicious squirty kernels. Corn will never taste the same again (and probably peanut butter also) once you've introduced them to each other with the intervention of a surprising but pleasant jolt of chilli and cumin heat. One caveat – it must be crunchy peanut butter, nothing else will do.

PREPARATION TIME: 15 minutes | **COOKING TIME:** 25 minutes | **SERVES:** 6

Preheat the oven to 200°C/400°F (fan 180°C/350°F).

Pull back the cornhusks without breaking them and remove the silky strands. Soak the corncobs in a bowl of cold water for 10 minutes.

In a separate bowl, combine the chillies, lime zest, peanut butter, garlic and cumin and smear generously over the drained corncobs. Rewrap the corn husks around the cobs and secure them with string if necessary. Arrange the cobs in a roasting pan and bake for 15–20 minutes, turning a couple of times until the corn is tender and the husks are scorched.

Serve with wedges of the limes used for zesting.

6 corncobs with husks
2 small red chillies, deseeded and finely chopped
grated zest of 2 plump limes
⅔ cup (185 g/6 oz) crunchy peanut butter, softened
1 garlic clove, crushed
1 teaspoon ground cumin

TIP Fresh corncobs quickly lose their sweetness if left at room temperature for too long. It's important to keep them refrigerated until just before you are ready to use them.

PAN-ROASTED SWEET POTATO AND BEETROOT WITH GRAPEFRUIT GLAZE

Aptly named, sweet potatoes turn remarkably sweet as they cook and caramelise. Roasted beetroot (beets) give colour contrast to the sweet potato and accentuate their candy-sweetness and intense earthiness. The sharp, sweet-sour glaze adds significantly to your vitamin P – pleasure that is. Lemon, blood orange or pomelo can be used instead of grapefruit, as you wish.

PREPARATION TIME: 15 minutes | **COOKING TIME:** 35 minutes | **SERVES:** 6

6 small beetroot (beets)
1 medium orange-fleshed sweet potato
2 medium red onions
⅓ cup (80 ml/2½ fl oz) balsamic
    vinegar
¼ cup (60 ml/2 fl oz) olive oil
1 tablespoon finely grated grapefruit
    zest
¼ cup (60 ml/2 fl oz) grapefruit juice
2 tablespoons currants
2 tablespoons toasted pine nuts

Preheat the oven to 200°C/400°F (fan 180°C/350°F).

Bring a large pot of water to the boil and blanch the beetroot for 10 minutes. Drain in a colander and when cool enough to handle, peel and halve. Peel the sweet potato and cut into chunks the size of the beetroot pieces. Slice the onion into thick wedges and put into a roasting pan with the beetroot, sweet potato, balsamic vinegar, oil, and grapefruit zest and juice.

Tumble everything together and roast for about 25–30 minutes, or until the vegetables are crisp-tender and slightly caramelised. Remove from the oven and sprinkle over the currants and pine nuts. Give the pan a few quick sharp tosses and serve.

TIP Roasting is one of the easiest and tastiest ways to cook autumn and winter veggies – simply toss everything with oil, throw in a baking dish and cook in a hot oven. The greater the exposed surface area of the veggies, the crisper they'll become.

SWEET POTATO, QUINOA, SPINACH AND RED LENTIL BURGERS WITH TAHINI-MINT YOGHURT

Mention burgers and barbecues, and suddenly vegetables seem to get sidelined. These burgers are anything but 'mock meat'. The sweet potatoes and slight crunch of lentils and quinoa give a heftier, satisfying texture to the burgers. If you prefer crispy-crusted burgers, lightly toss the patties in cornmeal (polenta) before cooking.

PREPARATION TIME: 20 minutes | **COOKING TIME:** 45 minutes | **MAKES:** 12

⅓ cup (60 g/2 oz) quinoa, rinsed

⅓ cup (70 g/2½ oz) red lentils, rinsed

1⅔ cups (420 ml/14½ fl oz) water

2 medium orange-fleshed sweet potatoes, cooked and mashed

3 cups (150 g/5½ oz) tightly packed chopped spinach

3 tablespoons chopped mint

2 tablespoons chopped chives

1 teaspoon ground cumin

sea salt flakes and freshly ground pepper

TAHINI-MINT YOGHURT

⅔ cup (170 g/6 oz) natural yoghurt

1 tablespoon tahini

½ teaspoon ground cumin

2 tablespoons chopped mint

2 tablespoons lemon juice

Preheat the oven to 200°C/400°F (fan 180°C/350°F). Line a baking tray with baking paper.

Put the quinoa, lentils and water and in a pan and bring to the boil over high heat. Reduce the heat to medium–low and simmer, covered, for about 12 minutes or until the quinoa and lentils are just tender. Drain well.

Put the sweet potato in a bowl with the spinach, quinoa, lentils, mint, chives and cumin. Season with salt and pepper to taste, and mix well. Scoop out about ⅓ cup of the mixture and, with wet hands, form into a ball. Repeat with the remaining mixture. Place on the baking tray and flatten slightly into patties. If you have time (and to prevent the patties from breaking up), refrigerate, uncovered, for about 1 hour before cooking.

Bake for 30 minutes, or until the patties are crisp and golden.

In a bowl, combine the yoghurt, tahini, cumin, mint and lemon juice, and spoon over the patties to serve.

FRESH TOMATO SAUCE FOR PASTA

Perfectly ripe red tomatoes are all soft juicy flesh and a balance of sweet, sour and richly savoury – perfect for a straight-up pasta sauce. Make a batch and freeze what you don't use for up to a month, but leave out the second addition of basil until you reheat the sauce.

PREPARATION TIME: 20 minutes | **COOKING TIME:** 20 minutes | **SERVES:** 6

Cut a small cross in the bottom of each tomato and drop them into a pot of rapidly simmering water for about 1 minute, or until the skin starts to peel. Drain and put the tomatoes in iced cold water. Using a small sharp knife, peel off the skins and cut in half. Remove the core and then use your fingertips to scoop out most of the seeds. Coarsely chop the tomatoes.

Heat the oil in a frying pan, add the onion and cook until soft and not coloured. Add the garlic and cook for 1–2 minutes, or until fragrant. Tip in the tomatoes, salt and pepper to taste and half the basil. Simmer for about 15 minutes or until the sauce has thickened to a soft ploppy consistency. Stir in the remaining basil and serve over cooked pasta. This sauce is also delicious as an accompaniment to grilled fish.

1.25 kg (2 lb 12 oz) ripe tomatoes
⅓ cup (80 ml/2½ fl oz) olive oil
1 medium onion, finely chopped
2 garlic cloves, finely chopped
sea salt flakes and freshly ground
    pepper
1 handful basil leaves

TIP Some food scientists claim that the seeds in the tomato jelly (the squidgy insides) have three times more flavour compounds (glutamates) than the flesh, so when you deseed tomatoes you're actually throwing out most of the flavour. The texture may be smoother, but it may not be as tasty. Our mothers and grandmothers didn't worry about seeds. You be the judge.

TOMATO AND FIG SALAD WITH BURRATA AND DATE-MINT DRESSING

All the tantalising tastes and colours of summer's best come together in this sublime salad with tomatoes and figs. The witlof – add a few small cos (romaine) leaves if you wish – is the crunchy base for the tomatoes, crowned with the cooling taste of mint to balance the rich creamy cheese. If your tomatoes are all different sizes, start by slicing the big ones into rounds, smaller ones into wedges and the cherry and grape varieties in half.

PREPARATION TIME: 25 minutes | **SERVES:** 6

To make the dressing, put the shallot, date syrup, lemon juice, oil with salt and pepper to taste, in a bowl. Give it a couple of whisks and then stir in the mint.

Arrange the witlof leaves on a platter. Cut the tomatoes into chunks and figs into quarters or both roughly the same size – and arrange casually over the witlof. Place the burrata in the centre of the platter. Give the dressing a good stir, spoon over the salad and scatter with the thyme.

TIP Burrata is a cow's milk cheese made with mozzarella curds and fresh cream. It has a very creamy texture and a sweet flavour. If you prefer, swap the burrata for fresh mozzarella, which if large can be torn into bite-size pieces. If date syrup is not on hand, blitz pitted medjool dates with a few splashes of water (enough for the consistency you want) in a blender. Begin on a low speed to allow the dates to break up, then increase to high and blitz until smooth, adding lemon juice to taste.

DATE-MINT DRESSING
1 shallot, very finely chopped
¼ cup (60 ml/2 fl oz) date syrup
juice of 1 plump lemon
¼ cup (60 ml/2 fl oz) extra virgin olive oil
sea salt flakes and freshly ground pepper
1 handful mint leaves, finely shredded

1 witlof (chicory), leaves separated
6 medium heirloom tomatoes
6 large fresh figs
1 burrata
2 teaspoons finely chopped lemon thyme

GREEN TOMATOES WITH A CHOPPED OLIVE AND HERB SAUCE

Green tomatoes are the end-of-season spoils when frosty weather arrives and vines shrivel leaving the green fruit. Their flavour is significantly different from fully ripened tomatoes. They are moist, not juicy, and sour to the point of astringency. We have a waste-not-want-not approach to pretty much everything nature delivers, and this scrumptious combination will convince you it's worth it.

PREPARATION TIME: 20 minutes | **SERVES:** 6

1 kg (2 lb 4 oz) firm green tomatoes
¼ cup (60 ml/2 fl oz) extra virgin
   olive oil
1 large shallot, finely chopped
3 anchovy fillets in olive oil, finely
   chopped (optional)
10 large pitted black olives, finely
   chopped
1 handful each mint leaves and
   parsley, roughly chopped
2 teaspoons finely chopped marjoram
sea salt flakes and freshly ground
   pepper
½ cup (70 g/2¼ oz) chopped raw
   almonds, lightly toasted

Slice the tomatoes thinly and arrange on a plate. Put the oil, shallot, anchovies, olives, mint, parsley, marjoram with salt and pepper to taste, in a bowl. Mix well and add to the tomatoes, gently turning the tomatoes through the herb mixture. Just before serving, sprinkle over the toasted almonds.

TIP Excess green tomatoes can be washed, cored and frozen to use in a pasta sauce. They will ripen eventually on the bench but the flavour will have slightly diminished.

SALMON CURRY WITH LYCHEES AND TOMATOES

Juicy and robust, with a gelatinous yet crisp creamy texture, fresh lychees are the key ingredient in this fragrant curry with luscious ripe tomatoes. Having just the right balance of not too sweet and not too tart, with a glorious floral-musky fragrance, they offset the richness of salmon and won't be bullied by the spices.

PREPARATION TIME: 15 minutes | **COOKING TIME:** 15 minutes | **SERVES:** 6

Cut the salmon into large chunks and put into a bowl. Add the salt flakes and turmeric and gently toss to coat the fish. Cover and refrigerate for 1–6 hours.

In a large pot combine the water, curry paste, coriander and cumin. Add the tomatoes, bring to the boil, then simmer gently for 5 minutes. Arrange the fish pieces in a single layer in the pot, cover and gently simmer for 5 minutes. Add the lychees and simmer for a further 2 minutes, just to heat through.

TIP This curry is lovely served with steamed brown basmati rice.

900 g (2 lb) thick skinless salmon fillet
½ teaspoon sea salt flakes
2 teaspoons ground turmeric
1½ cups (375 ml/13 fl oz) water
2 tablespoons Indian red curry paste
1 tablespoon ground coriander
2 teaspoons ground cumin
175 g (6 oz) ripe tomatoes, finely chopped
18 fresh lychees, peeled and deseeded

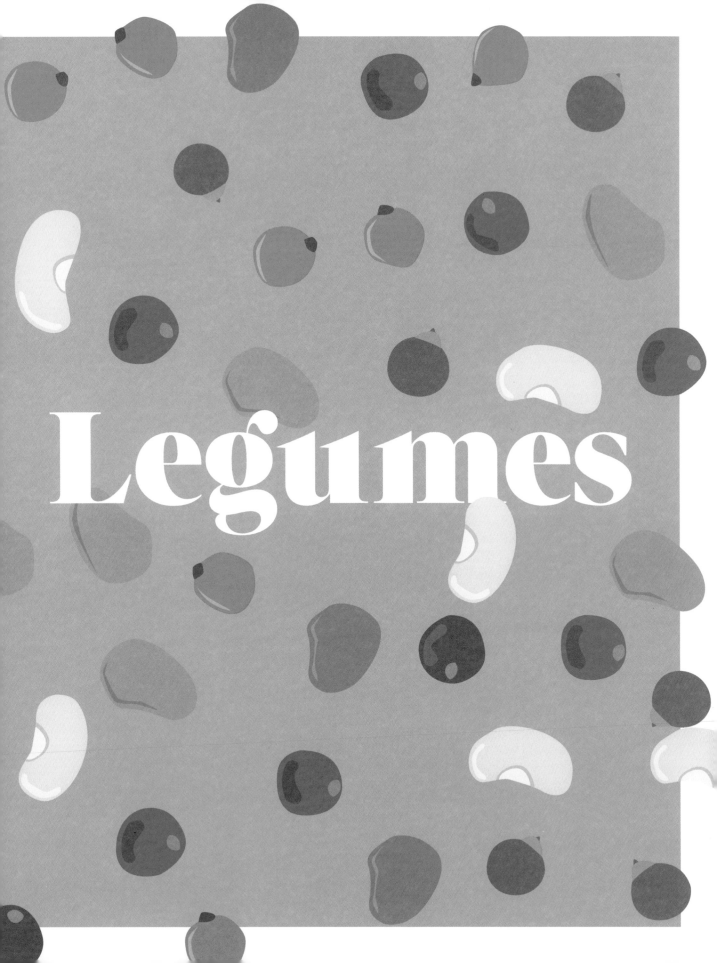

Legumes

Legumes belong in the Fabaceae family and include beans, peas and lentils as well as many related plants, like peanuts, and a few you probably didn't know were legumes, such as alfalfa, clover and lupins. When dried, beans, peas and lentils have a long shelf life. It's as if they don't have a use-by date. Archaeologists have found perfectly preserved seeds in Peru and Mexico dating back about 4000 years (they didn't eat them, they put them in a museum).

Filling bellies, tasting good and keeping for a long time, this family hits the trifecta. So it was only natural that people would want to grow beans, peas, chickpeas and lentils. Millennia ago, our forebears planted out their seeds in the Old World and the New – where they also came up with a multi-cropping system, growing beans along with maize and winter squash in their fields. This both boosted plant productivity and enriched the soil.

Some beans don't have to be cultivated. They grow on trees. Carob and mesquite pods are ripe for the picking. Mesquite, nowadays sold as a highly priced specialty organic flour, was a staple for North America's desert Apache, Pima, Cahuilla, Maricopa, Yuma, Yavapai, Mohave, Hualapai, and Hopi tribes.

Plant scientist Peter Felker tells us in *Mesquite Flour: New Life for an Ancient Staple* that: 'Many of the desert Cahuilla Indians of California stored the mesquite beans intact on the roofs of their dwellings in large elevated baskets woven of arrow weed or willow twigs and sealed with mud. The largest wicker baskets held ten to fifteen bushels each, a quantity sufficient to feed a family of six to ten people for a year. Some Maricopa Indians processed the pods before storage. Maricopa women pounded the pods into meal in a cottonwood or mesquite mortar, sifted the meal into fine and coarse grinds, and then poured the fine meal into an elliptical hole in the ground. The very hard seeds and the surrounding endocarp were usually discarded, as they were too difficult to grind and represented only about 10 per cent of each pod. Water was sprinkled onto the meal, layer by layer, a process that hardened the ground meal with its high sugar content into a firm, dry cake. The next day the women would remove the cakes from the hole. These cakes served as the long-term-storage form of the pods. Pieces were broken off and used for daily food preparation; they also served as dry rations for men going out to hunt.'

The bean family is a big, cosmopolitan family found on every continent except Antarctica. Although diverse – encompassing trees, shrubs, vines and herbs; food plants and flowering plants – it's united by those familiar pods, typically with one to twelve seeds.

What we call 'bean', the Romans called 'faba', and both words share a common ancestor in the Indo-European bhabh or bhabha, which means 'swollen' or 'swelling'. We think whoever had the naming rights was spot on – beans are very generous providers, swelling up in the cooking pan with one cup of dried beans giving us two or three cups of cooked beans to serve up. Not only do beans make great partners, they bulk things out, thicken, add texture and colour, absorb flavours, and are nourishing, frugal extenders making a little go a very long way. It's no wonder they appear in classic dishes around the world.

They also play a key role in fasting. The traditional Greek diet was influenced by the meatless-meals edict over Easter, Christmas, the Assumption of Mary and on Wednesday and Friday every week. That's around 200 days a year when only beans, fruit, vegetables, nuts and bread can be consumed. This doesn't sound like hardship. We think we could live very happily on such fare (accompanied by the Greek island that goes with it).

PROTEIN POWER

Beans, peas, chickpeas and lentils are packed with good things for good health, including slowly digested carbs, fibre, vitamins and minerals. What makes them stand out from the plant-food crowd is their protein – typically around 8–10 grams per ½ cup (100 g/3½ oz) cooked dried beans, peas or lentils (twice that of grains). If you don't want to, you don't need to eat meat, chicken and fish (or dairy) to top up your protein tank. However, you do need to make sure you're eating a variety of plant foods every day (beans, whole grains, nuts and seeds) to get the essential amino acids you need.

WIND POWER

Beans are renowned for farts (and jokes), and the main culprits are large indigestible sugars (raffinose, stachyose and verbascose), which zip through the digestive system and arrive in the large bowel intact, where the resident healthy bacteria ferment them and feast. That embarrassing gas is a natural outcome.

You may well have discovered that some beans are windier than others and that some people suffer more than others. Certainly eating small amounts regularly helps the body acclimatise. As the indigestible sugars responsible are water soluble, rinsing them several times before soaking and cooking helps wash the sugars away, and the quick, hot-soak method (page 86) leaches out the sugars more effectively than regular soaking.

A POT OF BEANS

There's a welcome place for canned convenience for quick meals, but don't shy away from buying dried beans and cooking them. It does take a bit of time and forethought.

THE FIXER

Our farming forebears didn't know about nitrogen-fixing bacteria, but they did know that growing beans, peas and lentils put food on the table and helped other crops grow and thrive. Here's how they do it. Plants need nitrogen to grow, make chlorophyll for photosynthesis and produce the flowers, fruits and seeds for new plants. Over thousands (probably millions) of years, beans, peas, lentils and other legumes have developed a special relationship with *Rhizobium* bacteria. These bacteria make themselves at home in root nodules, harvest nitrogen from the atmosphere (the plants can't) and convert it into a form of nitrogen that the plants can make use of. When legumes are dug in, they decay into the soil releasing a form of nitrogen that other plants can draw on. That's why they're renowned as 'nitrogen-fixing plants', though Rhizobium bacteria do all the work.

But you don't have to stand around stirring; they just get on with it and come out soft and intact. The cooking water doubles as an aromatic stock for soups and stews – if you can handle the indigestible sugars.

Regular bean cookers and eaters suggest cooking up a batch and freezing some for another time, which is eminently sensible. The only trouble with preparing a large batch of beans is fermentation, particularly if you use the quick, hot-soak method. If you leave them in the fridge for too long they become rather whiffy and that's when you need to bin them.

PREPARATION AND COOKING

CLEAN Pick through the dried beans, peas and lentils, discarding any discoloured or shrivelled ones and foreign matter such as tiny stones.

RINSE Always rinse them several times and then swirl them around in a bowl of cold water, discarding any floaters.

SOAK With the exception of split peas and lentils, all other legumes need soaking before cooking, one benefit being to speed up cooking time. Beans and peas will double or triple in size depending on which soaking method you choose, so it's important to use a large enough vessel.

COLD SOAK Pour room temperature water over the beans to cover and soak for 8 hours or overnight. (In particular, chickpeas have a better flavour if soaked overnight.) Discard the soaking water and rinse the beans in fresh cool water. They will appear wrinkled after soaking and will fully hydrate during cooking.

QUICK, HOT SOAK The warmer the water the faster the beans absorb it. This method reduces cooking time and produces consistently tender legumes. Put them in a large saucepan and add 4 cups (1 litre/35 fl oz) of water for every 1 cup of beans. Bring to the boil, reduce the heat and gently simmer for 10 minutes. Remove the pan from the heat, cover and let stand for 1 hour. Drain and rinse with fresh cool water before cooking.

COOKING ON THE STOVETOP

For each 1 cup of legumes allow 3–4 cups (750 ml–1 litre/25½–35 fl oz) of water or stock. In general, for every 1 cup dried legumes you should get 2–2½ cups of cooked legumes. The cooking time will depend on the type.

- Keep the cooking water at a gentle simmer to prevent split skins.
- Add warm water periodically during cooking to keep the beans covered.
- Stir the beans occasionally to prevent sticking.
- They are done when they are tender, but not mushy. Check by either biting one for tenderness or pressing between your thumb and forefinger, when it will break up easily.
- Drain immediately once the beans reach the desired tenderness to stop the cooking process and prevent overcooking.
- Hold the seasonings until the end of cooking. Acidic ingredients such as lemon juice, vinegar, wine or tomato sauce prevent softening, so don't add them until the beans are tender.

COOKING IN THE PRESSURE COOKER

Many people have a thing about using pressure cookers, but they are a real time saver with beans and give a great result. When using a pressure cooker, use about 2½ cups of water (625 ml/21½ fl oz) per 1 cup of soaked beans and cook for about 20 minutes (following the manufacturer's instructions). Make sure the pressure cooker is no more than half full of ingredients, including the cooking liquid.

WHAT BEAN IS THAT?

THE AMERICAS

Green bean, French bean, haricot bean, kidney bean, navy bean, pinto bean, black bean, borlotti bean, cannelloni bean, snap or string bean, frijoles (*Phaseolus vulgaris*)

Lima bean, butter bean, Madagascar bean (*Phaseolus lunatus*)

Runner bean (*Phaseolus coccineus*)

Lupin (tarwi) (*Lupinus mutabilis*)

AFRICA

Black-eyed pea, cowpea, yard-long bean (*Vigna unguiculata*)

EUROPE AND SOUTH-WEST ASIA

Chickpea, garbanzo bean, Bengal gram (*Cicer arietinum*)

Lentil (*Lens culinaris*)

Pea (*Pisum sativum*)

Broad bean, fava bean (*Vicia faba*)

Peanut, groundnut (*Arachis hypogaea*)

Lupin, white, yellow and sweet (*Lupinus albus, L. luteus, L. angustifolius*)

INDIA AND EAST ASIA

Soya beans (*Glycine max*)

Black gram, urd, woolly pyrol (*Vigna mungo*)

Mung bean, green gram, golden gram (*Vigna radiata*)

Adzuki bean (*Vigna angularis*)

Pigeon pea, red gram, Congo pea (*Cajanus cajun*)

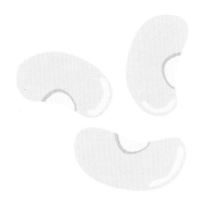

BEANS

Beans will be a big part of your life if you took Michael Pollan's tip to 'eat food, not too much, mostly plants' to heart. Sprouts, pods, fresh and dried, there's a tasty bean for all seasons and every meal. In our book, dried beans are in the five-star department, combining fibre and slowly digested carbs with plenty of protein and protective vitamins, minerals and phytonutrients. Take a tip for living longer from people who've lived the longest says *Blue Zones* author Dan Buettner: 'people who eat plenty of beans will be full of beans for longer with lower rates of heart disease and type 2 diabetes'. Typically, these people eat at least a cup of beans, peas, chickpeas or lentils a day. To help you get started and make beans more a centrepiece than sideshow, we've come up with a range of recipes showcasing them in soups, salads and sides, and leftovers. As for breakfast, baked beans on grainy toast ticks all the boxes.

WHAT TO LOOK FOR

For dried beans, look for smooth unwrinkled beans and check the best-before or use-by date; they lose moisture as they age, making them more time-consuming to cook. If you like to buy beans in bulk, make sure your provider has a good turnover.

When it comes to tinned beans, check the label and choose the reduced-salt ones if you can. Make sure you rinse and drain them well before using.

HOW TO STORE THEM

Dried beans should be stored in a resealable packet or airtight container in a cool, dry place. Tinned beans, once opened, should be stored in a non-metallic container in the fridge and used within 2–3 days.

WHAT'S IN THEM?

Half a cup (about 100 g/3½ oz) of cooked cannellini beans has about 365 kilojoules (87 calories), 7 g protein, 0 g fat, 12 g carbs (1 g sugars, 11 g starches), 6 g fibre, 2 mg sodium, 336 mg potassium, and a low GI (31) and GL (4).

WHAT ELSE?

Fresh soya beans (edamame) can be hard to find in the produce store. Check the freezer cabinet for snap-frozen edamame pods in large supermarkets and Asian produce stores.

HERO RECIPES

Glazed ginger soya beans (page 94)
Tuna, egg and seasonal vegetables with basil-lemon dressing (page 96)
Roasted snapper fillets with fennel and citrus on white bean purée (page 97)
Salmon, white bean and dill fishcakes (page 98)
Baked red kidney and butter bean ragout (page 100)

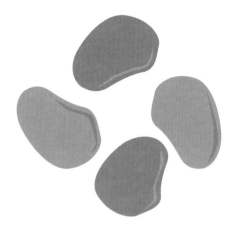

BROAD BEANS

The gentle, seasonal pleasure of podding beans and shelling peas seems to have been almost entirely replaced by the year-round convenience of frozen packets. It's perfectly understandable why, but it's rather a pity. Sitting at the kitchen table podding a pile of plump beans is one of those meditative chores providing something we all say we crave – time out. With mature broad beans, you could say we get extra 'time out'. Because the outer greyish skin is rather chewy, it pays to 'double pod', leaving behind the inner green bean.

WHAT TO LOOK FOR

Fresh broad beans make an all too brief appearance in the produce aisles and farmers' markets in spring. The good news is that snap-frozen podded broad beans are available all year round. Check the use-buy or best-before date.

HOW TO STORE THEM

Fresh broad beans are best eaten within a few days of picking. They can be stored in the refrigerator in a plastic bag for up to a week.

WHAT'S IN THEM?

Half a cup (about 95 g/3¼ oz) of podded and peeled broad beans has about 130 kilojoules (31 calories), 4 g protein, 0 g fat, 1 g carbs (0.5 g sugars, 0.5 g starches), 4 g fibre, 2 mg sodium, 138 mg potassium, and a moderate GI (63) and low GL (1).

WHAT ELSE?

Picked very young and tender straight from the vine, broad beans are a treat fresh or lightly cooked, just like regular runner beans. No podding necessary.

Broad beans are called fava in many parts of the world (from the Latin *faba,* which means bean, because those were the beans they had in their kitchens and gardens). In Greek cooking, fava refers to dried yellow split peas, and that's what you will need to have on hand to whip up a classic fava spread.

HERO RECIPES

Lamb and broad bean stew with silverbeet (page 101)
Spiced chickpea and broad bean soup (page 103)

CHICKPEAS

This large, wrinkled pea goes by numerous names on supermarket shelves – ceci, garbanzo beans, Bengal gram and chana dal depending on country of origin. Our word 'chickpea', like the Italian *ceci*, goes back to *cicer* (pronounced kiker), Latin for this particular pea and not the smaller round green one (*pisum*). Along with those regular peas, chickpeas have been a basic ingredient since the first farmers in the Fertile Crescent planted them around 10,000 years ago. They have had a long run as a pantry staple since those days without any need for marketing campaigns, because whole or split they have proven themselves one of the most versatile beans, making a meal of soups, and vegetable- or grain-based dishes. Toss them into a salad and a side dish becomes something satisfying, or roast them for a crunchy snack. Tinned chickpeas are a satisfactory substitute for home-cooked in many recipes, but for some traditional dishes like falafel, it's best to start from scratch with an overnight soak.

WHAT TO LOOK FOR

With dried chickpeas, you want those with a good colour. Check the best-before or use-by date on the pack, as they lose moisture as they age and take longer to cook. If you like to buy in bulk, make sure your provider has a good turnover. For tinned chickpeas, opt for reduced-salt varieties and rinse and drain well.

HOW TO STORE THEM

Dried chickpeas should be stored in a resealable packet or airtight container in a cool, dry place. Refrigerate tinned chickpeas in a non-metallic container and use within 2–3 days after opening.

WHAT'S IN THEM?

Half a cup (about 85 g/3 oz) of cooked chickpeas has about 490 kilojoules (117 calories), 7 g protein, 2 g fat, 14 g carbs (1 g sugars, 13 g starches), 5 g fibre, 9 mg sodium, 171 mg potassium, and a low GI (39) and GL (5).

WHAT ELSE?

Ever get confused about dal? In Indian cooking, dal (or dhal) describes both a dish (a soup or stew made with dried beans, peas or lentils) and an ingredient – split (and often hulled) beans, peas and lentils. Masoor dal, for example, is split red lentils; chana (or channa) dal, split chickpeas (also known as Bengal gram); and mung dal, split mung beans.

HERO RECIPES

Spiced chickpea and broad bean soup (page 103)
Fresh green herb hummus (page 104)
Smoked paprika, potato and chickpea salad (page 107)
Sumac-roasted chicken with chickpeas, barley and fruit stuffing (page 108)

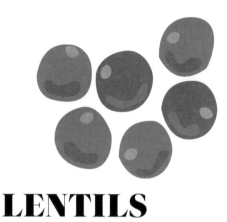

LENTILS

It wasn't long ago that you would hardly ever see a lentil dish on a menu. Now they are everywhere, and we like to think spruiking the benefits of healthy low-GI eating played a part in their rise in the ranks. Of course, lentils have other positives such as no soaking, and being fast cooking, versatile, good combiners, great flavour absorbers, and generally kinder to the digestive system than other members of the bean family. Don't default to rice or pasta for a speedy meal, try nutty-tasting lentils in soups, salads, sides, patties, pilafs and more.

WHAT TO LOOK FOR

Which lentil depends on what you plan to cook. Here's a quick guide:

- **Brown lentils:** The most common variety of lentil, ranging in colour from khaki to dark brown with a mild, earthy flavour. They retain their shape but will go mushy if overcooked. Best for soups, salads, casseroles and stuffing.
- **Green (puy) lentils:** Considered superior in taste and quality, these grey–green lentils have a robust, somewhat peppery flavour. They retain their shape and firm texture after cooking, and are best for cold or warm salads.
- **Red split lentils:** The sweetest and nuttiest of the lentils, these cook to a rich purée, making them perfect for dals, curries, soups and thickening casseroles.

- **Yellow lentils:** Similar to red split lentils, they are great for adding colour and texture to dishes.

With dried lentils, check the best-before or use-by date on the pack, as they take longer to cook if they are old. If you buy in bulk, make sure your provider has a good turnover. For tinned lentils, opt for reduced-salt varieties if you can, and rinse and drain well.

HOW TO STORE THEM

Dried lentils should be stored in a resealable packet or airtight container in a cool, dry place.

Refrigerate tinned lentils after opening in a non-metallic container and use within 2–3 days.

WHAT'S IN THEM?

Half a cup (about 90 g/3¼ oz) of cooked red lentils has about 420 kilojoules (100 calories), 7 g protein, 0 g fat, 15 g carbs (0.5 g sugars, 14.5 g starches), 2 g fibre, 1 mg sodium, 177 mg potassium, and a low GI (25) and GL (2).

WHAT ELSE?

Lentils will have varied cooking times depending on their variety and age, but as a rough guide to cooking times:

- brown and green lentils: 20–35 minutes
- yellow and red split lentils: 10–20 minutes.

Do not add salt or acid (vinegar, lemon, tomato) to lentils at the beginning of cooking or they won't soften.

Note that some manufacturers don't recommend cooking lentils in a pressure cooker, so it's best to check the instruction manual.

HERO RECIPES

Spiced lentil with roasted vegetables (page 109)
Baked fish with lentils, tomatoes and olives (page 111)

PEAS

Eating the youngest, most tender peas shelled straight after picking is a truly sweet experience. Peas are easy to grow and in the right spot and with the appropriate TLC are generous providers from late spring through the summer months. You keep picking, they keep providing. Most of us outsource the growing and shelling and buy frozen peas, which are just as nourishing. Using frozen means we can make the most of peas all-year round as a side dish or in soups, salads, stir-fries, fritters, frittatas, rice dishes and more. As for dried peas (whole or split), if you were in the line-up for a blind taste test, you would find it hard to imagine this starchy staple is a relative of that sweet pea. But they are one and the same family and have been providing stick-to-the-ribs pottages before the deliciously green, pick-and-eat 'garden' pea was even a twinkle in a gardener's eye. Don't just stick to pea and ham soup, they make delicious patties, and are a great addition to salads, stews and curries.

WHAT TO LOOK FOR

When it comes to fresh, bright pea-green unwrinkled pods in season with no splits or blemishes is what you want. Avoid prepacked trays of shelled peas.

Snap frozen peas are a great standby to have in the freezer year round and are just as nutritious. Check the use-by or best-before date.

Dried whole and split peas are available, but split peas are perhaps more common in recipes. Green split peas tend to have a slightly earthier taste than the milder yellow. Check the use-by or best-before date on the pack as dried peas lose moisture as they age and will take longer to cook.

HOW TO STORE THEM

Fresh peas in the pod are best the day you buy (or pick) them. They will keep in a plastic bag in the fridge for up to a week. Store dried peas in a resealable packet or airtight container in a cool, dry place.

WHAT'S IN THEM?

Half a cup (about 80 g/2¾ oz) of cooked fresh green peas has about 200 kilojoules (48 calories), 4 g protein, 0 g fat, 5 g carbs (2 g sugars, 3 g starches), 4 g fibre, 1 mg sodium, 112 mg potassium, and a low GI (51) and GL (3).

Half a cup (about 90 g/3¼ oz) of cooked dried split peas has about 245 kilojoules (58 calories), 6 g protein, 0 g fat, 7 g carbs (0.5 g sugars, 6.5 g starches), 4 g fibre, 8 mg sodium, 126 mg potassium, and a low GI (25) and GL (2).

WHAT ELSE?

Note that some manufacturers don't recommend cooking dried peas in a pressure cooker, so it's best to check the instruction manual.

HERO RECIPES

Dal with curry spices (page 112)
Sweet spiced lamb with avocado pea crush (page 115)
Spiced beef with onions and yellow split peas (page 116)
Omelette with garden peas, feta and mint (page 119)

GLAZED GINGER SOYA BEANS

Sometimes simple is astonishingly good. Edamame – the Japanese word for sweet unripe soya beans, glinting bright green in their pods – are exquisite served with a subtle ginger pungency, sweet soy and hint of chilli heat.

PREPARATION TIME: 15 minutes | **COOKING TIME:** 10 minutes | **SERVES:** 6

2 cups (310 g/11 oz) podded fresh or
    frozen edamame (soya beans)
3 tablespoons soft brown sugar
⅓ cup (80 ml/2½ fl oz) soy sauce
⅓ cup (80 ml/2½ fl oz) water
2 teaspoons sesame oil
2 teaspoons finely grated fresh ginger
2 garlic cloves, crushed
¼ teaspoon crushed red chilli flakes

Steam the edamame for no longer than 5 minutes, until just tender and then pat dry with paper towel.

Whisk the brown sugar, soy sauce and water in a small bowl. Put the sesame oil, ginger and garlic in a non-stick pan over medium heat and sizzle for about 30 seconds. Add the brown sugar mixture along with the chilli, and gently simmer and stir for 3–5 minutes, or until the sauce is reduced and the consistency of thick pouring cream. The sauce needs to be thick enough to glaze the beans. If not, continue to cook until reduced further. Add the edamame and toss well to coat.

TIP Steaming the edamame locks in more of the nutrients as it reduces contact with water. Don't put the lid on the steamer or they'll lose their natural vibrant green colour.

TUNA, EGG AND SEASONAL VEGETABLES WITH BASIL-LEMON DRESSING

It could appear that this is a Niçoise salad that has left home and created its own identity in culinary circles. With glistening green beans and spring-fresh asparagus, this is a stunning salad. The tiny new potatoes have thin skins so there's no need to peel them – call them rustic if you want to.

PREPARATION TIME: 25 minutes | **COOKING TIME:** 15 minutes | **SERVES:** 6

12 tiny potatoes, scrubbed
3 eggs
small butter lettuce, or your favourite
    lettuce or salad greens
200 g (7 oz) green beans, trimmed
12 thin asparagus spears, trimmed
12 large pitted black olives
400 g (14 oz) tin tuna in oil, drained

BASIL-LEMON DRESSING
1 small shallot, finely chopped
1 teaspoon Dijon mustard
2 tablespoons lemon juice
⅓ cup (80 ml/2½ fl oz) olive oil
2 tablespoons chopped basil
sea salt flakes and freshly ground
    pepper

Put the potatoes in a large pot of salted water and cook at a lively simmer for 8 minutes, or until just tender. Drain and plunge them into a bowl of iced water to stop the cooking process. When the potatoes are cool, halve and put in a large bowl.

Put the eggs in a small pot of cold water and gently bring to the boil. Simmer for 7½ minutes. Drain and place the eggs in a bowl of iced water for 15 minutes before peeling them.

Separate the lettuce leaves, rinse gently and pat dry. Wrap them in paper towel and refrigerate until needed.

Drop the beans into a pan of boiling salted water and cook for about 3 minutes, until just tender. Lift out with a strainer and drop into a bowl of iced water to stop the cooking process. Add the asparagus to the pan and gently boil for 2 minutes. Drain and put into iced water. Drain the vegetables well and tumble them into the bowl with the potatoes. Add the olives and tuna.

For the dressing, whisk the shallot, mustard, lemon juice, olive oil and basil in a bowl. Add salt and pepper to taste, tip the dressing over the salad and toss lightly. Arrange the lettuce leaves on plates and top with the salad. Garnish with sliced boiled eggs to serve.

TIP For a more substantial meal, add sliced cherry tomatoes, cucumber and cooked double-podded broad beans.

ROASTED SNAPPER FILLETS WITH FENNEL AND CITRUS ON WHITE BEAN PURÉE

This dish has clean flavours and a simple garnish of briny clams and bright herbs. The bean purée contrasts perfectly with the fish.

PREPARATION TIME: 30 minutes | **COOKING TIME:** 20 minutes | **SERVES:** 6

Preheat the oven to 200°C/400°F (fan 180°C/350°F).

Cut the zest off the oranges in wide strips. Remove the peel and pith from both citrus fruits and, using a small sharp knife, cut the flesh between the membranes into segments over a bowl to catch the juices. Cut the orange zest into very thin strips and add them to the bowl. Put the garlic, fennel (keeping the fronds as a garnish) and leek in a sturdy pot. Add the oil and butter, and cook gently for about 8 minutes, or until softened.

Add the orange and lemon segments with the reserved juices, ginger, and add salt and pepper to taste. Tip into a shallow ovenproof dish about 12 cups (3 litres/101 fl oz) capacity. Arrange the fish fillets on top, skin side up, in a single layer. Pour over the wine and roast for 8–10 minutes, or until a toothpick meets no resistance when piercing the fish flesh. In the last 5 minutes of cooking, spoon the clams on top.

To make the white bean purée, put the garlic and oil in a frying pan and cook gently until the garlic is soft but not coloured. Rinse the beans, drain and add them to the pan along with the stock and lemon juice. Stir gently, just to heat through, and then pour into a food processor or blender. Blitz to a purée, then add salt and pepper to taste.

To serve, divide the bean purée between serving plates. Arrange a roasted fillet of fish on each and then spoon over the clams, citrus, fennel and juices from the pan. Garnish with the coriander, parsley and reserved fennel fronds.

2 oranges
2 lemons
1 plump garlic clove, crushed
1 fennel bulb with fronds, thinly sliced
1 small leek (white part only) thinly sliced and rinsed
2 tablespoons fruity olive oil
2 tablespoons butter
1 tablespoon finely grated ginger
sea salt flakes and freshly ground pepper
6 large snapper (or bream) fillets, skin on
1 cup (250 ml/9 fl oz) white wine or chicken stock
500 g (1 lb 2 oz) small clams (optional)
1 handful coriander (cilantro) leaves, roughly chopped
1 handful parsley, roughly chopped

WHITE BEAN PURÉE
2 garlic cloves, crushed
¼ cup (60 ml/2 fl oz) olive oil
2 × 400 g (14 oz) tins cannellini beans, drained
½ cup (125 ml/4 fl oz) hot chicken stock
juice of ½ lemon
sea salt flakes and freshly ground pepper

SALMON, WHITE BEAN AND DILL FISHCAKES

The appeal of fishcakes never diminishes, and if they look and taste as good as these, and are as good for you, may the appeal intensify. It is a delicate mixture naturally held together without egg, and therefore can easily break if not handled gently. A non-stick frying pan also helps prevent crumbling.

PREPARATION TIME: 25 minutes | **COOKING TIME:** 10 minutes | MAKES: 8

500 g (1 lb 2 oz) best market value skinless salmon
1 teaspoon tiny salted capers, rinsed
2 tablespoons finely chopped dill or parsley, plus extra to serve
1 tablespoon Dijon mustard
400 g (14 oz) tin butterbeans, drained and rinsed
sea salt flakes and freshly ground pepper
1 cup (175 g/6 oz) fine burghul (bulgur)
¼ cup (60 ml/2 fl oz) olive oil
lemon wedges

Roughly cut the salmon into chunks, check for fine bones and put in a food processor with the capers, dill, mustard, butterbeans, salt and pepper, and pulse until just combined. Shape the mixture into patties using about ⅓ cup of the mixture for each, and press into the burghul to coat.

Heat 1 tablespoon of the oil in a large non-stick pan over medium heat. Cook the fishcakes in batches, adding more oil as necessary, for about 3 minutes on each side or until golden brown. Remove and drain the fishcakes on paper towel.

Serve with lemon wedges, extra dill and, if liked, yoghurt flavoured with lemon juice and finely chopped chives.

TIPS Fishcakes are the perfect example of a marriage of convenience when using tinned fish and beans. Tinned salmon can be a time-saving substitute, but make sure to drain it very thoroughly before using otherwise the mixture may crumble.

You can use polenta or panko breadcrumbs instead of burghul if you prefer.

BAKED RED KIDNEY AND BUTTER BEAN RAGOUT

The method may seem fiddly (it really isn't), but it's vital for the lovely smooth, almost creamy and chunky final texture. Large tender leaves of English spinach can replace the more robust silverbeet (Swiss chard).

PREPARATION TIME: 20 minutes | **COOKING TIME:** 1¾ hours | **SERVES:** 8

1½ cups (250 g/9 oz) butterbeans, soaked overnight and drained

1¼ cups (250 g/9 oz) red kidney beans, soaked overnight and drained

sea salt flakes and freshly ground pepper

1 cup (250 ml/9 fl oz) olive oil

1 large handful parsley, finely chopped

4 garlic cloves, finely chopped

1 medium onion, chopped

½ small fennel bulb, finely sliced

¼ large celeriac (celery root), peeled, cut into 1 cm (½ in) pieces

1 celery stalk, finely chopped

2 bay leaves

4 silverbeet (Swiss chard) or kale stems

½ cup (30 g/1 oz) panko crumbs, lightly toasted

TIP Instead of butterbeans, you can use cannellini beans bearing in mind they will take less time to cook. Celeriac (celery root) is a lovely alternative to carrot.

Place both types of beans in a large heavy pot and cover with cold water by 2.5 cm (1 in). Bring to the boil over medium–high heat, reduce the heat to low, cover and simmer, skimming occasionally, for about 1 hour, or until the beans are tender enough to be easily smashed with the back of a spoon. Add salt (you will need about 1 teaspoon) and stir in half the oil.

Meanwhile, put the parsley, half the garlic, and the remaining oil in a small food processor and blitz until smooth. Cover the parsley sauce with plastic wrap to prevent it discolouring.

Heat 2 tablespoons of the oil in a large pan and when hot add the onion, fennel, celeriac, celery, bay leaves and remaining garlic, and cook, stirring occasionally over medium heat, for about 15 minutes, or until the vegetables are very soft but not coloured. Remove the bay leaves and add the vegetables to the pot of cooked beans.

Preheat the oven to 200°C/400°F (fan 180°C/350°F).

Put 3 cups of the bean mixture (and its liquid) in a blender. Blitz to make a smooth and creamy purée and then tip it back into the remaining bean mixture. Wash, trim and chop the silverbeet leaves (keep the stalks for using in soups or stir-fries), then tear into bite-sized pieces and stir through the bean mixture. Add salt and pepper to taste. Pour the mixture into a 8–12 cup (2–3 litre/68–101 fl oz) capacity casserole dish and bake for about 25 minutes, until the ragout is thick and bubbling, and the top is browned. Leave it to cool for 10 minutes before serving.

Serve the ragout drizzled with the parsley sauce and sprinkled with toasted panko crumbs.

LAMB AND BROAD BEAN STEW WITH SILVERBEET

An ode to spring comes to mind with this impressive dish. First there is tender lamb, then the vibrant green colour of silverbeet and the sweet, mild grassy flavour of tender broad beans – colours and tastes of spring.

PREPARATION TIME: 20 minutes | **COOKING TIME:** 1¾ hours | **SERVES:** 6

Put the lamb in a large, sturdy pot with the oil and onion. Cook over medium heat, stirring often, until the meat is slightly browned, making sure the onion does not burn. Add the tomato and harissa pastes, and stir for about 2 minutes to coat the meat. Add the garlic and stock, with salt and pepper to taste. Cover the pot and cook over medium–low heat for about 1½ hours, or until the lamb is tender.

Trim off and discard the stalk ends of the silverbeet and wash well. Roughly chop the leaves and thinly slice the remaining stems. Add to the pot with the beans and cook for a further 15 minutes, adding more stock if necessary to keep the meat and vegetables moist. Stir in the parsley and more salt and pepper to taste. If liked, serve generously sprinkled with chopped mint.

TIP When they are young and tender, eat broad beans in their tight thin paper skins. When the skins become more mature, thick and green–grey, they will be unpleasantly tough to eat. Blanch, drain and then pop the beans out of their skins.

¼ cup (60 m/2 fl oz) olive oil

1.25 kg (2 lb 13 oz) boned lamb shoulder, cut into medium-sized chunks

1 large onion, chopped

2 tablespoons tomato paste (concentrated purée)

1 tablespoon harissa paste

2 garlic cloves, crushed

at least 2 cups (500 ml/17 fl oz) chicken stock

sea salt flakes and freshly ground pepper

6 stems young silverbeet (Swiss chard), washed

about 3 cups (450 g/1 lb) podded broad beans

2 handfuls parsley leaves, chopped

SPICED CHICKPEA AND BROAD BEAN SOUP

The wonderful contrast between the nutty, slightly grainy texture of chickpeas and the creamy texture of young broad beans is a perfect foil for the assertive spiciness of the harissa. Do use tender young beans, as the older beans can be a little starchy in texture.

PREPARATION TIME: 20 minutes | **COOKING TIME:** 20 minutes | **SERVES:** 6

Heat the oil in a large pan and when hot add the onion and celery. Gently cook for 10 minutes or until vegetables softened, stirring frequently. Add the garlic and cumin and fry for 1 minute, or until fragrant.

Increase the heat to medium–high, add the stock, tomatoes with their juices and chickpeas with salt and pepper to taste. Simmer for 8 minutes. Add the broad beans, harissa to taste and lemon juice, and simmer for a further 2 minutes. Serve topped with lemon zest and coriander leaves.

TIPS Rinsing the tinned chickpeas in cold water removes a lot of the preserving salt, makes them easier to digest and helps reduce the wind effect.

When making soup there's no shortcut to good flavour. The very first step – gently cooking the celery and onion together – is important. When these veggies heat up, their intense jostling releases flavour compounds that react with each other, ensuring a mellower, more balanced aroma and a slightly sweeter flavour. You won't achieve the same depth of flavour if you simply throw all your ingredients in the pot at once and simmer.

1 tablespoon olive oil
1 medium onion, chopped
2 celery stalks, chopped
2 garlic cloves, crushed
2 teaspoons ground cumin
6 cups (1.5 litres/52 fl oz) hot chicken stock
400 g (14 oz) tin chopped tomatoes
400 g (14 oz) tin chickpeas, rinsed and drained
sea salt flakes and freshly ground pepper
1½ cups (275 g/9¾ oz) double podded broad beans
2–3 teaspoons harissa paste
grated zest and juice ½ lemon
1 large handful coriander (cilantro) leaves

FRESH GREEN HERB HUMMUS

It would be a mistake to confine this lively green fresh herb mixture to dips. Swirl it through cooked pasta, add large spoonfuls to soups, use as a scrumptious pillow for grilled or pan-fried fish and other meat, wrap large dollops in rice paper, or use as a sandwich filling with tomatoes.

PREPARATION TIME: 20 minutes | **SERVES:** 6

¼ cup (60 g/2 oz) tahini
juice of 1 lemon
⅓ cup (80 ml/2½ fl oz) olive oil
1 handful parsley, roughly chopped
3 tablespoons roughly chopped
    coriander (cilantro)
3 tablespoons chopped chives
1 handful salad spinach leaves
2 garlic cloves, crushed
400 g (14 oz) tin chickpeas, drained
    and rinsed
1–2 tablespoons water
sea salt flakes

Put the tahini, lemon juice and 3 tablespoons of the olive oil in a blender or food processor and pulse to a smooth paste. Add the parsley, coriander, chives, spinach leaves and garlic. Blitz for about 1 minute, pausing as necessary to scrape down the bowl. Add the chickpeas and blitz again until the hummus is thick and quite smooth. If it's too thick, drizzle in the water a little at a time, with the motor running, until it reaches the consistency you want.

Store the hummus in an airtight container and refrigerate for up to 1 week.

To serve, drizzle with the remaining olive oil and, if liked, sprinkle with extra chopped herbs.

TIP Use any combination of your favourite herbs such as tarragon, basil and mint, or use one herb and blend with rocket (arugula).

SMOKED PAPRIKA POTATO AND CHICKPEA SALAD

This salad is the sum of very democratic ingredients – they all give and take agreeably to balance in perfect harmony. The blandness of the potato is important for offsetting all the other flavours. Nutty and slightly grainy chickpeas make a wonderful contrast to other textures and keep the paprika in check. The sweet fire of the onion perfectly balances the eggs. There is no cloying mayo dressing – instead, a slightly sharp-sweet herbal concoction.

PREPARATION TIME: 15 minutes | **COOKING TIME:** 40 minutes | **SERVES:** 8

Preheat the oven to 200°C /400°F (fan 180°C/350°F).

Place the potatoes in a large pot, cover with water, add a large pinch of salt and bring to the boil. Reduce the heat and simmer for about 12 minutes, or until the potatoes are just tender. Add the eggs in the last 6 minutes of cooking time. Drain and cool slightly. When the eggs are cooled, peel off the shells. Cut the potatoes into uniform medium chunks, put into a large bowl with the paprika and toss.

Pour the oil into a sturdy roasting pan and put in the oven for 5 minutes to heat up. Toss the potatoes in the oil and roast them for about 20 minutes, or until crisp and golden. About 5 minutes before the end of cooking, tip in the chickpeas and lightly toss to warm through.

Tip the potato mixture into a large bowl. Cut the eggs into quarters and add to the bowl with the onion, mint and rocket. Whisk together the ingredients for the dressing, pour over the salad, toss together lightly and serve.

TIP Sweet smoked paprika increases the earthiness of a dish. However, you might consider swapping or combining another spice with paprika: warming cumin, or fennel with its slightly aniseed flavour and sweet aroma.

2 kg (4 lb 8 oz) baby potatoes
sea salt flakes
6 eggs
2–3 teaspoons smoked sweet Spanish paprika
½ cup (125 ml/4 fl oz) olive oil
400 g/14 oz tin chickpeas, drained and rinsed
1 medium red onion, thinly sliced
2 handfuls mint leaves
2 handfuls baby rocket (arugula) leaves
freshly ground pepper

DRESSING
¼ cup (60 ml/2 fl oz) red wine vinegar
2 tablespoons honey
1 teaspoon Dijon mustard
1 garlic clove, finely chopped

SUMAC-ROASTED CHICKEN WITH CHICKPEAS, BARLEY AND FRUIT STUFFING

If you've never used sumac before, let this roast chook be your seductive introduction – you may never look at the old spice favourites in your pantry the same way again. Sumac is astringent and brings a tingling fresh lemony twist. The stuffing has its own twist, too: it sings with fruity, nutty, starchy, herbal notes – another delicious surprise.

PREPARATION TIME: 20 minutes | **COOKING TIME:** 1½ hours | **SERVES:** 8

2 kg (4 lb 8 oz) free-range chicken
2 tablespoons ground sumac
finely grated zest of 1 lemon, plus
    1 extra small lemon
2 tablespoons olive oil
2 garlic cloves, crushed
1 small onion, finely chopped
⅔ cup (125 g/4½ oz) cooked chickpeas
    or rinsed and drained tinned
    chickpeas
⅔ cup (200 g/7 oz) cooked pearl barley
⅓ cup (40 g/1½ oz) chopped toasted
    walnuts
6 dates, pitted and chopped
1 tablespoon chopped parsley
sea salt flakes and freshly ground
    pepper
1 tablespoon soft butter

TIP: Chopped prunes, dried apricots or raisins can be swapped with dates. Pine nuts can replace walnuts.

Preheat the oven to 200°C/400°F (fan 180°C/350°F).

Pat the chicken all over with paper towel. Combine the sumac and lemon zest in a small bowl. Loosen the skin over the chicken breasts and thighs by gently running your fingers underneath it and push the sumac mixture between the skin and flesh.

Heat the oil in a frying pan, add the garlic and onion, and cook over medium heat for about 5 minutes or until soft.

Put the chickpeas and pearl barley in a bowl. Add the onion mixture, walnuts, dates, parsley, and salt and pepper to taste. Mash lightly and then stuff the chicken cavity with the mixture until about three-quarters full. Push the whole lemon into the cavity entrance to 'seal' it off.

Place the chicken in a roasting pan and smear all over with the butter, then season with salt and pepper. Roast for 10–15 minutes, until the chicken becomes golden and crisp, then reduce the temperature to 180°C/350°F (fan 160°C/315°F) and roast for about 1 hour, or until the chicken is cooked. To check if it's cooked, use a fine skewer to pierce the thigh close to the bone – if the juices run clear it's ready.

Remove the lemon from the cavity, cover the chicken with foil and leave to rest for 10–15 minutes before serving.

SPICED LENTILS WITH ROASTED VEGETABLES

The panic when culinary creativity grinds to a halt! The answer? Look no further than a medley of like-minded veggies tumbled together and roasted to unbelievable sweetness and colours. While they are roasting, whip up some toothsome spice-spiked lentils. Dinner's ready.

PREPARATION TIME: 20 minutes | **COOKING TIME:** 30 minutes | **SERVES:** 6

Soak the lentils in a bowl of water for 20 minutes (this halves the cooking time). Preheat the oven to 220°C/425°F (fan 200°C/400°F).

Bring a pot of water to the boil and blanch the beetroot for 15 minutes, then drain and cool. Peel away the skins and cut the beetroot into thick wedges. Scrape the carrots and trim the green tops. Cut the parsnips into four pieces lengthways and quarter four of the onions.

Place all the vegetables in a roasting pan and sprinkle with salt and pepper. Pour over 3 tablespoons of the oil and toss to coat. Roast the vegetables for about 30 minutes, or until browned and crisp. In the last 5 minutes of roasting, place the cavolo nero leaves, if using, on top of the vegetables to crisp.

While the vegetables are roasting, simmer the lentils in a pot of salted water for 5 minutes, (they should still be firm), then drain and cool. Do not rinse.

Put the remaining oil in a sturdy pan over medium heat. Dice the remaining onion and add with the garlic and bacon, and gently cook for about 10 minutes, until the onion softens. Add the almonds, lentils, cumin, cayenne and oregano. Toss and cook gently for 5 minutes, then add the stock. Bring to the boil and simmer for about 5 minutes, uncovered, or until the liquid has evaporated. Add salt and pepper to taste.

To serve, pile the lentils in the middle of a large platter and surround with roasted vegetables and the cavolo nero.

1 cup (200 g/7 oz) green lentils
3 medium beetroot (beets)
12 small bunched carrots
3 small parsnips, peeled
5 medium onions
300 g (10½ oz) peeled butternut pumpkin (squash), cut into chunks
sea salt flakes and freshly ground pepper
100 ml (3½ fl oz) olive oil
6 stems cavolo nero (optional)
1 teaspoon crushed garlic
2 shortcut rindless bacon rashers, finely chopped
½ cup (80 g/2¾ oz) chopped raw almonds
1 teaspoon ground cumin
¼ teaspoon cayenne pepper
1 teaspoon dried oregano
1 cup (250 ml/9 fl oz) chicken stock

TIP Sweet potato, turnip, fennel or swede can be added to the mix of roast vegetables.

BAKED FISH WITH LENTILS, TOMATOES AND OLIVES

Lentils have gone from a kind of hippie wholefood ghetto to a year-round staple, perfect for cosying up a soup in the winter, and never better than in this consoling dish. The tiny, mottled greeny-blue pellets of puy lentils introduce a spicy earthiness and an incomparable nutty texture. When added to other ingredients at the still-warm stage, they soak up flavours beautifully.

PREPARATION TIME: 15 minutes | **COOKING TIME:** 35 minutes | **SERVES:** 6

Preheat the oven to 180°C/350°F (fan 160°C/315°F).

Rinse the lentils and put in a large pot of water. Bring to the boil, reduce the heat and simmer for about 35 minutes, or until the lentils are tender. Drain well.

Meanwhile, put the tomatoes with their juices, stock, olives, garlic and capers in a casserole dish and gently cook on the stovetop for 10 minutes. Place the fish fillets in the dish with the cooked lentils and spoon over the tomato sauce, making sure the fish is covered completely in the sauce to prevent it from drying out. Loosely cover with foil and bake for 10 minutes, or until the fish is just cooked. Use the point of a small knife to peek inside the thickest part of the fish. It should gently resist flaking and if it appears almost opaque, the fish is cooked. The trick is to take it off the heat just before you think it's fully cooked, as fish continues to cook for a couple of minutes off the heat. Serve the fish with the sauce spooned over and garnish with basil leaves.

⅔ cup (125 g/4½ oz) small green (puy) lentils
2 × 400 g (14 oz) tins chopped tomatoes
1 cup (250 ml/9 fl oz) stock
1 cup (155 g/5½ oz) pitted black olives
3 garlic cloves, crushed
1 tablespoon capers, drained
6 thick white fish fillets (about 155 g/5½ oz each)
1 handful small basil leaves

TIPS Use a sustainable best-value fish. Instead of the basil, try pairing parsley with some dill, which is a natural choice of herb for fish.

DAL WITH CURRY SPICES

Curries are a playground for spices. Here the chana dal provides a neutral backdrop to let them play and sing to mellow perfection. Tadka (tempering) is the process of roasting spices briefly to release their flavour into hot oil. It is poured into dal just before serving to intensify flavour and create tantalising aromas.

PREPARATION TIME: 30 minutes | **COOKING TIME:** 1 hour | **SERVES:** 6

1½ cups (300 g/10½ oz) chana dal
    or yellow split peas
1 teaspoon ground turmeric
1 small onion
6 cups (1.5 litres/52 fl oz) water
3 whole cloves
1 cinnamon stick
2 small red chillies, split lengthways
400 g (14 oz) tin chopped tomatoes
1 teaspoon sea salt flakes

TADKA
½ cup (125 ml/4 fl oz) vegetable oil
1 teaspoon cumin seeds
2 medium onions, thinly sliced
2 teaspoons finely grated ginger
2 small dried red chillies, finely
    chopped
3 garlic cloves, crushed
10 curry leaves (optional)
small handful coriander (cilantro), torn

Rinse the chana dal and put in a large pot with the turmeric, whole onion and water (if you prefer a thick dal, use 5 cups/1.25 litres/44 fl oz of water). Bring to the boil over medium–high heat, stirring occasionally to prevent the peas from lumping. Reduce the heat to low and simmer, partially covered, skimming occasionally, for about 35 minutes or until the peas are tender and break up under pressure from the back of a spoon.

Remove from the heat and discard the onion. Beat the mixture with a wooden spoon. If you prefer a coarse texture, purée half the mixture in a blender or food processor and mix it with the rest of the of the mixture. Return the dal to the pot with the cloves, cinnamon stick, chillies, tomatoes and salt. Simmer for about 10 minutes, stirring now and then to prevent sticking.

For the tadka, heat the oil in a small frying pan and when very hot add the cumin seeds. Fry the seeds for 10 seconds, or until they turn dark brown. Add the onions and fry for about 10 minutes, stirring constantly. This is an important step. Browning the onions is what will give the dal its magnificent aroma and flavour. First, the onions will steam, then they will gradually change to a deep caramel brown. Add the ginger, chillies, garlic and curry leaves, if using (but they do 'make' the dish), and cook for a further 5 minutes.

Divide the dal between warm bowls, top with the tadka, and garnish with coriander and, if liked, extra curry leaves.

SWEET SPICED LAMB WITH AVOCADO PEA CRUSH

This is the ideal special occasion meal where everything can be prepared in advance, and refrigerated. For a start, the cooked chilled lamb will be easier to slice thinly. The blitzed avocado and pea mixture will need plastic wrap patted firmly down on the surface to keep air out and to retain its emerald brilliance.

PREPARATION TIME: 25 minutes | **COOKING TIME:** 5 minutes | **SERVES:** 6

Put the lamb into a bowl with the cumin, paprika, garlic, parsley and oil. Use your hands to thoroughly coat the lamb, then cover and refrigerate for 15 minutes.

Heat a sturdy pan over medium–high heat and when hot add the lamb (in batches, if necessary, to avoid cramming the pan). Cook for 2 minutes on each side for medium rare, or longer to your liking. Remove the lamb and leave to rest for 10 minutes.

Cut the avocado in half, remove the stone, and scoop out and roughly chop the flesh. Put into a food processor with the peas (if using frozen peas there is no need to thaw them before using), lemon juice, mint, cumin, and salt and pepper to taste. Pulse-blend until it has a medium texture.

Slice the lamb crossways into strips and serve on top of a big spoonful of the avocado pea crush.

1 kg (2 lb 4 oz) lamb backstraps
3 teaspoons ground cumin
3 teaspoons sweet paprika
4 garlic cloves, crushed
1 tablespoon chopped parsley
2 tablespoons olive oil
1 large ripe avocado
1½ cups (235 g/8½ oz) fresh or frozen peas
1 tablespoon lemon juice
small handful mint leaves
1–2 teaspoons ground cumin
sea salt flakes and freshly ground pepper

TIPS Hass avocado holds its buttery smooth texture better than other avocado varieties and does not discolour as quickly.

The avocado pea crush is also excellent with chops, fish, prawns, burger and grills. Instead of cumin and paprika you may like to try using sumac. Lamb backstrap is also known as eye of loin and is a cut from the side of the loin chop. It's a premium lean, sweet and tender cut that is ideal for quick pan cooking.

SPICED BEEF WITH ONIONS AND YELLOW SPLIT PEAS

Split peas have long been a soup stalwart, but here they play the contemplative companion to the lively flavour combinations in this meat dish, a shadow of a fragrant light curry. Do use allspice (not mixed spice or a blend of 'all spices'), which takes its name from its aroma – a combination of spices, especially cinnamon, cloves, ginger and nutmeg. In much of the world, allspice is called pimento.

PREPARATION TIME: 25 minutes | **COOKING TIME:** 2 hours | **SERVES:** 6

¼ cup (60 ml/2 fl oz) olive oil

¼ cup (60 ml/2 fl oz) tomato paste (concentrated purée)

2 large onions, chopped

1 teaspoon ground turmeric

1 kg (2 lb 4 oz) beef chuck, cut into 3 cm (1¼ in) cubes

1 teaspoon ground cinnamon

1 teaspoon ground allspice (optional)

sea salt flakes and freshly ground pepper

2 × 400 g (14 oz) tins crushed tomatoes

4 cups (1 litre/35 fl oz) water

1 cup (185 g/6½ oz) dried yellow split peas, rinsed and drained

¼ cup (60 ml/2 fl oz) lemon juice

2 radishes, very thinly sliced

1 handful mint leaves

In a small pan, heat 1 tablespoon of the oil over medium heat, add the tomato paste and cook, stirring, for 2–3 minutes just until the tomato paste turns slightly darker. Remove from the heat and set aside.

In a large sturdy pot, heat the remaining oil over medium heat. Add the onions and cook for about 8 minutes or until the onions are golden. Add the turmeric, stir well, then toss in the meat and brown all over. Add the cinnamon, allspice (if using), and salt and pepper to taste. Tip in the tomatoes and water, cover and simmer gently for 1¼ hours. Stir in the split peas and simmer, covered, stirring occasionally, for about 30 minutes, or until the meat is tender and the peas cooked. Stir in the lemon juice and serve garnished with sliced radishes and mint leaves, or very young mint sprigs if you grow your own.

TIP Choose an inexpensive cut of beef that suits slow cooking. Chuck, from the neck and shoulder, has a great full flavour and a fantastic gelatinous texture. Other good cuts to use are blade, round or boneless shin.

OMELETTE WITH GARDEN PEAS, FETA AND MINT

There are times when the yearning for an omelette is overwhelming. But for some reason many cooks shy away from this gloriously simple light meal. The best technique is practice. And don't be too fussed about how it looks when turned out. The refreshing lively filling makes up for any imperfection. Be comforted by the wisdom of Elizabeth David who wrote in *French Provincial Cooking* that 'there is only one infallible recipe for the perfect omelette: your own'.

PREPARATION TIME: 15 minutes | **COOKING TIME:** 8 minutes | **SERVES:** 2

Put the peas in a bowl with the oil, lemon zest, spring onions, and add salt and pepper to taste.

Whisk the eggs with salt and pepper in a bowl. Heat the butter in a large non-stick pan over medium heat until foaming and golden. Add the eggs and gently cook, without stirring, for about 3 minutes or until large curds form. Reduce the heat to medium-low and, using a broad spatula, gently push the eggs around in the pan until they are almost set. Spoon the peas, feta and mint mixture over the top and, with the aid of the spatula, gently roll the omelette up and over the filling. (This is easier if you hold the pan at a slight angle to assist the rolling.) Cook for 1 minute more and then slide the omelette onto a plate. Divide between two to serve. If liked, garnish with extra mint and spring onion.

TIP Change the filling as you fancy: prawns (shrimp), flaked cooked fish, diced tomato and plenty of chopped fresh herbs are all delicious options.

⅔ cup (100 g/3½ oz) cooked peas
1 tablespoon olive oil
1 teaspoon finely grated lemon zest
2 spring onions (green onions/ scallions), finely sliced
sea salt flakes and freshly ground pepper
6 eggs
2 tablespoons butter
½ cup (65 g/2 oz) crumbled feta
3 tablespoons shredded mint leaves

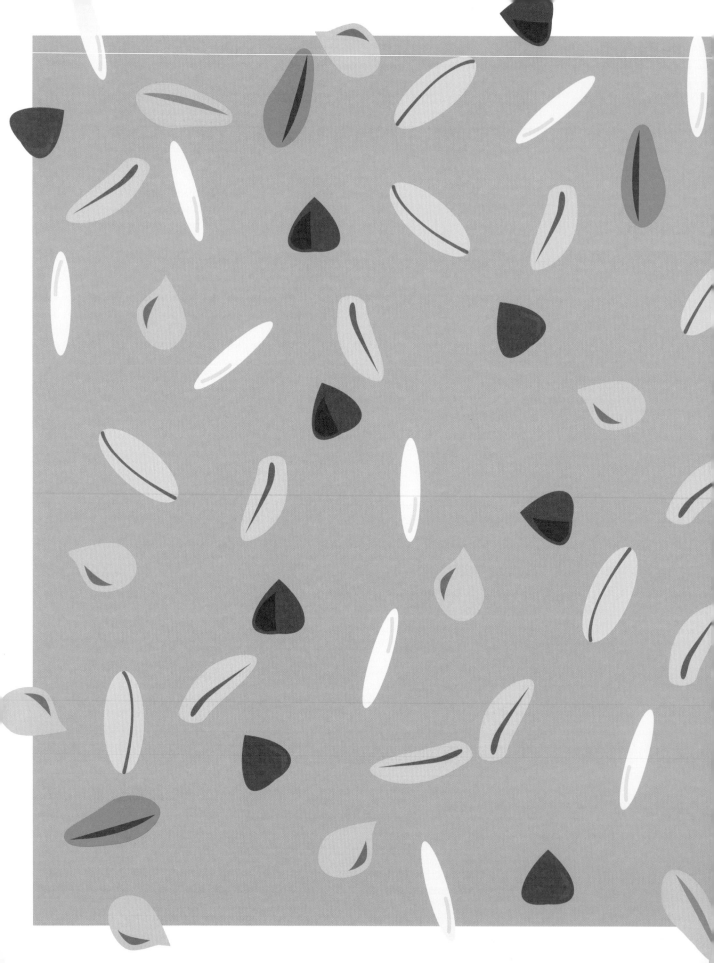

Grains

We have been going with the grain for a long time. Food diaries weren't around, so we can't put a date on when our forebears began pounding and grinding the tough little seeds they gathered, adding a bit of water and making gruel or porridge or kneading dough to bake bread. We know it was many thousands of years before we became farmers. Our genes provide telling evidence for this. 'We have evolved multiple copies of the salivary amylase gene, AMY1, which kicks off the digestion of starch in cooked foods. AMY1 has no other function. Amylase cannot act on raw starch, only starch that has been gelatinised by the action of heat and water,' says Prof. Jennie Brand-Miller in her foreword.

What's exciting about digging around in buried villages is that it gives us very early pictures of the range of foods on a 'Paleo' menu. In the remains of the 23,000-year-old lakeshore camp submerged under the Sea of Galilee (Ohalo II, in present-day Israel) scientists found charred seeds and bones revealing that the fisher-hunter-gatherers who spent much of the year there hunted gazelle and fallow deer, and occasionally fox, hare and wild pig; fished in the lake and caught migratory birds – the great crested grebe a favourite if bone count is any indication. And they certainly tucked in to grains, including wild barley, wheat and oats, as the scientists found these seeds all over the campsite along with a grinding stone with starchy traces of barley. They also ate acorns, legumes and wild fruit, and may have used their oven-like hearth to bake bread.

But they hadn't yet found their green fingers. Seed planting came later. Around 11,000 to 10,000 years ago our ancestors made a major lifestyle change. We don't really know why, but in various parts of the world they settled down, built houses and villages and became farmers. We can only imagine the trial and error involved in the early days, but at some point they discovered that

INSIDE THE NOURISHING SEED

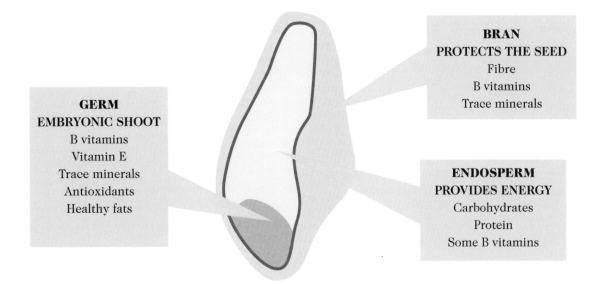

GERM
EMBRYONIC SHOOT
B vitamins
Vitamin E
Trace minerals
Antioxidants
Healthy fats

BRAN
PROTECTS THE SEED
Fibre
B vitamins
Trace minerals

ENDOSPERM
PROVIDES ENERGY
Carbohydrates
Protein
Some B vitamins

along with beans and lentils, eager-to-sprout grass seeds made an ideal crop to produce food for the table.

For a long time, seeds were lumped under the general heading 'grain' or 'corn'. At some point 'grain' was reserved for grass seeds – barley, corn (maize), millet, oats, rice, rye, sorghum, wheat and wild rice – while the sustaining seeds from leafy plants such as amaranth, quinoa and buckwheat were sidelined into a 'pseudograins' category. There's no culinary reason for this bureaucratic A-list-B-list approach and we take no notice of it.

Food guru Harold McGhee says, 'Seeds are our most durable and concentrated foods. They are the rugged lifeboats designed to carry a plant's offspring to the shore of an uncertain future. Tease apart a whole grain, or bean, or nut, and inside you find a tiny embryonic shoot.' And this is why they are so nourishing: they are a baby plant's pantry. And that's also why we along with insects, birds and mammals seek them out. And on top of that, we grow them.

If you look inside these small, hard dried seeds (or fruit), you'll see there are three distinct parts:

- the fibre-rich bran, which is the outer skin and protects the seed from predators
- the starchy endosperm, which nourishes the embryonic shoot during germination (the potential baby plant's pantry)
- the nutrient-rich germ, which becomes the plant's offspring if pollinated.

The process of milling and refining grains consists of separating and removing the bran and germ. This gives us a more shelf-stable and quicker-cooking end product, but means it lacks many of the vitamins, minerals, fats and fibre of the original grain.

Grains are at their most nourishing when we eat them as whole as possible or as the minimally processed staples our forebears enjoyed. They certainly figure prominently in the diets of the long-living Blue Zones folks, and observational studies around the world suggest that eating plenty of wholegrain staples may reduce the risk of developing certain types of cancer, heart disease and type 2 diabetes. That's why health professionals tend to worship at the altar of wholegrains and the words 'consume more wholegrains' is in all dietary guidelines around the globe.

If we really want to go 'paleo', we should probably eat a much wider variety of seeds than we do currently. Scientists identified around 150 different types of seeds and fruits at that fisher-hunter-gatherers' camp now submerged under the Sea of Galilee. If we choose the less refined versions such as pearl barley, brown rice or quinoa that have just been hulled and/or washed, digesting them will give our whole system a really good work out.

Our policy is to stick to the traditional staples our ancestors enjoyed and cooked from scratch. This means bypassing the more processed or highly refined products despite any glowing health claims on the packaging.

While many 'wholegrain' or 'wholemeal' products in the bread and ready-to-eat breakfast cereals aisle do contain much of the grain's germ, endosperm and bran, what's actually inside tends to have been milled, cooked, flaked, toasted, puffed and popped beyond recognition, so it won't behave on our insides like the original. In fact, such highly refined and reconstituted 'wholegrain' products will tend to slip through the system, be digested in a flash and send blood glucose levels rocketing.

GRAIN COOKING 101

Grains and seeds (such as quinoa) retain a lot of water when you cook them, and because they are very wet, it takes a long time for them to drain and become dry enough to be combined with other ingredients without clumping. The following method is the quickest way to cool cooked grains and works with all the grains featured in this chapter. If you have the time, prepare them the day before.

Cook the grains, tip them into a strainer large enough to prevent the grains being compressed (which will make them soggy) and run cold water through them before draining. After straining them for a minute or two, spread them evenly in a thin layer on a tray. Don't be tempted to leave them outside to dry otherwise the birds will feast on them! The inside of a frost-free refrigerator has a cold dry atmosphere that is ideal for drying cooked grains and seeds on uncovered trays.

WHAT'S GLUTEN GOT TO DO WITH IT?

Gluten (Latin for 'glue'), a protein found in wheat, rye, barley and triticale, helps give bread dough and cake batter elasticity to help them rise and hold their shape.

Some people can't tolerate gluten and need to eliminate it completely from their diet. This includes anyone with coeliac disease or dermatitis herpetiformis (a distressing gluten-sensitive chronic skin condition). People with gluten intolerance (non-coeliac gluten sensitivity) can tolerate small amounts of gluten but they may have to cut back significantly, depending on how sensitive they are.

WHAT HAPPENS?

When someone with coeliac disease eats something that contains gluten, they have an immune reaction in their small intestine that damages the intestinal villi (small finger-like projections that line the small intestine), reducing its ability to absorb nutrients from food. This may lead to deficiencies in certain vitamins and minerals the body needs for growth, health, healing and energy. If you suspect you or someone in your family may have coeliac disease, seek advice from a health professional and get tested.

COELIAC DISEASE CAN BE SERIOUS

It's actually the most common and one of the most under-diagnosed hereditary autoimmune diseases affecting children and adults. Around one in every 100 people in Australia and New Zealand suffer from it.

WHO GETS IT?

Genes play a part: around one in ten of all parents, brothers, sisters or children (first-degree relatives) of someone with coeliac disease will also have it. And if one identical twin has coeliac disease, there is about a two in three chance the other twin will, too.

WHAT ABOUT OATS?

Oats don't actually contain gluten but are frequently grown, harvested, stored, milled and processed alongside gluten-containing grains, so they may be contaminated with gluten. They also contain a protein very similar in structure to gluten, which some people with coeliac disease react to.

BARLEY

Those first farmers in the Fertile Crescent knew they were onto a good thing with barley. It didn't seem to mind poor soils or dry conditions, had a rapid growing season, and produced lots of large seeds. They ground them to bake bread or make gruel, and along the way discovered the magic of malting. As towns grew and people prospered, however, barley was more often on the plates of the ruled rather than the rulers. Romans didn't eat much of it, but it was on the menu for the gladiators (who were nicknamed *hordearii* or 'barley eaters'). These days, barley is seen as a traditional pantry staple to bring out to add texture and substance to winter-warming soups or give risottos a different spin, but to leave it out for everyday fare as it takes too long to cook. We challenge you to take the time and pick that packet of pearl (or pearled) or pot barley off the shelf to enjoy its natural nuttiness and bite in some classic dishes with a contemporary twist.

WHAT TO LOOK FOR

Pearl barley is one of the most widely available wholegrain products. You'll find it in the soup section of every supermarket. Look for other barley products, too: pot (hulled barley, which takes a little longer to cook) and black (purple) barley. Check the use-by or best-before date.

HOW TO STORE IT

Store in a cool dry place in a resealable packet or airtight container.

WHAT'S IN IT?

Half a cup (about 95 g/3¼ oz) of cooked barley has about 400 kilojoules (96 calories), 3 g protein, 1 g fat, 17 g carbs (0 g sugars, 17 g starches), 3.5 g fibre, 10 mg sodium, 65 mg potassium, and a low GI (28) and GL (5).

WHAT ELSE?

For a speedy wholegrain to add to your meals, try barley couscous. You are more likely to find it in specialty and health food stores than in the supermarket.

HERO RECIPES

Hot and sour mushroom and barley soup with broccolini (page 132)
Lamb shanks with barley, garden peas and mint (page 135)

BUCKWHEAT

With so many grains competing for attention on supermarket shelves, buckwheat doesn't get much of a look-in unless you want soba noodles or buckwheat pancakes. Its reputation for being an acquired taste with a robust and assertive flavour is not exactly encouraging for the novice. 'Buckwheat, like Marmite and durian, is a seriously divisive foodstuff, so it needs a capable defence team if it's going to make it on to most people's dinner tables,' says our favourite cookbook writer–chef, Yotam Ottolenghi. In fact, untoasted, the groats have a rather mild flavour and make a nutty addition to grainy salads and sides, or a speedy option for risottos – especially with mushrooms. Don't overcook them or use too much liquid, as they tend to go mushy.

WHAT TO LOOK FOR

There are a variety of gluten-free buckwheat products in supermarkets and health food stores, including:

- buckwheat groats or kernels (hulled whole buckwheat)
- roasted buckwheat groats or kasha (roasted hulled whole buckwheat)
- creamy buckwheat or cream of buckwheat (hulled and milled to a fine grain for porridge)
- buckwheat flour (milled and sieved whole buckwheat; light, medium and dark grades depending on amount of hull retained)
- buckwheat or soba noodles (typically contain up to 50 per cent wheat flour and are not gluten free).

Check the use-by or best-before date.

HOW TO STORE IT

Store in a cool dry place in a resealable packet or airtight container. For fresh soba noodles, store in the refrigerator following the manufacturer's instructions.

WHAT'S IN IT?

Half a cup (about 90 g or 3¾ oz) of cooked groats has about 370 kilojoules (88 calories), 3 g protein, 0.5 g fat, 17 g carbs (0.5 g sugars/ 16.5 g starches), 1 g fibre, 4 mg sodium, 78 mg potassium, and a low GI (45) and GL (8).

WHAT ELSE?

Toasting wholegrains such as buckwheat, barley, brown rice or wheat berries gently and evenly on the stovetop in a sturdy pan or in the oven boosts flavour. It may seem like an extra step, but it doesn't add extra time, as the dry heat begins the cooking process, cracking the outer bran layer. It may even speed things up when it comes to those slow-cooking kernels. Don't overdo it though, and only toast the grains until they are warm, nutty and aromatic – 5 or 6 minutes.

HERO RECIPES

Crispy cauliflower with buckwheat and pine nuts (page 136)
Buckwheat pikelets (page 139)
Chilli-ginger peanut butter soba noodles with silken tofu (page 140)

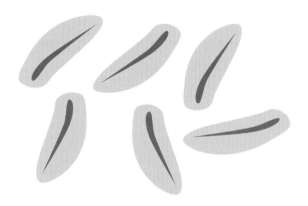

OATS

Oats make great porridge. They become comfortingly thick and soothingly creamy when you cook them, thanks partly to their soluble fibre. Exuding a friendly health halo, they are so successful at kick-starting the day for porridge people and muesli fans alike that they have become confined to the breakfast cereal aisle. But oat groats (dehulled oat grain) have a place at the table for other meals, too. You can use them in salads, pilafs and soups instead of pearl barley or spelt. It's worth remembering that the word 'porridge' comes from 'pottage' from the French *potage*, which simply means something cooked in a pot. Think of them as early versions of soups. Originally they were based on the locally available grain, but cooks would add vegetables, herbs and beans to make them a meal in themselves or to serve as an accompaniment to meats.

WHAT TO LOOK FOR

The range of wholegrain oat products includes: steel-cut oats (also called pin-head or Irish oats), Scottish or stone-ground oats, traditional rolled oats (old-fashioned oatmeal) and instant oats (quick oats). Instant oats are pre-cooked so you just add boiling water to make porridge. Some also have flavourings and sweeteners added, so read the ingredient list. Check the use-by or best-before date.

HOW TO STORE IT

Store in a cool, dry place in a resealable packet or airtight container.

WHAT'S IN IT?

Half a cup (about 130 g/4½ oz) of cooked oats has about 270 kilojoules (65 calories), 2 g protein, 1.5 g fat, 10 g carbs (0 g sugars, 10 g starches), 1 g fibre, 0 mg sodium, 48 mg potassium, and a low GI (55) and GL (5).

WHAT ELSE?

Plant 'milks' are popular these days, and are, in essence, milky-coloured water. The ingredients in oat milk (GI 69) are water (typically about 85 per cent), steamed or heat-treated oat flakes or oat flour, sunflower oil and sea salt. Some brands (not all) are boosted with calcium to match the calcium content of regular milk.

HERO RECIPES

Mixed mushroom buttermilk soup with rolled oats and peas (page 141)
Garlicky mushrooms with onions and thyme on oat mash (page 142)

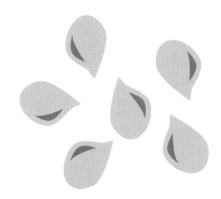

QUINOA

While quinoa may currently be the trendiest grain on the block, not so long ago none of us outside the Altiplano had heard of it. But it has always been the Americas' other major grain. Unlike corn (maize), the rest of the world forgot about it for several hundred years until three enthusiastic Americans – Stephen Gorad, Don McKinley and David Cusack of the Quinoa Corporation (now the Ancient Grains brand) – put quinoa back on our plates. They planted the first test field in Colorado, imported the first grain, and offered it to the American public for the first time at a health food store in Boulder in 1983. The rest is history (though not without hiccups). Quinoa ticks so many boxes: it's tasty, quick cooking, packed with nutrition, gluten free, versatile and colourful, and it has its place in soups, salads, sides, mains, desserts and snacks. It's now grown around the world. What a success story.

WHAT TO LOOK FOR

Cream (ivory), tan, red (purple) and black quinoa (sold separately and in colourful combinations) and mixed grain combinations such as quinoa and rice are available. You'll also find quinoa pasta, flakes and flour on the shelves, especially in health food and produce stores. Check the use-by or best-before date.

HOW TO STORE IT

Store in a cool, dry place in a resealable packet or airtight container.

WHAT'S IN IT?

Half a cup (about 95 g/3¼ oz) of cooked quinoa has about 400 kilojoules (96 calories), 4 g protein, 2 g fat, 15 g carbs (1 g sugars, 14 g starches), 2 g fibre, 4 mg sodium, 150 mg potassium, and a low GI (53) and GL (8).

WHAT ELSE?

To rinse or not to rinse? Like many seeds, quinoa arms itself with bitter-tasting compounds in its outer skin to deter insects and birds. In this case, the said compounds are saponins. Most quinoa has been treated in some way to remove the saponins before being packaged for sale, but it's a good idea to pop the grains in a sieve and run them under cold water first.

Saponins are a group of phytochemicals that occur in certain veggies (such as peas, edamame (soya beans)) and herbs, albeit in very small amounts. They tend to pass straight through us, as they are poorly absorbed by our bodies. Heating destroys them. The naming rights come from the soapwort plant (*Saponaria officinalis*) – its root was used as soap (from the Latin *sapo* 'soap') because of its natural foaming tendency. With natural cleaning products making a comeback, there's growing interest in using saponins for making natural detergents.

HERO RECIPES

Mixed grains salad with marinated zucchini (page 145)
Quinoa 'risotto' with pumpkin, carrots and hazelnuts (page 146)

RICE

Rice is the go-to grain. It's the starchy staple you can tuck into day in, day out without tiring of it. It has also made itself at home in kitchens everywhere. In a wok, pot or bowl, or on a plate, it soaks up the flavours from stocks and sauces, and partners with meat, chicken, fish, seafood, tofu, vegetables, nuts or fruit and so much more. Those early farmers who planted the first seeds some 8,000 to 10,000 years ago in southern China would be gobsmacked at the number of varieties that have evolved. It's estimated that there are more than 100,000 kinds, ranging in colour, size, shape, aroma, stickiness and starchiness. And gobsmacked, too, at all the things we make with the grains, from flour, noodles and crackers to syrup, alcohol, oil and puffed breakfast cereals shot out of a gun.

WHAT TO LOOK FOR

Nutty-tasting brown rice with just the inedible hull removed is the rice with the serious nutritional wholegrain credentials and these days we can buy 2-minute microwave options to help get meals on the table fast. Refined, popular, palatable white rice is still a good choice, especially combined with lots of veg. Look for lower-GI varieties such as basmati. For speedy meals rice noodles are good to have on hand. Check the use-by or best-before date.

HOW TO STORE IT

Store in a cool, dry place in a resealable packet or airtight container.

WHAT'S IN IT?

Half a cup (about 90 g or 3¼ oz) of cooked basmati rice has about 395 kilojoules (95 calories), 2 g protein, 0.5 g fat, 20 g carbs (0 g sugars, 20 g starches), 0.5 g fibre, 6 mg sodium, 50 mg potassium, and a moderate GI (58) and GL (12). The GI of rice can range from low (47) to very high (98) depending on variety, so it's impossible to generalise.

WHAT ELSE?

The starch in raw food is stored in hard, compact granules our bodies find hard to digest, which is why starchy foods usually need to be cooked. Water and heat expand the starch granules during cooking to different degrees; some actually burst and free the individual starch molecules (this is gelatinisation). Rice is a great grain for getting to know the starches in our foods – amylose and amylopectin:

- Amylose is a string of glucose molecules that tend to line up in rows and form tight, compact clumps that are harder to gelatinise and digest. The lower-GI rices have a higher proportion of amylose.
- Amylopectin is a string of glucose molecules with lots of branching points, such as you see in some types of seaweed. Amylopectin molecules are larger and more open, and the starch tends to be easier to gelatinise and digest. Higher-GI rices have a higher proportion of amylopectin.

HERO RECIPES

Fish soup with Thai flavours and rice noodles (page 147)
Golden rice with peas and cashews (page 149)
Brown rice risotto with peas and prawns (page 150)
Wild rice pilaf with mushrooms and almonds (page 153)

WHEAT

Gluten helped wheat rise to the top of the crops. Bread made from other grains tended to be on the stodgy side, while bread from wheat rose because its gluten proteins trapped the bubbles of carbon dioxide produced by the baker's yeast and caused the dough to rise. Wheat was prized and bread became the staff of life – no food was more basic, more essential or more universal. But wheat is versatile and has provided our table with numerous traditional staples, including pasta, noodles, fregola and couscous of all kinds.

WHAT TO LOOK FOR

We're not going to confuse you with the ancient versus modern talk. Look for wholegrain when it comes to wheat products. There's quite a range, from wheat kernels (berries) including spelt, Kamut and farro; freekeh (roasted green immature wheat); and cracked wheat and burghul (bulgur) available in a variety of grades of fineness, to the traditional staples (preferably wholegrain or wholemeal) made from wheat flour – bread, pasta, noodles and couscous. White bread and pasta are fine but don't make them the default setting. Check use-by or best-before dates.

HOW TO STORE IT

Store grains and staples in a cool dry place in a resealable or airtight container. Bread is best kept in the refrigerator.

WHAT'S IN IT?

Half a cup (about 130 g/4½ oz) of prepared bulgur has about 525 kilojoules (125 calories), 4 g protein, 0.5 g fat, 23 g carbs (0 g sugars, 23 g starches), 6 g fibre, 13 mg sodium, 64 mg potassium, and a low GI (47) and moderate GL (11).

WHAT ELSE?

We are fans of quick-cooking burghul. Made from whole wheat grains that have been hulled and steamed before grinding to crack the grain, it's ideal for tabbouleh, or adding to pilafs, burgers (meaty and veggie), stuffings, stews, salads and soups.

HERO RECIPES

Burghul and red lentil soup with sizzling mint and chilli (page 154)
Spaghetti with green tomatoes and fresh herbs (page 155)
Ribbon pasta with broad beans and pancetta (page 156)
Fregola and blood orange salad with fennel (page 159)
Jerusalem artichokes with farro, spinach and oyster mushrooms (page 160)
Farro with roasted winter vegetables, prunes and walnuts (page 161)
Farro and green lentils with cherry tomatoes and marinated feta (page 162)
Lamb, feta and burghul meatballs (page 165)
Roasted beetroot purée and burghul with mixed fresh herbs (page 166)

HOT AND SOUR MUSHROOM AND BARLEY SOUP WITH BROCCOLINI

There's something that clicks inside us all the minute the temperature drops to real winter chill. The click happens and then it's soup season. This soup, with its broth of tantalising sweet and sour flavours underpinning the earthy mushrooms is the answer. Barely cooked vegetables provide crunch, and the barley adds creamy richness. And what's the best way to achieve the perfect, personal-preference balance of sweet and sour? Taste and taste again. It's an instinctive way of cooking.

PREPARATION TIME: 15 minutes | **COOKING TIME:** 10 minutes | **SERVES:** 6

⅓ cup (80 ml/2½ fl oz) olive oil
1 large onion, finely chopped
4 garlic cloves, crushed
1 tablespoon finely grated ginger
400 g (14 oz) mixed mushrooms, roughly chopped
sea salt flakes and freshly ground pepper
¾ cup (150 g/5½ oz) pearl barley
6 cups (1.5 litres/52 fl oz) chicken stock
2 cups (500 ml/17 fl oz) water
1 bunch thin broccolini, thick ends trimmed
juice of 1 plump lime
1 handful bean sprouts, trimmed
1 handful coriander (cilantro) leaves

Heat the oil in a large pot over medium heat. Add the onion and cook for about 8 minutes, stirring occasionally, or until softened but not coloured. Stir in the garlic and ginger and cook for about 1 minute, or until fragrant. Add the mushrooms, season with salt and pepper, and cook, stirring occasionally, until their liquid is released. (Add 1–2 tablespoons of water if the mushrooms begin to stick to the bottom of the pot.) Add the pearl barley, stock and water. Bring to the boil then lower the heat to a simmer and cook, covered, for about 30 minutes, or until the barley is tender. Add the broccolini in the last 10 minutes of cooking – it should be just tender. Add the lime juice, and salt and pepper to taste. Ladle into bowls and garnish with the bean sprouts and coriander.

TIP Try enoki mushrooms, with their almost sweet taste and crunchy texture, which are best used raw or added to dishes at the last moment. Grown and packaged in clusters, they need to be picked apart from the main cluster before using, then woody parts of the stems trimmed. Choose mushrooms that are firm and white, and reject any that are discoloured or slimy-looking.

LAMB SHANKS WITH BARLEY, GARDEN PEAS AND MINT

Add a touch of spring to the day with braised lamb shanks in a soupy, risotto-like combo of barley, garden peas and refreshing fresh mint. Lamb and pearl barley are a natural pairing. This is a one-pot meal that you can prepare quickly and then leave to gently cook. Pearl barley is a gentle way to bolster the sustenance of a slow-cooked meat dish and is an excellent alternative to potatoes, rice or pasta.

PREPARATION TIME: 15 minutes | **COOKING TIME:** 2 hours | **SERVES:** 6

Preheat the oven to 180°C/350°F (fan 160°C/315°F).

Place a large casserole dish on the stovetop over medium–high heat. Pour in the oil and, when hot, add the shanks and brown`all over, turning occasionally, for about 8 minutes. Push the shanks to the side of the dish slightly and reduce the heat. Add the onion and cook for about 8 minutes, or until golden. Pour in the stock, bring to a lively simmer, cover and place in the oven for about 1½ hours, or until the shanks are tender.

Rinse the barley, drain and add it to the casserole dish, making sure it is covered in liquid. If not, add a little more stock. Cover and cook for about 25–30 minutes, or until the barley is al dente, adding the peas in the last 5 minutes of cooking. Roughly chop half of the mint and stir it in with the orange zest and juice, and salt and pepper to taste. Using forks, pull the meat from the bone and serve with the barley and pea mixture, garnished with the remaining mint leaves.

1 tablespoon olive oil
4 large lamb shanks
1 brown onion, chopped
about 4 cups (1 litre/35 fl oz) chicken stock
1½ cups (300 g/10½ oz) pearl barley
1½ cups (235 g/8½ oz) garden peas
1 handful mint leaves
grated zest and juice of 1 large orange
sea salt flakes and freshly ground pepper

TIPS Depending on the size, one large shank is usually enough for two people.

Tiny whole carrots, peeled garlic cloves and extra onions can be added with the barley if you like.

CRISPY CAULIFLOWER WITH BUCKWHEAT AND PINE NUTS

The earthy, nutty and slightly smoky flavour of buckwheat's amazing tiny pyramid shapes, makes a robust addition to dishes.

PREPARATION TIME: 10 minutes | **COOKING TIME:** 30 minutes | **SERVES:** 6

1 medium cauliflower
2 tablespoons olive oil
sea salt flakes
¾ cup (135 g/4¾ oz) raw buckwheat groats, rinsed
⅔ cup (90 g/3¼ oz) medium pitted black olives, roughly chopped
2 tablespoons salted capers, rinsed and drained
3 tablespoons toasted pine nuts
2 tablespoons currants

DRESSING
1 garlic clove, crushed
1 handful parsley, chopped
⅓ cup (80 ml/2½ fl oz) olive oil
2 tablespoons lemon juice
sea salt flakes and freshly ground pepper

Preheat the oven to 190°C/375°F (fan 170°C/325°F). Line a baking tray with baking paper.

Rinse the cauliflower and cut through the thick core into quarters. Cut each quarter into thick slices and put into a bowl. If you prefer, cut them into large florets. Pour over the oil, sprinkle with a little salt and toss. Arrange the cauliflower on the tray and roast for 20–25 minutes, or until crispy and slightly charred. Set aside to cool.

While the cauliflower is roasting, bring a pot of water to the boil, tip in the buckwheat and simmer for 8–10 minutes, or until al dente. Drain, rinse and leave to cool to room temperature.

Whisk together the dressing ingredients, adding salt and pepper to taste, to make a chunky thick dressing. Watch the amount of salt you use, as both the capers and olives will provide a briny tang.

Put the cauliflower, buckwheat, olives, capers, pine nuts and currants in a bowl. Pour over the dressing and lightly tumble together. Serve at room temperature.

BUCKWHEAT PIKELETS

One of the first recipes many children cook is pikelets. Pouring batter in to large spreading blobs in a hot pan and then anxiously waiting to see tiny bubbles appear on the surface before flipping them over to cook golden brown on the other side was a lesson in learning to be patient for the good things in life.

PREPARATION TIME: 10 minutes | **COOKING TIME:** 12 minutes | **MAKES:** 24

Using an electric mixer, whisk the egg whites in a squeaky-clean bowl until they form soft peaks. Gradually add the sugar, whisking until it is dissolved and the mixture stiff. (Because buckwheat flour can sometimes become dense and slightly chewy in baked goods, egg whites are whisked separately and folded into the batter at the end to incorporate air and produce fluffy pikelets.)

In another bowl, sift together the flour and salt. Make a hollow in the centre and add the egg yolks and buttermilk. Using a large metal spoon, stir from the inside outwards to incorporate the flour until just combined, not smooth. Quickly and lightly fold through the egg whites and avoid overmixing. The mixture will look lumpy but this indicates the batter has large air bubbles trapped, which will create soft fluffy pikelets. Cover the batter with plastic wrap and rest for 10 minutes.

Heat a non-stick pan over medium heat, add 1 teaspoon of the butter and swirl the pan to spread evenly. Add tablespoons of batter to the hot pan, allowing room for spreading. Cook the pikelets for about 30 seconds or until they are set and tiny bubbles appear on the surface, then flip them over to cook for a further 1–2 minutes or until golden. Remove to a plate and cover with foil to keep warm. Repeat the process, adding more of the butter, until all the batter is used.

3 eggs, separated
1 tablespoon soft brown sugar
1 cup (150 g/5½ oz) buckwheat flour
pinch salt
1 cup (250 ml/9 fl oz) buttermilk
about 2 tablespoons butter

VARIATIONS For sweet, add chopped nuts, sultanas, grated citrus, blueberry and/or other berries, cooked pear, banana, grated apple, ground cinnamon or star anise to the batter. Topping ideas include yoghurt, berries, fresh figs and honey-sweetened ricotta. For savoury, omit the sugar from the batter and add corn kernels, chopped spinach, herbs, mushrooms, grated cheese, pine nuts or diced red capsicum. Topping ideas include pesto, scrambled egg, prawns, avocado, flaked cooked salmon, hummus and whipped ricotta. For both sweet and savoury, add a slight textural crunch by replacing half of the flour with ½ cup (65 g/2¼ oz) finely ground toasted buckwheat groats, which also adds a subtle smoky, nutty taste.

CHILLI-GINGER PEANUT BUTTER SOBA NOODLES WITH SILKEN TOFU

This slurp-worthy noodle dish will convert those who decry the marvellousness of silky smooth tofu. Blot the tofu gently, as it breaks easily, requiring the careful handling of a poached egg.

PREPARATION TIME: 25 minutes | **COOKING TIME:** 5 minutes | **SERVES:** 6

½ cup (140 g/5 oz) crunchy peanut butter

¼ cup (60 ml/2 fl oz) light soy sauce

1 tablespoon red wine vinegar

2 tablespoons vegetable oil

1 small red chilli, deseeded and finely chopped

2 teaspoons finely grated fresh ginger

1 teaspoon sesame oil (optional)

4 garlic cloves, crushed

¼ cup (60 ml/2 fl oz) warm water

50 g (1¾ oz) dried soba noodles

100 g (3½ oz) firm silken tofu

⅓ cup (40 g/1½ oz) thinly sliced spring onions (green onions/ scallions)

3 teaspoons toasted sesame seeds

1 Lebanese cucumber, thinly sliced

Put the peanut butter, soy sauce and vinegar in a bowl and blend well. Stir in the vegetable oil, chilli, ginger, sesame oil, if using, and garlic. Add enough of the warm water to blend the mixture into a sauce with the consistency of pouring cream.

Cook the noodles fully according to the instructions on the packet. Drain well and divide between serving bowls. Blot the tofu with paper towel and roughly break up with a fork. Spoon the sauce over noodles and top with spring onions, sesame seeds, cucumber and tofu.

TIP When buying soba noodles, check the packet to make sure they are made from only buckwheat flour. To prevent the noodles from sticking together when cooked, dump them in a big bowl of cold water and drain.

MIXED MUSHROOM BUTTERMILK SOUP WITH ROLLED OATS AND PEAS

The backbone of this soup is buttermilk, the slightly sour-tasting liquid made by fermenting milk or from making butter. Its sharpness underpins the complex mushroom flavours and makes for a brighter, tastier soup. Mushroom varieties have, well, mushroomed in recent years and the dominance of the squeaky-clean white button is now challenged by all kinds of shapes, colours, textures and flavours. Be adventurous.

PREPARATION TIME: 20 minutes | **COOKING TIME:** 45 minutes | **SERVES:** 6

Put the onion and butter in a pot and cook gently for about 8 minutes, or until the onion is soft. Add the mixed mushrooms and cook for 5 minutes, or until they start to release their juices. Add the oats, stock and buttermilk, and simmer for at least 30 minutes; the oats should be soft but still slightly chewy and nutty. Add the snow peas with salt and pepper to taste. Serve garnished with a few enoki mushrooms and lots of parsley.

TIPS Mushrooms that have been in the fridge for slightly longer than they should (just 'on the edge' but not soggy) are perfect for soup and ragouts. They have an evocative woodsy scent and an almost wild-mushroom flavour.

Any green veg can be added, including chopped spinach, broccoli florets, double-shelled broad beans or sugarsnap peas.

Make your own buttermilk by stirring together 1 cup (250 ml/9 fl oz) of whole milk with 4 teaspoons of white vinegar or lemon juice. Let it sit for 10–15 minutes, or until it looks slightly curdled, and it's ready to use.

½ cup (80 g/2¾ oz) finely chopped onion

2 tablespoons butter

2 cups (180 g/6 oz) finely sliced mixed mushrooms

⅔ cup (70 g/2½ oz) traditional rolled oats

6 cups (1.5 litres/52 fl oz) chicken stock

2 cups (500 ml/17 fl oz) buttermilk

60 g (2¼ oz) snow peas (mangetout), trimmed and thinly sliced

sea salt flakes and freshly ground pepper

50 g (1¾ oz) enoki mushrooms, to garnish

1 handful parsley, coarsely chopped, to garnish

GARLICKY MUSHROOMS WITH ONIONS AND THYME ON OAT MASH

There's no requirement to use just the one variety of mushroom if you prefer a more sophisticated, rich and earthy flavour. Toss in a few toasted chopped hazelnuts for textural pleasure. The flavours in this dish may be gutsy and uncompromising, but the finish is undeniably light.

PREPARATION TIME: 20 minutes | **COOKING TIME:** 20 minutes | **SERVES:** 6

3 cups (750 ml/26 fl oz) water
1½ cups (240 g/8½ oz) steel-cut oats
about ¼ cup (60 ml/2 fl oz) olive oil
2 medium onions, finely sliced
5 garlic cloves, crushed
about 450 g (1 lb) crimini mushrooms, sliced
5 thyme sprigs (or tarragon, dill or chervil)
½ cup (60 g/2¼ oz) finely grated smoked cheese (gouda or cheddar)
sea salt flakes and freshly ground pepper
thyme (or tarragon) leaves

Bring the water to the boil in a large pot over medium–high heat. Add the oats, reduce the heat and simmer, covered, and cook for about 20 minutes or until the oats are tender.

Meanwhile, heat the oil in frying pan over medium heat, add the onions and garlic, and cook for 3–5 minutes. Add the mushrooms and thyme sprigs, and cook about 5 minutes or until the mushrooms turn golden brown. Drizzle in a little more oil if necessary to stop the mushrooms from drying out. Take off the heat and remove the thyme sprigs.

Stir the cheese through the cooked oats, mixing well and seasoning with salt and a little pepper if necessary. Spoon large dollops in each serving dish and top with the mushroom mixture. Garnish with thyme leaves.

> **TIPS** In place of smoked cheese you might prefer mozzarella, goat's cheese or parmesan.
>
> Rolled or old-fashioned oats can be used instead of steel-cut oats. They cook faster than steel-cut oats, absorb more liquid and form a soft thick mixture. Steel-cut oats are coarser, smaller and tougher than your ordinary rolled oats. They look almost like rice that's been cut into pieces, take longer to cook and have a nutty, chewy texture.

MIXED GRAINS SALAD WITH MARINATED ZUCCHINI

Slow-cooking barley combines with quick-cooking quinoa in this refreshing and vibrantly coloured salad influenced by Italian and Greek cuisine. The grains soak up the bold flavours, giving the dish bite and substance.

PREPARATION TIME: 40 minutes | **COOKING TIME:** 30 minutes | **SERVES:** 6

To make the marinated zucchini, wash, trim and cut the zucchini lengthways into 8 mm (⅜ in) thick slices. Working in batches, heat 2 tablespoons of the oil in a sturdy non-stick frying pan over medium–high heat. Arrange the zucchini in a single layer in the pan and cook for about 3 minutes on each side, until well browned. Remove from the pan, arrange in a shallow dish and sprinkle lightly with salt and pepper. Warm the garlic, vinegar and sugar in a small pan and pour over the zucchini. Scatter with mint and parsley, toss lightly and leave at room temperature for 1 hour before serving.

For the salad, put the barley, quinoa, tomatoes, olives, walnuts, radicchio and curly endive in a large bowl, adding salt and pepper to taste. Whisk the oil and vinegar together until emulsified, pour over the salad and toss lightly. Serve the salad topped with marinated zucchini.

TIP Cook the pearl barley in stock to pump up the flavours.

MARINATED ZUCCHINI
6 small zucchini (courgettes)
about ¼ cup (60 ml/2 fl oz) olive oil
sea salt flakes and freshly ground
  pepper
2 garlic cloves, crushed
¼ cup (60 ml/2 fl oz) red wine vinegar
1 tablespoon caster (superfine) sugar
3 tablespoons torn mint leaves
3 tablespoons torn parsley

MIXED GRAINS SALAD
1 cup (200 g/7 oz) pearl barley, cooked
1 cup (200 g/7 oz) quinoa, rinsed and
  cooked
1 cup (150 g/5½ oz) halved red cherry
  tomatoes
1 cup (150 g/5½ oz) halved yellow
  cherry tomatoes
½ cup (60 g/2¼ oz) pitted black olives
½ cup (60 g/2¼ oz) walnut halves
4 large radicchio leaves, roughly torn
2 handfuls torn pale inner leaves of
  curly endive or rocket
sea salt flakes and ground pepper
⅓ cup (80 ml/2½ fl oz) extra virgin
  olive oil
1 tablespoon red wine vinegar

QUINOA 'RISOTTO' WITH PUMPKIN, CARROTS AND HAZELNUTS

This cheesy, creamy, aromatic faux risotto studded with veggies is just as soothing and satisfying as the real deal. If you're not keen on constant pot stirring, add the stock all at once, cover, turn the heat down to medium–low and cook until the quinoa is tender.

PREPARATION TIME: 20 minutes | **COOKING TIME:** 25 minutes | **SERVES:** 6

350 g (12 oz) pumpkin (squash), peeled and cut into 1 cm (½ in) cubes
3 medium carrots, scraped and cut into 1 cm (½ in) cubes
1½ cups (300 g/10½ oz) quinoa
¼ cup (60 ml/2 fl oz) olive oil
1 large shallot, finely chopped
3 cups (750 ml/26 fl oz) hot vegetable stock
1 handful mint leaves, finely chopped
1 handful parsley, finely chopped
½ cup (45 g/1½ oz) grated mozzarella
½ cup (130 g/4½ oz) natural yoghurt
finely grated zest and juice of 1 plump lemon
sea salt flakes and freshly ground pepper
1 cup (120 g/4½ oz) coarsely chopped roasted hazelnuts

Bring a large pot of water to the boil, add the pumpkin and carrot and cook at a lively simmer for 8 minutes. Drain.

Rinse the quinoa (this step is essential as it removes the bitter coating on the tiny seed) and drain. Wipe the pot dry, add the oil and the shallot and gently cook for 5 minutes. Add the quinoa and cook, stirring occasionally, until glossy. Start adding the stock about ½ cup (125 ml/4 fl oz) at a time, stirring after each addition and keeping the mixture gently bubbling. When the stock is nearly evaporated, add more. Continue cooking and adding enough stock for about 15 minutes, until the mixture becomes softened – it shouldn't be too dry or soupy.

Add the vegetables, mint, parsley, cheese, yoghurt, lemon zest and juice, and season with salt and pepper. Stir lightly until the cheese melts, then serve with a generous sprinkle of hazelnuts.

TIP Other cheeses, including ricotta, cheddar and gruyere, also work very well in this dish. Chicken stock can be used for added depth of flavour.

FISH SOUP WITH THAI FLAVOURS AND RICE NOODLES

The allure of this soup depends entirely on a deep-flavoured, perfectly balanced and spiced broth. Snap the dry noodles before cooking to make the soup less messy.

PREPARATION TIME: 20 minutes | **COOKING TIME:** 10 minutes | **SERVES:** 6

Put the stock, chilli, lemongrass, ginger, fish sauce and kaffir lime leaves in a large pot and bring the boil over medium–high heat. Reduce the heat to low and gently simmer for 3–4 minutes to infuse the flavours. Taste and adjust as you like, adding more chilli and fish sauce; it should be hot, sour and salty. Add the tomato, salmon (make sure all the fine bones are removed) and noodles, and gently simmer for no longer than 4–5 minutes – just until the salmon has turned opaque. (The cooking time depends on the thickness of the noodles and they can become mushy very quickly, so add them just before serving – and watch carefully.)

Ladle the soup into bowls and serve sprinkled with coriander and some lime juice.

TIP This is a very forgiving soup, as you can adjust the flavours to suit your own taste by adding more chilli or Thai chilli paste, some cooling mint or sliced lime in place of the kaffir lime leaves.

- 6 cups (1.5 litres/52 fl oz) chicken stock
- 1 small red chilli, finely chopped
- 2 lemongrass stalks, trimmed and bruised
- 4 slices peeled ginger
- ¼ cup (60 ml/2 fl oz) fish sauce
- 3 kaffir lime leaves
- 1 medium tomato, diced
- 600 g (1 lb 5 oz) thick skinless salmon fillet, cut into large chunks
- 125 g (4½ oz) rice noodles, 5 mm (¼ in) wide
- 8 long coriander (cilantro) sprigs, chopped
- ¼ cup (60 ml/2 fl oz) fresh lime juice

GOLDEN RICE WITH PEAS AND CASHEWS

Delicate and aromatic basmati is the undisputed king of long-grain rice. This dish, with fragrant and warming spices, deserves the best.

PREPARATION TIME: 10 minutes | **COOKING TIME:** 25 minutes | **SERVES:** 6

Wash the rice several times and drain well.

Heat the oil in a large sturdy pot with a tight-fitting lid, add the cloves, cinnamon, cardamom pods and cumin seeds, and gently fry for 1 minute. Add the turmeric and drained rice, and stir over medium heat for about 3 minutes. Add the hot stock and salt. Bring quickly to the boil, then reduce the heat to very low and cook, covered, for 25 minutes, adding the peas in the last 5 minutes of cooking.

Remove the pot from the heat, take the lid off and leave to stand for 3 minutes to allow the steam to escape. Remove the whole spices at this stage, if you like. Add the cashews, fluff the grains lightly with a fork and serve.

TIP It is essential to rinse basmati – even soak it for 10–15 minutes to allow the grains to absorb water and cook evenly without breaking. The peas are very soft after 25 minutes' cooking, so if you prefer, cook them separately. Jasmine rice, which has a more floral fragrance, or long-grain rice can be substituted but cooking times will vary.

1½ cups (300 g/10½ oz) basmati rice
1 tablespoon vegetable oil
4 whole cloves
1 small cinnamon stick
4 cardamom pods, cracked
1 teaspoon cumin seeds
1 teaspoon ground turmeric
3½ cups (875 ml/30 fl oz) hot chicken stock
1 teaspoon sea salt flakes
1½ cups (235 g/8½ oz) garden peas
1 cup (155 g/5½ oz) raw cashews

BROWN RICE RISOTTO WITH PEAS AND PRAWNS

In a world where dazzling white is lauded – think teeth – brown rice is a standout grain, richly deserving bragging rights. After all, white rice started out as brown rice, but has been refined, processed and polished to shiny white brightness, into a grain with depleted nutritional appeal.

PREPARATION TIME: 20 minutes | **COOKING TIME:** 25 minutes | **SERVES:** 6

1 cup (200 g/7 oz) brown rice, rinsed
¼ cup (60 ml/2 fl oz) olive oil
1 medium onion, finely chopped
about 4 cups (1 litre/35 fl oz) hot chicken stock
200 g (7 oz) raw small prawns (shrimp), peeled and deveined, tails intact
1 cup (155 g/5½ oz) garden peas
2 tablespoons extra light sour cream
1 handful parsley, chopped
1 teaspoon finely grated lemon zest
sea salt flakes and freshly ground pepper

Bring a large pot of salted water to the boil, add rice and stir well. Reduce the heat to low and gently simmer, without stirring, for about 10 minutes or until the rice is swollen and half-tender. Drain well.

Heat the oil in a wide, deep pan over medium heat. When hot, add the onion and cook for about 8 minutes, stirring occasionally, or until softened but not coloured. Add the well-drained rice and cook for 5 minutes, stirring occasionally, until it is glossy and coated with oil. Start adding the stock about ½ cup (125 ml/4 fl oz) at a time, stirring after each addition. Allow the rice to absorb the stock before adding more. Keep the heat level at medium to medium–high, stir frequently, and cook for about 20 minutes or until the rice is almost tender and the mixture creamy. Stir in the prawns and peas, and continue to cook, adding more hot stock, if needed, until the rice is tender. (The mixture should not be too soupy or too dry.) Quickly stir though the sour cream, parsley and lemon zest, along with some salt and pepper to taste. Serve immediately.

TIP Don't stir rice when it's boiling, as this activates starch and will make the rice gluggy. With risotto, however, stirring the rice makes it creamy.

WILD RICE PILAF WITH MUSHROOMS AND ALMONDS

This is a sensational combination of nutty, chewy brown rice and toothsome wild rice – the wild card in this pilaf. (It's neither a rice or wild – it's a native grass.) Choose several mushroom varieties to intensify the flavour: brown mushrooms for dense texture and robust flavour; delicate buttons; slightly spongy shiitake with their distinct aroma; or shell-shaped succulent oyster mushrooms.

PREPARATION TIME: 20 minutes | COOKING TIME: 1¼ hours | SERVES: 8

Heat the oil and butter in a large sturdy pot with a tight-fitting lid. Add the onion, carrot, celery and garlic, and gently cook for 5 minutes, or until the vegetables soften. Add the mushrooms, increase the heat to medium and cook for 5 minutes, stirring often. Rinse both types of rice, drain well and add to the pot. Stir until the grains are well coated in oil. Pour in the stock, bring to the boil and then reduce the heat to as low as possible. Put the lid on (if it does not fit tightly, cover the pan with foil and then ram the lid on) and cook for 50 minutes. (Don't be tempted to lift the lid during this time.)

Remove the pan from the heat and take off the lid. Check the rice – it should be al dente. If not, replace the lid and cook for a further 10 minutes. Season with salt and pepper to taste, and add the lemon zest and juice. Replace the lid, remove from the heat and leave the rice to rest for 10 minutes. To serve, add the parsley and almonds and fluff the rice through with a fork.

TIP It may seem costly to buy wild rice, but a little really does go a long way – it swells up to four times its size as it cooks. Unlike long-grain rice, there's no fixed cooking time. It's ready when most of the grains split to reveal a creamy interior, and they open at different rates. Because wild rice won't always absorb all the water when it has finished cooking, simply drain it.

2 tablespoons olive oil
1 tablespoon butter
1 small onion, very finely chopped
1 small carrot, scraped and finely chopped
1 small celery stalk, finely chopped
2 garlic cloves, crushed
3 cups (270 g/9½ oz) sliced mushrooms
1 cup (200 g/7 oz) brown rice
1 cup (190 g/6¾ oz) wild rice
4 cups (1 litre/35 fl oz) chicken or vegetable stock
sea salt flakes and freshly ground pepper
2 teaspoon lemon zest
1 tablespoon lemon juice
2 tablespoons chopped parsley
½ cup (80 g/2¾ oz) coarsely chopped raw almonds

BURGHUL AND RED LENTIL SOUP WITH SIZZLING MINT AND CHILLI

Make heaps of this soup and freeze it for those times when you're too tired to do anything more than reheat in a pot while you make the sizzling browned butter. Serve with hunks of sourdough bread.

PREPARATION TIME: 15 minutes | **COOKING TIME:** 55 minutes | **SERVES:** 6

3 medium tomatoes
¼ cup (60 ml/2 fl oz) vegetable oil
1 teaspoon ground cumin
1 teaspoon ground turmeric
2 garlic cloves, finely chopped
1 medium onion, chopped
1 tablespoon tomato paste
    (concentrated purée)
4 cups (1 litre/35 fl oz) chicken stock
⅔ cup (125 g/4½ oz) red lentils, rinsed
    and drained
⅔ cup (135 g/4¾ oz) burghul (bulgur)
4 cups (1 litre/34 fl oz) water
sea salt flakes and freshly ground
    pepper
2 tablespoons butter
1 tablespoon dried mint
1 teaspoon ground aleppo pepper

Remove the core from the tomatoes using a fine-bladed small knife, cut a small wedge out from around the stem end of the tomatoes. Drop into a pot of gently boiling water. After 3 minutes scoop the tomatoes out and when cool enough to handle, peel the skins off. Halve the tomatoes, remove the seeds and chop the flesh finely.

Heat the oil in a large sturdy pot over medium heat, add the cumin, turmeric, garlic and onion, and cook, stirring occasionally, for about 8 minutes, or until the onions soften. Stir in the tomato paste and simmer for 3 minutes. Add the tomatoes and cook at a lively simmer for 3 minutes. Add the stock, lentils, burghul and water. Bring to the boil, reduce the heat and cook at a medium simmer for about 40 minutes, or until the soup has thickened. Add salt and pepper to taste, being careful with pepper, bearing in mind you are adding chilli at the end. Remove the pot from the heat and cover.

Melt the butter in a small frying pan over medium–high heat for about 3 minutes or until foaming and starting to brown, remove from the heat and stir in the mint and aleppo pepper. To serve, ladle the soup into bowls and drizzle with the chilli-mint browned butter.

TIP Aleppo pepper is a highly desirable variety of chilli with a moderate heat level, a fruity flavour and slight vinegary, salty taste. As a substitute, combine four parts sweet paprika with one part cayenne pepper.

SPAGHETTI WITH GREEN TOMATOES AND FRESH HERBS

There are two options for sourcing the tomatoes for this lively sauce: end of harvest when the sun's ripening rays are no more, or early in the season for those impatient for their homegrown fruit to ripen. Their sharp flavour and crisp texture offer a fresh perspective on ripe tomatoes we all know and love. Don't hold back on the fresh herbs – measure with a large hand.

PREPARATION TIME: 15 minutes I **COOKING TIME:** 12 minutes I **SERVES:** 6

Put the mint, basil, parsley, tomatoes, garlic and olive oil in a food processor and pulse-blend for a few seconds to form a chunky mixture. Add salt and pepper to taste.

Cook the pasta in a large pot of salted boiling water for about 9 minutes, or until al dente and then drain, reserving about ½ cup (125 ml/4 fl oz) of the cooking water. (The salty starchy water adds flavour, helps thicken the sauce and binds everything together.) Return the pasta to the pan with the reserved water, tip in the sauce and stir until well combined. Serve immediately, topped with blobs of ricotta.

1 large handful mint leaves, chopped
1 large handful basil leaves, chopped
1 large handful parsley, chopped
6 medium green tomatoes, roughly chopped
2 garlic cloves, chopped
½ cup (125 ml/4 fl oz) olive oil
sea salt flakes and freshly ground pepper
500 g (1 lb 2 oz) spaghetti
⅔ cup (165 g/6 oz) ricotta

TIP Choosing green tomatoes can be tricky, as some varieties have a greenish tinge but are almost ripe. The best tomatoes for this dish are very firm and very green.

RIBBON PASTA WITH BROAD BEANS AND PANCETTA

You don't have to know the difference between farfalle, fettuccine and fusilli, but you should know that pasta brings people together. It is cheap, versatile and convenient, and an excellent pantry staple for when you need a quick meal.

PREPARATION TIME: 15 minutes | **COOKING TIME:** 20 minutes | **SERVES:** 6

500 g (1 lb 2 oz) ribbon pasta (pappardelle, fettuccine, tagliatelle)
½ teaspoon sea salt flakes
1½ cups (255 g/9 oz) podded small fresh broad beans
⅓ cup (80 ml/2½ fl oz) olive oil
2 garlic cloves, crushed
2 rashers short-cut rindless bacon, chopped
3 tablespoons chopped parsley
½ cup (50 g/1¾ oz) grated pecorino

Bring a large pot of water to the boil, and then add the pasta and salt. Cook for 8–10 minutes, or according to the packet instructions, until al dente.

Meanwhile, drop the broad beans into a pot of simmering salted water. Cook for 3 minutes or until just tender. Drain and refresh under cold water. If the beans are not young tender beans (and if you can be bothered), after they are cooked and cooled, slip off the grey–green tough outer skins.

Heat the oil in a frying pan over medium heat, then add the garlic and bacon, and cook for about 8 minutes, or until crisp. Add the broad beans, toss and heat through.

Drain the pasta, reserving about ½ cup (125 ml/4 fl oz) of the cooking water. Put the pasta and reserved cooking water in a large serving bowl with the bean mixture. Sprinkle over the parsley and pecorino and toss well before serving.

TIP For a vegetarian option, replace the bacon with peas, sliced mushrooms or asparagus tips.

FREGOLA AND BLOOD ORANGE SALAD WITH FENNEL

Every ingredient in this lively salad says Italy. Fregola is a type of Sardinian semolina pasta, not dissimilar to couscous. During processing, it is mixed with water, rolled into tiny pebbles, sun-dried and roasted, giving it a rustic quality. Red-fleshed blood oranges were developed in Sicily, while subtly-scented aniseedy fennel is everywhere in Italy.

PREPARATION TIME: 25 minutes | **COOKING TIME:** 12 minutes | **SERVES:** 6

Bring a pot of salted water to the boil and add the fregola. Boil for about 10–15 minutes, or until cooked through. Drain, refresh under cold water and set aside to drain and dry.

Slice the peel and white pith from the oranges and slice the flesh into thin rounds. Arrange in a circle on a serving dish.

For the dressing, mash the anchovies with the garlic and chilli flakes and then whisk in the lemon juice and oil.

Put the well-drained and cooled fregola and the fennel in a bowl, add the dressing and toss lightly. Pile the mixture on top of the oranges and season generously with pepper. Garnish with fennel fronds.

TIP The flavour is improved if the fregola is cooked in a flavoursome stock. It should take no more than 15 minutes of cooking, until al dente. You can replace fregola with Israeli (pearl) couscous or orzo if you wish.

2 cups (400 g/14 oz) fregola
4 blood oranges
1 medium fennel bulb, trimmed and thinly sliced
freshly ground pepper

ANCHOVY-LEMON DRESSING
4 anchovy fillets, drained
1 garlic clove, peeled
½ teaspoon dried chilli flakes
¼ cup (60 ml/2 fl oz) lemon juice
¼ cup (60 ml/2 fl oz) olive oil

JERUSALEM ARTICHOKES WITH FARRO, SPINACH AND OYSTER MUSHROOMS

Texturally, this is a masterstroke: chewy farro, velvety oyster mushrooms, creamy starchiness of artichokes and tender spinach. They all earn a prime spot of real estate in the fridge.

PREPARATION TIME: 20 minutes | **COOKING TIME:** 35 minutes | **SERVES:** 6

⅔ cup (120 g/4¼ oz) farro
500 g (1 lb 2 oz) Jerusalem artichokes, scraped or thinly peeled
¼ cup (60 ml/2 fl oz) olive oil
2 garlic cloves, crushed
1 small red onion, thinly sliced
150 g (5½ oz) small oyster mushrooms
2 handfuls (50 g/1¾ oz) baby spinach leaves
1 handful parsley, chopped
1 teaspoon finely grated lemon zest
juice of ½ small lemon
sea salt flakes and freshly ground pepper

Put the farro in a pot and cover with 5 cm (2 in) of water. Bring to the boil, cover and cook over low heat for about 20 minutes, or until the farro is tender. Drain well.

Thickly slice the artichokes and put them in a large pot of lightly salted water. Simmer for about 3 minutes, or until just tender and then drain.

Heat 2 tablespoons of the oil in a sturdy pan and when hot, add the garlic, onion and artichokes and cook over medium heat for about 8 minutes, or until the onion is soft and golden. Increase the heat to high, add the remaining oil with the mushrooms and spinach and toss. Cook for 2–3 minutes, or until the spinach just starts to wilt. Add the farro, parsley, lemon zest and juice, with salt and pepper to taste. Give the pan a few quick tosses for a couple of minutes to heat through. Serve immediately.

TIP Salt has the habit of hardening grains if it's added at the beginning of cooking.

FARRO WITH ROASTED WINTER VEGETABLES, PRUNES AND WALNUTS

Here, farro is the chewy counterpoint to caramelised roasted veggies and squidgy prunes. Try to avoid replacing the malt vinegar here as its assertive yet sweet nature adds a lively note to the dish, melding the flavours.

PREPARATION TIME: 15 minutes | **COOKING TIME:** 25 minutes | **SERVES:** 6

Preheat the oven to 200°C/400°F (fan 180°C/350°F).

Trim the bottoms off the brussels sprouts and cut into quarters. Peel the pumpkin and cut into medium dice. Break the cauliflower into large florets and cut each one in half or into thick slices. Place all the vegetables in a roasting pan with the olive oil and toss. Roast for about 20 minutes, or until tender and browned.

Meanwhile, put the farro in a large pot of boiling water over medium heat and cook for about 20 minutes, or until al dente. Drain well.

When the vegetables are cooked, cool slightly and then tip into a large bowl. Add the well-drained farro, spring onions, parsley, prunes and walnuts. Whisk together the vinegar and extra virgin olive oil, and add salt and pepper to taste. Pour into the bowl and gently toss to mix. If liked, garnish with parsley and serve immediately.

300 g (10½ oz) brussels sprouts
250 g (9 oz) pumpkin (squash)
250 g (9 oz) cauliflower
⅓ cup (80 ml/2½ fl oz) olive oil
1½ cups (270 g/9½ oz) farro
4 spring onions (green onions/ scallions) trimmed, sliced
1 handful parsley, chopped
½ cup (90 g/3¼ oz) chopped pitted prunes
½ cup (60 g/2 oz) coarsely chopped walnuts
2 tablespoons malt vinegar
⅓ cup (80 ml/2½ fl oz) extra virgin olive oil
sea salt flakes and freshly ground pepper

TIPS Brussels sprouts are wonderful when roasted. Use them on their own or team them with your favourite winter vegetables.

Prunes can be swapped for sultanas (golden raisins), seeded raisins or dried apricots.

FARRO AND GREEN LENTILS WITH CHERRY TOMATOES AND MARINATED FETA

This is a crunchy–squishy salad, for which the lentils and farro can be prepared ahead of time and, at the last minute, everything tossed together. Unlike some other grains, farro is hard to overcook.

PREPARATION TIME: 20 minutes | **COOKING TIME:** 40 minutes | **SERVES:** 6

1 cup (180 g/6 oz) small green lentils

1 cup (180 g/6 oz) farro

¼ cup (60 ml/2 fl oz) lemon juice

3 garlic cloves, crushed

½ cup (125 ml/4 fl oz) extra virgin olive oil

sea salt flakes and freshly ground pepper

400 g (14 oz) ripe cherry tomatoes, halved

1 small red onion, finely diced

1 large handful mixed herbs (parsley, thyme, chives), chopped

¾ cup (90 g/3¼ oz) crumbled marinated soft feta

Bring a large pot of lightly salted water to the boil. Add the lentils and simmer for about 20 minutes. Rinse the farro and add to the pan. Simmer for 20 minutes or until the farro and lentils are tender. Drain well.

Meanwhile, whisk together the lemon juice, garlic and oil, and add salt and pepper to taste. Put the cherry tomatoes in a large bowl.

Tip the lentils and farro into the bowl with the tomatoes, pour over the dressing with the onion and herbs and gently toss. Pile on a large serving dish with the feta spooned over the top and garnished with extra herbs.

TIPS Use as many herbs as you fancy – marjoram, tarragon or chervil.

Instead of marinated feta, a soft goat's cheese or a large ball of mozzarella torn into pieces would be a nice substitute.

Brighten the flavour even more by cooking the lentils and farro in two parts water and one part apple cider with a couple of bay leaves thrown in.

LAMB, FETA AND BURGHUL MEATBALLS

Burghul (bulgur/bulgar/bulghul) is wheat that's been dehusked, parboiled, dried and cracked into nibbly bits. Don't confuse it with cracked wheat, which is simply that – cracked wheat – and can take up to an hour to cook. As burghul has been parboiled, it needs little cooking and, in most cases, nothing more than a good soak in hot water.

PREPARATION TIME: 25 minutes | **COOKING TIME:** 45 minutes | **SERVES:** 6

Put the beef, one finely chopped onion, feta, mint, cinnamon, burghul and half the garlic in a bowl with salt and pepper to taste. Clump the mixture together with your hands to mix well and then cover and set aside for 1 hour. Scoop out pieces of the mixture and shape into small balls about the size of golf balls.

Heat the oil in a deep, non-stick pan over medium heat. Slice the remaining three onions, add to the pan and cook for about 7 minutes, or until the onions are soft but not coloured. Stir in the remaining garlic and cook for a further 1 minute. Add the tomatoes with the water, and add salt and pepper to taste. Bring the mixture to a gentle simmer and then place the meatballs evenly on top. Pour in enough water to come about two-thirds of the way up the contents of the pan. Cover the pan, reduce the heat to low and gently simmer for about 35 minutes, or until the meatballs are tender and cooked.

500 g (1 lb 2 oz) lean minced (ground) beef
4 large onions
⅔ cup (90 g/3¼ oz) crumbled feta
2 tablespoons chopped mint
1 teaspoon ground cinnamon
1 cup (175 g/6 oz) fine burghul (bulgur)
2 garlic cloves, crushed
sea salt flakes and freshly ground pepper
¼ cup (60 ml/2 fl oz) olive oil
400 g (14 oz) tin chopped tomatoes
1 cup (250 ml/9 fl oz) water

TIP Play with the seasonings to add punchy colourful flavours: add a little heat with chilli, bump up the mint or use cumin instead of cinnamon.

ROASTED BEETROOT PURÉE AND BURGHUL WITH MIXED FRESH HERBS

Burghul is a refreshing alternative to rice and couscous. It's best known in green tabbouleh, but when introduced to beetroot blushes a fuschia colour. Serve spoonfuls on the witlof leaves for a meal starter, or on mixed platters of mezze, tapas or antipasti.

PREPARATION TIME: 20 minutes | **COOKING TIME:** 25 minutes | **SERVES:** 6

3 medium beetroot (beets), scrubbed
⅔ cup (170 ml/5½ fl oz) olive oil
2 cups (500 ml/17 fl oz) water
sea salt flakes and freshly ground pepper
1 cup (200 g/7 oz) medium burghul (bulgur)
⅓ cup (80 ml/2½ fl oz) red wine vinegar
2 teaspoons Dijon mustard
⅓ cup (80 ml/2½ fl oz) vegetable oil
3 handfuls mixed herbs, roughly chopped
2 spring onions (green onions/ scallions), trimmed and finely sliced
½ cup (60 g/2¼ oz) finely chopped celery
1 witlof (chicory), leaves separated
⅓ cup (95 g/3 oz) natural yoghurt

Preheat the oven to 220°C/425°F (fan 200°C/400°F).

Cut the beetroot in half and arrange in a roasting pan. Drizzle with 1 tablespoon of the oil and splash with 2 tablespoons of the water. Sprinkle with salt and pepper, cover with foil and bake for about 20 minutes, or until tender. Cool the beetroot and then peel and dice.

Put the beetroot in a pot with the remaining water over medium–high heat, bring to the boil and simmer for 2 minutes. Strain the beetroot, reserving the liquid. Put the burghul in a bowl, measure 1½ cups (375 ml/13 fl oz) of the reserved beetroot liquid and pour this over the burghul. Cover with plastic wrap and leave for about 45 minutes, or until the burghul has absorbed the liquid.

Blitz the beetroot with the vinegar, mustard and remaining oil in a blender (or use a hand-held blender), until it becomes a coarse purée. Add salt and pepper to taste. Tip the mixture into the burghul, add the herbs, spring onions and celery, and mix well. Serve immediately (or refrigerate for up to 1 day), with witlof leaves and dotted with yoghurt. Alternatively, serve the yoghurt on the side.

TIP Herbs that complement beetroot include dill, tarragon, thyme, basil and chives.

Fruit

We take as much pleasure biting into fruits and berries as we have for thousands of years. As the 'eaters', we think we're the winners. But it's a two-way relationship. The 'eaten' wins, too. If you are rooted to the spot, you need something that's mobile to help you disperse your seeds. Sweet, ripe, juicy flesh is an inducement; it tempts us (and animals, birds and insects) to tuck in and, one way or another, disperse seeds. This successful strategy has seen seeds become the original globe trotters.

If seed dispersal was an Olympic sport, it's unlikely we would make the finals. As competitors, we are outclassed. A thirsty hyena can chomp through 18 tsamma melons in a night then disperse seeds over a home range of some 400 square kilometres (150 square miles). This is impressive, but possibly pales alongside a black bear sitting around gorging up to 30,000 berries in a day, then distributing thousands of seeds over its territory.

There's a smart evolutionary explanation for our sweet tooth. Hunting and gathering are hard work, day in, day out. Discovering that the sweet, ripe fruits dangling on a branch or bright berries on a bush were safe to pick and eat was a no-brainer. Bitterness, on the other hand, helped us steer clear of plants with potentially tummy-upsetting toxins.

The sweetness in fruits and berries that spells 'safe to eat' comes from natural sugars – typically fructose (or fruit sugar), glucose and sucrose. Amounts range from a mere trace in limes to almost 60 per cent in dates. And although sugars in themselves aren't a health food, in fruits they are accompanied by really good stuff, such as fibre, vitamins, minerals and phytonutrients including eye-catching carotenes in orange-fleshed fruits like mangoes, papaya and peaches and anthocyanins in all blue–purple berries. And, of course, vitamin C.

WASTE NOT, WANT NOT

'Fruit is a most important item in the economy of health; the epicurean can scarcely be said to have any luxuries without it; therefore, as it is so invaluable, when we cannot have it fresh, we must have it preserved.' said Mrs Beeton in her *Book of Household Management* (1861).

Ever since we became farmers, we've preserved summer's harvest one way or another to make sure we had food to put on the table through the winter. We made the most of the sun to dry fruit and, according to archaeological records, fire and hot sand mounds did the same job. Drying keeps bacteria at bay by reducing water content (from around 90 per cent to 5–35 per cent) and concentrating the sugars. Sun-drying is still carried out in many parts of the world, Turkish sun-dried apricots, for instance.

However, the dried fruits on supermarket shelves – from tree fruit such as apples, apricots, dates, figs, muscatels, peaches, pears, prunes (dried plums) and vine fruits including sultanas (golden raisins), raisins, and currants – are generally dried in dehydrators. Processors typically add sulphur dioxide (E220) to ensure fruits keep their appealing colour and texture and prevent them from oxidising and browning. Organic versions may not have good looks on their side (they are often darker) but they are equally delicious if not more so. Some very tart fruits are sweetened before drying. Regular dried cranberries (sometimes called craisins) can have quite large amounts of added sugar.

If you want to try your hand at drying fruit, you will need about 4 kilograms of fresh grapes to produce 1 kilogram of sultanas and 6 kilograms of ripe tree fruits for 1 kilogram dried. If you get enthusiastic and invest in an electric dehydrator, don't limit yourself to fruit. Try drying tomatoes, capsicums (peppers), chillies, mushrooms and even kale.

At some point, our forebears discovered that storing fruit in honey meant it lasted longer. Boosting the sugar content prevents bacterial growth because sugar is hygroscopic, meaning it has a tendency to absorb moisture, reducing the amount of water available for encouraging microorganisms. This method of preservation also tends to draw water from microbes, thus dehydrating and killing them.

Preserving whole fruit or fruit pieces so they kept their shape without having to add any sugar came with the discovery of sterilisation in the 19th century and the availability of affordable reusable containers you could sterilise such as the Mason jar. Many of us remember our mothers and grandmothers in steamy kitchens at summer's end busily transforming nature's abundance into glistening jars of fruit, preserves, jams and chutneys.

BOTTLING

In Kate's mum's kitchen, it was all hands on deck for bottling and jam making. It was not just about providing for the winter months. It was a highly competitive local sport. In her story-packed country cookbook, *Apple Blossom Pie*, Kate describes how 'the noble art of fruit bottling culminated at local agricultural shows where intricate pieces of edible art were showcased in tall Fowlers jars with brass-coloured lids, clipped by a spring to the neck, or with taut, concave cellophane throttled by a rubber band'. Her mum and nan bottled vegetables, too. She remembers many a late night, knitting needle in hand, fastidiously trying to arrange a decorative slice of carrot in a mosaic pattern with green beans and peas. Kate still bottles fruit. It's the habit of a lifetime living by the seasons.

APPLES

Crisp, juicy and filling, apples are long-time tempters. 'It is remarkable how closely the history of the apple tree is connected with that of man,' wrote Henry David Thoreau. Roman legions munched them and marched; Silk Road travellers snacked on them and trekked; *Mayflower* pilgrims stocked on them as did Captain Arthur Phillips heading off to Botany Bay. Thanks to all this seed dispersing, apples grow on every continent apart from Antarctica, which is why we can pack this affordable hero fruit into lunchboxes, grate it over muesli, slice it into salads, serve it with pork and lovingly make it into muffins, pies and tarts.

WHAT TO LOOK FOR

Although available year round, new-season apples appear in the produce aisles from late summer through autumn. And that's when they are at their best.

Shop where apples are kept cold otherwise they may be mealy and insipid. Skip the pre-packed apples and hand-pick firm to hard apples with tight, well-coloured, unblemished skin and a delicate sweet aroma. Farm fresh apples are not shiny. Shiny apples have been prepared to catch your eye.

Apples that look imperfect are often perfectly good for eating and cooking, although you may have to cut out the odd blemish on the skin.

HOW TO STORE THEM

Keep apples cold to prevent them from ripening further. Since most apples are picked at peak ripeness, additional 'ripening' actually means 'decaying', and this process speeds up tenfold if the fruit is left at room temperature. To enjoy the texture, store them in plastic bags in the crisper drawer of the refrigerator, where they will keep for many weeks. Check them often and remove any decayed apples, since one rotten apple can indeed spoil the whole barrel. Apples absorb odours easily and they also affect nearby produce such as lemons, avocados and tomatoes because of the natural ripening gas they emit.

WHAT'S IN THEM?

1 small apple (about 110 g/3¾ oz) has about 240 kilojoules (57 calories), 0.5 g protein, no fat, 13 g carbs (all sugars), 2 g fibre, 110 mg potassium, and a low GI (40) and GL (5).

WHAT ELSE?

Wash apples before using and if you are slicing or peeling lots of them, drop the apple slices or peeled apples into cold water with a squeeze of lemon juice to prevent discolouration.

There's a variety of apple for every purpose and sometimes a combination works best. For a pie, the more varieties you use the richer the flavour. Once you know which apples to look for, mix and match to find your tastiest combination. The best baking apples offer a balance of sweet and tart flavours as well as flesh that doesn't break down in the oven.

HERO RECIPES

Apple sponge pudding (page 204)
Apple rose tart (page 205)

BANANAS

Bananas are the world's number-one fruit when it comes to tonnage shipped – an impressive achievement given they have only been widely available for a hundred years or so. They have so many pluses – affordability, portability, easy-peel skin, creamy flavour and versatility. But ripeness is all. Their not-so-digestible starch turns to sugars as they ripen, and they become so easy to eat that mums often mash them as a first food for babies. The rest of us enjoy them raw or cooked, whole, sliced or mashed, as a snack, in baking, as dessert, in fruit salad or as part of a meal and, of course, in creamy smoothies.

WHAT TO LOOK FOR

The taste and texture of a banana is directly related to its stage of ripeness. Very green bananas are hard with an astringent taste, whereas fully ripened yellow bananas are soft, sweet and creamy. Bananas that are yellow and flecked with just a few brown spots will be at their peak flavour, but their texture verges on mushy. Look for plump bananas that have unspotted yellow skins and green tips with no splits or bruising. We think it's a good idea to select both ripe and underripe fruit so you have a steady supply. Bananas bruise easily, so handle them with care.

HOW TO STORE THEM

Keep them in the fruit bowl, away from heat or direct sun, as they will ripen at room temperature. Once ripened to your liking, refrigerate for up to 2 weeks to prevent further ripening. The skin will blacken, but they are still perfectly edible. Never refrigerate unripe bananas. If they become overripe, we suggest you freeze them (skin and all) and take them out as you need them for baking or whizzing to make a smoothie. Another idea is to freeze them on a stick, making natural fruit popsicles.

WHAT'S IN THEM?

A small banana or ½ a larger one (about 100 g/3½ oz) has 410 kilojoules (98 calories), 1.5 g protein, no fat, 22 g carbs (5 g starches, 17 g sugars), 2.5 g fibre, 345 mg potassium, a low GI (49–53) and a moderate GL (12).

WHAT ELSE?

Ever wondered about the difference between bananas and plantains? Generally speaking, banana refers to the types we eat raw and plantain to the ones we cook. But in fact you can cook bananas and eat some ripe plantains raw. Green, starch-rich plantains are a staple in tropical countries, cooked and eaten very much the way we would serve up potatoes – steamed, boiled or fried. They are also dried and made into a meal (flour), as are green bananas.

HERO RECIPE

Banana and peanut ice cream (page 207)

BERRIES

What's not to like about berries. Some are sweet, others are tart and all of them are packed with vitamins, minerals and phytonutrients. We don't see the point of saying this one's a superfood and that one isn't. They are all fine fare. Enjoy your favourites in season when the price is right. How better to start the day than with a strawberry-blueberry-raspberry combo to lift muesli or porridge from the mundane to the magical? And berry muffins, trifles, cheesecakes, pies, tarts, crisps and crumbles, or berry sauces and salsas with sweet or savoury dishes, always have the family lining up for seconds.

WHAT TO LOOK FOR

When buying, check the punnet of berries closely (top and bottom) to make sure they all look well formed, fresh and dry (moisture attracts mould), have a uniform bright colour, aren't squashed or damaged and there's no oozing juice or fermenting smell. Strawberries should have their green caps attached. Fresh blueberries should be deep blue and covered with a chalky white 'bloom', which is a sign of freshness.

If you are planning on using them to make jam, or want to freeze your own berries for the coming months, it is worth visiting a berry farm and picking your own.

HOW TO STORE THEM

Berries wait for no one. They are among the most perishable of fruits and can turn soft and mouldy within 24 hours. Sort and remove any bruised or damaged berries and store them in the refrigerator for 2–3 days in the punnet. With strawberries, it is a good idea to place them on a paper-towel-lined plate in a single layer and cover with plastic wrap. Blueberries are the least perishable of all berries and will last for 7–10 days if refrigerated.

WHAT'S IN THEM?

Most berries have very few calories or carbs. Five medium-sized strawberries (70 g/2½ oz) have about 70 kilojoules (17 calories), 1 g protein, no fat, 2 g carbs (all sugars), 1.5 g fibre, 90 mg potassium, and a low GI (40) and GL (1). Blueberries have more carbs – about ½ cup (80 g/2¾ oz) has 9 g carbs, and a low GI (53) and GL (5).

WHAT ELSE?

Don't rinse berries until you are ready to use them. The easiest way is to put them in a colander, gently rinse with cold water and blot gently with kitchen paper.

Be careful with fragile berries such as raspberries, and don't hull strawberries until after rinsing.

HERO RECIPES

COCONUT

The coconut has to be a top contender for 'gold' in the world's most useful fruit category. It provides us with a food to eat, water to drink, fibre to spin into rope or coir, and a hard shell to turn into a cup or into charcoal for fuel. And if you ever need help to stay afloat, one or two could come in handy. It's not a nut but rather a type of stone fruit (technically it's a 'dry drupe') that can be processed one way or another to give us pantry staples such as coconut milk, cream or yoghurt, coconut oil, coconut butter, coconut flour and desiccated, flaked or shredded coconut. It doesn't give us coconut sugar or vinegar. These are processed from sap that's tapped from the inflorescence or flowering spike – as is alcoholic toddy or arrack.

WHAT TO LOOK FOR

Fresh coconuts should be heavy for their size and have no splits or cracks. Don't buy coconuts that don't have any slosh when you shake them – the more water the better.

A medium coconut will give you about ½ cup (125 ml/4 fl oz) of milk and 3 cups (255 g/9 oz) of freshly grated coconut. When buying desiccated, shredded or flaked coconut, keep in mind that because they are oil rich they can easily go rancid – check the use-by or best-before date on the packaging.

HOW TO STORE THEM

Store fresh coconuts in a cool, dry place. Once cut, place the chunks in an airtight container in the refrigerator for up to 2 weeks.

Store dried coconut products in a resealable packet or airtight container in a cool, dry place. Some brands recommend storing in the refrigerator or freezer.

WHAT'S IN THEM?

A small piece of coconut (45 g/1½ oz) has 530 kilojoules (127 calories), 1 g protein, 12 g fat (includes 11 g saturated fat), 2 g carbs (all sugars), 3 g fibre and 150 mg potassium. It will have little effect on blood glucose levels, as it is mostly fat and has very little carbohydrate.

WHAT ELSE?

Trendy coconut water, the liquid in a green coconut, has long been the beverage du jour in tropical climes. With its high potassium content, it's sometimes promoted as a rehydration option for athletes, but it lacks the sodium they need to replace what's lost in sweat. And although marketed as 'nature's tropical hydrator', it's no replacement for a glass of water as it's not calorie free. A 330 ml (12 fl oz) container of plain coconut water has 300 kilojoules (72 calories), less than a gram each of protein and fat, 17 g carbs (all sugars), no fibre, 60 mg potassium and a low GI (55).

HERO RECIPES

Mango, fresh coconut and avocado salad with Thai dressing (page 196)
Mango salad with fresh coconut and apple (page 197)

DATES

Fresh dates 'are so remarkably luscious that there would be no end to eating them, were it not for fear of the dangerous consequences that would be sure to ensue' noted Pliny the Elder about 2000 years ago. In moderation, however, they make the perfect snack, and they bring moist deliciousness to fruit breads, cakes, cookies, muffins, stuffing, crumble toppings, salads or combined with meats in tagines. They can also be used to make pastry and a topping treat for ice cream. And there's even more: thick, sticky date syrup has been enjoyed as a sweetener for thousands of years in the Middle East and North Africa, drizzled over tahini or yoghurt. For our hero date recipe, however, we slipped over to the savoury side with a salad that pairs dates with grated parsnip and spices up the relationship with a zesty dressing.

WHAT TO LOOK FOR

There are hundreds of varieties of dates, dried, semi-dried and fresh, pitted and unpitted. Dried dates are an inexpensive and nourishing snack (long ago they sustained Arab sailors during long voyages of trade and discovery) and are ideal for snacking, cooking and baking.

Unpitted dates will have better flavour than pitted as they stay moister. Fresh dates should be plump and moist with glossy skins. Dried dates, though a little wrinkly, shouldn't look withered, and should still be plump and glossy, with an even colour. Avoid those with crystallised sugar on their skins, as this means they are not quite as fresh as you might like. When buying packaged dates, check the use-by or best-before date.

If using pitted dates, check as you chop, as there can sometimes be traces of stones (also called pits). Fresh or soft dates such as the large plump fleshy Medjool dates have a chewy toffee-like taste and are sold loose and prepacked (often pricy but worth it). Medjool dates are particularly delicious in salads and desserts.

HOW TO STORE THEM

Fresh or dried, dates keep well for a few months in an airtight container in a cool, dry cupboard. They freeze very well, and this prevents the sugars in them from drying out and creating white sugar spots.

WHAT'S IN THEM?

Five regular dried dates (about 25 g/1 oz) have 300 kilojoules (72 calories), 0.5 g protein, no fat, 17 g carbs (16.5 g sugars, 0.5 g starches), 2.5 g fibre, 180 mg potassium, and a low GI (39–45) and GL (7).

WHAT ELSE?

There's also date sugar. Although resembling a brown sugar, it is simply powdered dried dates. As it does not dissolve or melt and tends to clump, it is not ideal as a sugar substitute in baking. But it comes into its own as a tangy, sweetish topping over porridge or yoghurt, or in crumbles.

HERO RECIPE

Parsnip, yoghurt and date salad (page 188)

GRAPEFRUIT

Grapefruit is a shining example of citrus doing what comes naturally – cross-pollinating. In this case, it took place (apparently) in Barbados. Parents were new arrivals (in the seventeenth century) from Asia themselves the pomelo and orange. Little did Odet Philippe know it was the beginning of a billion-dollar American success story when he planted the country's first grapefruit seeds in Florida in 1823. Numerous fad diets extolling grapefruit's miraculous 'fat-burning' powers certainly boosted business. And no, they don't have special fat-burning powers, and nor do they eliminate toxins. But if you do need to lose a few kilos, then half a grapefruit starts the day with a zing as part of an overall healthy diet. But there's much more. Grapefruit perks up fruit and vegetable salads; is perfect for marmalades, granita, marinades and sauces; replaces water in bread, pikelets or scone making; and is ideal with oily fish, shellfish and avocado salsa.

WHAT TO LOOK FOR

Grapefuit, like all citrus fruit, is ripe and ready when it's picked. Look for round, smooth, evenly coloured firm fruits that are heavy for their size (they will be juicy) and with no soft spots or blemishes. Glossy fruit with slightly flattened ends are preferable, and avoid those with puffy skins. They should have a mildly sweet fragrance at room temperature.

HOW TO STORE THEM

Grapefruit will keep well at room temperature for a week and are juiciest when slightly warm rather than chilled. If you want to store them longer, put them in the refrigerator for 6–8 weeks. If doing this, give them a chance to come up to room temperature before eating or juicing.

WHAT'S IN THEM?

A small grapefruit (about 210 g/7½ oz) has 240 kilojoules (57 calories), 2 g protein, no fat, 10 g carbs (all sugars), 1 g fibre, 250 mg potassium, and a very low GI (25) and GL (2).

WHAT ELSE?

Med alert. Some compounds in grapefruit can interact with some medicines, making the dose stronger or weaker than it should be. So if that new diet you have started recommends you eat a lot of grapefruit or you are just a grapefruit enthusiast, check with your doctor or pharmacist about potential problems with any prescription medicines you take.

HERO RECIPE

Grapefruit, orange and Aperol granita
(page 214)

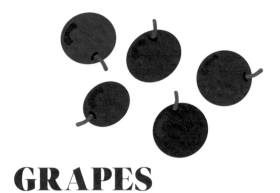

GRAPES

Wine is generally destiny for the grape. Perhaps this is why we first began cultivating them and (mostly) why we still do. Some 76,000 square kilometres (about 29,000 square miles) of the Earth's surface is dedicated to grape growing, and over 70 per cent of the harvest is for wine-making. In the kitchen, grapes are typically treated as a garnish rather than the main event, but you can make delicious jams, jellies, cakes and tarts with them, too. Most of us are happy to pick them from the bunch, serve them with cheese or add them to salads and fruit salads. It's the dried grapes (sultanas, raisins and currants) that we use for sweetness and zing in compotes, pilafs and biryanis, numerous desserts including plum pudding, and in all kinds of baking from breads and buns to Christmas fruit mince, cakes and nut bars.

WHAT TO LOOK FOR

New season grapes start arriving in the produce aisles in late summer. Taste one to check for sweetness as they won't ripen once picked. Be careful when handling grapes, as the thin skins are easily damaged.

Look for bunches as inviting as those in a still-life painting: plump fruit attached to moist flexible stems. The powdery bloom, more visible on dark-coloured grapes than on pale ones, is an important sign of freshness; it fades with time and handling. Avoid any sticky, split or wrinkled grapes on withered or limp stems. Give them a sniff to make sure they aren't starting to ferment.

When buying sultanas, raisins, muscatels or currants, check the best-before date.

HOW TO STORE THEM

Store unwashed grapes in a plastic bag in the refrigerator and rinse just before using or eating. They should keep for about a week. It's fun to freeze little bunches to make 'grape blocks' for children to snack on.

Dried fruit can be stored in an airtight container (preferably glass) in a cool, dry place, and will keep well for 6 months to a year.

WHAT'S IN THEM?

A small bunch of grapes (80 g/2¾ oz) has 215 kilojoules (51 calories), 0.5 g protein, no fat, 12 g carbs (sugars), 1 g fibre, 155 g potassium and a low GI (53) and GL (6). Raisins (GI 49) and sultanas (GI 56) are much more concentrated sources of calories and carbs. About 2 tablespoons of sultanas (30 g/1 oz) have 400 kilojoules (95 calories) and 22 g carbohydrate.

WHAT ELSE?

Grape syrup or molasses, what is it? Slowly reducing unfermented grape juice, or grape must, is a way to make the most of the harvest, providing velvety syrups (saba, vino cotto or vincotto, pekmez or petimezi) with just a hint of tartness. Try replacing your balsamic vinegar with one of these velvety concoctions in dressings and glazes, or give tahini, hummus or plain yoghurt a lift with a drizzle.

HERO RECIPES

Pork meatballs with fresh grapes (page 191)
Wild rice with fresh grapes, walnuts and feta (page 192)

LYCHEES

According to their legions of fans, lychees with their delicate fragrance and sweet clean flavour are 'most delightful to eat'. Rewind about 1000 years back to 1094, and we read that Chinese poet Su Shih certainly found solace tucking into '300 a day' when exiled from court. A native of southern China, the lychee is cultivated worldwide, making it easy for us to pass on the syrupy tinned ones nowadays and relish them fresh. As for cooking, keep it simple. Peel, deseed, and combine with leaves or with tropical fruits in a salad. Or add them to stir-fries at the last minute, just heating them through.

WHAT TO LOOK FOR

Don't be put off by the dimpled leathery exterior – underneath is fleshy, translucent and juicy fruit with a floral fragrance. Choose pinkish-red, heavy, uncracked fruit with a small piece of the stem attached; the redder the skin, the fresher the lychee. If you get the chance, taste before you buy, as they don't continue to ripen once they have been picked. When canned, lychees lose their distinctive perfume and their taste is diminished. Canned lychees are very sweet and better suited to desserts.

HOW TO STORE THEM

Store unpeeled fruit in a plastic bag in the refrigerator for up to a week. Lychees can also be frozen for up to 6 months.

WHAT'S IN THEM?

Ten fresh lychees (100 g/3½ oz) have 296 kilojoules (71 calories), 1 g protein, no fat, 16 g carbs (all sugars), 1.5 g fibre, 150 mg potassium, and a medium GI (57) and low GL (9).

WHAT ELSE?

Dried lychees, or 'lychee nuts' as they are sometimes labelled, are also available and make a tasty snack.

HERO RECIPES

Thai red duck curry with lychees (page 193)
Salmon, lychee and sugar snap pea salad (page 194)

LYCHEE BLOSSOM HONEY

'Great quantities of honey are harvested from hives near lychee trees,' botanist Julia Morton tells us. 'Honey from bee colonies in lychee groves in Florida is light amber, of the highest quality, with a rich, delicious flavour like that of the juice that leaks when the fruit is peeled, and the honey does not granulate.'

MANGO

It is hard to imagine summer without luscious mangoes. Originally from south and south-east Asia, where they have been cultivated for some 4000 years, they are now grown worldwide in tropical climates. When ripe, the flesh is soft and exceptionally juicy, to the point where eating a mango can be messy. But the taste is matchless, somewhere between a peach and a pineapple, only sweeter than either. 'With these beautiful objects, it is best to leave them as they are,' says Jane Grigson. We agree they are best eaten fresh. But they do make rather stunning desserts, and along with flavours such as lime juice, chilli and coriander (cilantro), you can happily marry them with fish, meat, and poultry. And they are hard to beat when it comes to creating a palate-refreshing salad.

WHAT TO LOOK FOR

The size and colour of a mango depends on the variety. Colour is not an indicator of quality or ripeness, as there are numerous varieties ranging from pale yellow–green to blushing pinky gold. So look for fruit with smooth, unwrinkled skin and no black spots, and that yields just a little when gently pressed in the palm of your hand. A perfectly ripe mango will have an intense, flowery fragrance.

Frozen mango pieces are available year round. Check the use-by or best-before date on the package. Tinned mango slices or cheeks have a very different flavour, texture and aroma, and are no substitute for fresh.

HOW TO STORE THEM

Ripe mangoes are for eating, not storing. If you can't use them immediately, store them, away from other food, in the refrigerator in a plastic bag for only a day or two. Leave underripe mangoes at cool room temperature for a few days to soften and sweeten. (Note that very warm temperatures can cause an off flavour to develop.) Peeled, sliced mangoes freeze very well and can be used in sorbets, ice cream, smoothies, sweet and sour sauce, desserts and baked items.

WHAT'S IN THEM?

One cheek (about 90 g/3¼ oz) has 220 kilojoules (53 calories), 1 g protein, no fat, 11 g carbs (sugars), 1.5 g fibre, 220 mg potassium and a low GI (51) and GL (6). Eat the whole mango and the GL will shoot up to moderate.

WHAT ELSE?

To deal with the drips, some mango lovers urge you to eat them in the shower. But there are easier ways to avoid drips and mess. Simply slice the unpeeled mango lengthways down each side of the stone with a paring knife, score the fleshy cheeks in a criss-cross pattern, flip inside out and go for it.

HERO RECIPES

Mango, fresh coconut and avocado salad with Thai dressing (page 196)
Mango salad with fresh coconut and apple (page 197)

ORANGES AND LEMONS

The golden glow of oranges and lemons and the perfect green of limes in the midst of a grey winter is uplifting. With oranges, it's not just colour. Their sweet acidity makes them a versatile ingredient in the kitchen (variety doesn't matter so much, although some recipes specify blood oranges or Seville oranges for colour or flavour). Whole citrus fruit (skin and all), segments, juice and zest are used in every category of cooking, from salads, soups, sauces, red meat, fish and poultry to desserts and baking. Mouth-puckering lemons, with their fragrance and aromatic sourness, are indispensable to the cook – the sharpness of their zest and juice heightens flavour.

WHAT TO LOOK FOR

Oranges and lemons should be firm, glossy and bright. Citrus fruit doesn't ripen further once it has been picked. Smell the fruit, as there should be no hint of fermenting aromas. Oranges will be at their best during the midpoint of their growing seasons. Heavy fruits with fine-grained skin are juiciest. Avoid soft, bruised or wrinkled fruit, as well as spongy soft ones. Be wary of pre-packaged citrus, and always check the best-before date.

HOW TO STORE THEM

Lemons look wonderful in the fruit bowl and will stay fresh at room temperature for up to 2 weeks. In very hot weather, it's a good idea to put them in a plastic bag and store them in the refrigerator, where they will keep well for 6 weeks.

Oranges keep almost as well at room temperature, and will be juicier. They don't require wrapping: avoid storing them in plastic bags as this may encourage mould growth.

WHAT'S IN THEM?

One medium orange (about 130 g/4½ oz) has 225 kilojoules (54 calories), 1.5 g protein, no fat, 10 g carbs (all sugars), 2.5 g fibre, 190 mg potassium, and a low GI (42) and GL (4).

1 small lemon (about 60 g/2 oz) has 67 kilojoules (16 calories), 0.5 g protein, no fat, 1 g carbs (1 g sugars), 1.5 g fibre, 70 mg potassium and no effect on blood glucose levels.

WHAT ELSE?

Before zesting oranges, lemons and other citrus, make sure the fruit has not been waxed. If it has, you need to wash and dry the fruit well first.

To get the most juice from a lemon, the fruit should be at room temperature or warmer. Roll the fruit under your palm on the worktop until it feels softened.

HERO RECIPES

Lemon passionfruit pudding (page 217)
Almond-crusted flourless 'boiled' citrus cake – two ways (page 218)

PAPAYA

As you tuck into a tangy Thai papaya salad, you may be surprised to find the fruit's original home was the tropical Americas. The Spanish took this so-called 'tree melon' to the Philippines in the sixteenth century, from where it made its way to India and down through South-East Asia, flourishing in tropical climes and making itself at home in local cuisines. In some areas, the flowers, leaves and stems are also eaten and the seeds used as a spice. You can use the fruit to make desserts, jams, chutneys and relishes, but they are best fresh in savoury and fruit salads. And they are unrivalled served on their own or with a dash of lime. 'Breakfast in Dar es Salaam never varied,' says Roald Dahl in his wartime autobiography *Going Solo*: 'It was always a delicious ripe paw paw picked that morning in the garden by the cook, on to which was squeezed the juice of a whole fresh lime ... It is the healthiest and most refreshing breakfast I know.'

WHAT TO LOOK FOR

Papayas turn from green to yellow–orange as they ripen, and it's best to choose fruits that are at least half yellow; the colour change begins at the bottom and progresses towards the stem end. At peak ripeness, they'll give slightly when pressed gently between your palms, but shouldn't be soft and mushy. Look for fruit with smooth, firm, unbruised and unshrivelled skin and no dark spots. Light, superficial blemishes may be disregarded.

Completely green papayas with no tinge of yellow have been picked too soon and may never ripen properly. Uncut papayas have no aroma, and cut papayas should smell fragrant and sweet, not harsh or fermented.

HOW TO STORE THEM

A semi-ripened papaya will ripen in 2–4 days if left at room temperature. Store ripe fruit in the refrigerator in a plastic bag for up to a week, but the delicate flavour will fade, so ideally use within 1–2 days. If you have cut it into halves or segments, plastic wrap the pieces before storing.

WHAT'S IN THEM?

A slice of papaya (about 70 g/2½ oz) has 100 kilojoules (24 calories), 0.5 g protein, no fat, 5 g carbs (all sugars), 1.5 g fibre, 100 mg potassium and a moderate GI (56) and GL (3).

WHAT ELSE?

In Thailand, green papayas are grated and used in many mouthwatering dishes, such as the famous sweet, sour and spicy papaya salad laced with peanuts.

HERO RECIPES

Charred spiced fish with chopped papaya salsa (page 199)
Shredded chilli ginger chicken and papaya salad (page 200)

PEACHES

When peaches first arrived in Europe, no one had any idea that they had come all the way from China. The Romans thought they came from Persia and called them 'Persian apple' (*Malum persicum*), which became then *pêche* in French and eventually 'peach' and a handy way to describe a colour, a flavour, a complexion (with cream), a desirable person and utter perfection.

Peaches certainly set the juicy–sweet sublime bar high. If you have a tree in your garden, you can choose the perfect moment to pick a peach to enjoy fresh, serve on a platter or toss into a salad. The rest of us have to rely on trays of overripe and underripe fruit with signs declaring 'Do not squeeze me'. Peaches are good cookers, and although the flavour and texture are not the same as fresh, they are equally delicious poached, halved, stuffed and grilled, or baked for desserts. They make wonderful jams and conserves, chutneys and relishes, salsas and sauces.

WHAT TO LOOK FOR

Peaches are picked when they are ripe but still firm. They will soften after being picked but will not ripen further (or get sweeter). Choose medium to large plump fruit with unwrinkled skins. When determining ripeness, pay attention to colour, not the red 'blush' on their cheeks, which depends on the variety. You want to look for the background colour of yellow to cream, particularly around the stem. If there is a bit of green, it means the fruit is not yet ripe. Gently press or squeeze the shoulder and tip (where the stem was) – if it just starts to give, it's ripe and ready to eat. If you can, buy freestone peaches (and nectarines), they are so much easier to use in your cooking than clingstone.

Tinned peaches are popular. Look for brands in water or natural juice with no added sugar.

HOW TO STORE THEM

Store firm peaches and nectarines stem side down in the fruit bowl at room temperature, out of sunlight, for a few days until they soften. Eat them or use them right away because they are highly perishable. They will keep for 2–3 days in the refrigerator but they should never be refrigerated until they are fully ripe. Chilling them before that will result in fruit that is mealy and flavourless.

WHAT'S IN THEM?

One small peach (about 145 g/5¼ oz) has about 210 kilojoules (50 calories), 1.5 g protein, no fat, 9 g carbs (all sugars), 2 g fibre, 270 mg, potassium a low GI (42) and GL (4).

WHAT ELSE?

To remove the stone from nectarines, apricots, peaches and plums, use a small serrated knife to cut along the seam from top to bottom, twist and hopefully the stone will pop out. If it doesn't, cut small wedges of flesh through to the stone and then continue cutting around the stone until it comes away.

HERO RECIPE

Baked peaches bombe Alaska (page 223)

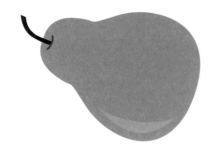

PEARS

The pear that first fired popular imagination and made its way into art and literature is the pear-shaped European pear (*Pyrus communis*). It gave its shape to pottery, pearls, sonorous tones and situations that don't turn out quite as expected. In the kitchen, pears are a remarkably versatile ingredient. Check out any fruit cookbook and you'll likely find more recipes with pears than other fruits. They are a natural for salads, be it with cabbage or crispy cos (romaine) leaves and blue cheese; an ideal accompaniment to roasts, especially pork or lamb; great for baking (pies, tarts, cobblers and cakes), and delicious in countless desserts.

WHAT TO LOOK FOR

Pears are stocked in produce aisles all year round, but the new season ones only appear from late summer through autumn. Pick out plump, firm and well-coloured pears that have undamaged skin. Some varieties won't develop full colour until the fruit ripens. Ripe pears will give to gentle pressure at the stem end, depending on the particular variety. Do not purchase pears that are soft at the bottom, shrivelled at the stem end, or that have nicks or dark, soft spots. Small surface blemishes can be ignored. They will continue to ripen in the fruit bowl.

Of all the tinned fruits available, pears are one of the most popular. Look for brands in water or natural juice with no added sugar.

HOW TO STORE THEM

The pear is one of the few fruits that does not ripen on the tree. It is harvested when it is mature, but not yet ripe, and, if left at room temperature, it slowly reaches a sweet maturity as it ripens from the inside out.

To ripen pears, there are two options. You can ripen them at room temperature first, then put them loose in the crisper drawer of the refrigerator for no longer than a day or two before eating them. Or refrigerate the pears until you are ready to ripen them; the cold will slow, but not stop, the ripening process. Just remove the pears from the refrigerator several days before you plan to eat them, and let them ripen at room temperature.

Never store pears, either in or out of the refrigerator, in sealed plastic bags, as the lack of oxygen will cause the fruit to brown at the core.

WHAT'S IN THEM?

One medium pear (about 190 g/6¾ oz) has about 390 kilojoules (93 calories), 1 g protein, no fat, 21 g carbs (20 g sugars, 1 g starch), 4 g fibre, 245 mg potassium, and a low GI (38) and GL (8).

WHAT ELSE?

The crisp nashi or Asian pear (*Pyrus pyrifolia*) is pear through and through. It is not a cross with an apple. '*Nashi*' means 'pear' in Japanese.

HERO RECIPES

No-bake poached pear flan with lime cream (page 224)
Winter fruit poached in mulled wine topped with granita (page 227)

PINEAPPLE

When Christopher Columbus stumbled upon them in 1493, pineapples had spread from their original home in Brazil and Paraguay to the West Indies. He named this coalesced berry of a tropical bromeliad 'pina' (pine). Back home, serving them was a serious status symbol. For starters, you needed an estate and a greenhouse to grow them. Then bingo, it all went pear shaped. Steamships and canneries put the 'king of fruits' on our tables, and we found there's nothing like them in fruit salads, and that they are equally at home in burgers, pizzas (the faithful ham and pineapple combo), Boston baked beans and sweet and sour dishes. Pineapple's lush, tropical sweetness is reason enough to enjoy it any way you can.

WHAT TO LOOK FOR?

Choose pineapples that are firm, plump and heavy for their size, with fresh-looking skin and good green leaves. Avoid pineapples with bruises or soft spots, especially at the base or those that have a sour or fermented smell. They don't ripen further after picking, but they do develop a more mellow flavour as the acids turn to esters.

Tinned pineapple isn't a substitute for fresh in recipes, as it has a different flavour and texture, but it does make a quick and easy dessert. Look for brands that use natural juice or water with no added sugar.

HOW TO STORE THEM

A pineapple will get softer and juicier if left at room temperature for a day or two before serving. Fresh pineapple is best eaten as soon as possible; alternatively, store in the refrigerator for 3–5 days, but no longer otherwise the fruit may be spoiled by the cold. Store in a plastic bag to help conserve its moisture content, leaving the leaves exposed. Cut pieces of pineapple can be stored in an airtight container where they will keep for about a week.

WHAT'S IN THEM?

Two thin raw slices (about 110 g/3¾ oz) have 195 kilojoules (47 calories), 1 g protein, no fat, 9 g carbs (sugars), 2.5 g fibre, 200 mg potassium and a moderate GI (59) and low GL (5).

WHAT ELSE?

Ripeness is all. But how do you know? The colour of a pineapple does not indicate ripeness. The skin naturally varies depending on the season, so you can't judge a pineapple by its cover. Nor can you test it by sniffing it, squeezing it or pulling a leaf from the crown; this will only be a guide to the age, not the sweetness of the fruit. In summer, look for greener fruit and check that there's a just-turning-yellow ring of colour around the base. In winter, you want fruit that's at least pale–golden green as it's a different variety.

HERO RECIPES

Carpaccio of pineapple with chilli syrup (page 228)

PLUMS

It's the tart tang that sets plums apart, and they retain this edgy sharpness when made into preserves or poached or baked in desserts. As for dried plums (prunes), their reputation for keeping us regular is well deserved, but they bring much more to the table. They plump up in compotes, add flavour and moisture to baking, and enliven savoury dishes including lamb, pork, chicken and game. But it wasn't a plum Little Jack Horner pulled out of his Christmas pudding, it was a raisin. Up until the nineteenth century, 'plum' referred to dried fruit. And the plum season was long gone by the first Sunday before Advent in the northern hemisphere, when the puddings for Christmas were boiled and hung. Plums are a summer fruit, and that's the time to make the most of them – fresh, poached or baked in desserts. Or bring out the preserving pan and stock the pantry shelves with bottled plums, homemade plum jam, chutney or sauce to serve with pork.

WHAT TO LOOK FOR

Fresh plums are difficult to gauge for ripeness. Plums are picked when they are ripe (mature) but still firm. They will soften after this but won't actually ripen any more, so they won't get sweeter. If the fruit yields to gentle pressure, it's ready to eat. Look for plump fruit with good colour for their variety and avoid fruit with splits, wrinkles or soft spots. A few rings around the stem end is fine, as this can be a sign of sweetness in a plum. If you are not planning to use them straight away it's better to buy plums that are a little firm.

HOW TO STORE THEM

Store hard plums in the fruit bowl at room temperature but out of sunlight for 1–2 days. When softened, use them right away or transfer to the fridge for up to 3 days.

WHAT'S IN THEM?

A small plum (about 65 g/2¼ oz) has about 110 kilojoules (26 calories), 0.5 g protein, no fat, 4.5 g carbs (4 g sugars, 0.5 g starches), 1.5 g fibre, 100 mg potassium and although not yet GI-tested, we estimate that fresh plums will have a low GI and GL like other stone fruit. Prunes (dried plums) have a low GI (40), but are a more concentrated source of calories and carbs. Four moist pitted prunes (30 g/1 oz) have 320 kilojoules (76 calories) and 17 g carbs.

WHAT ELSE?

The chalky white bloom on plums is natural and is a good sign that they haven't been handled too much from orchard to store.

To remove the stone use a small, sharp knife to cut a small, v-shaped wedge through the flesh to the stone and then continue cutting around the stone until it comes away.

HERO RECIPES

Plumped walnut prunes with orange in spiced port (page 220)
Oven-roasted plums with couscous crumble (page 229)

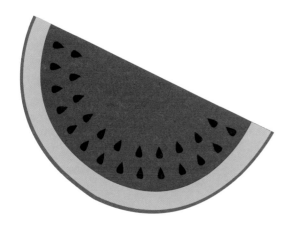

WATERMELON

Nothing says summer more than watermelon. It's big, mostly water and one of the most refreshing fruits in salads, soups or sorbets. It's also a popular addition to juices, especially with ginger and lemon or strawberries. You can eat it all. The rind can be pickled or sliced and added to stir-fries, the seeds processed for oil or roasted and snacked on, and the flesh used in sweet and savoury preparations alike. The top-selling watermelons today are seedless varieties, but traditional watermelons have many fans and spitting their seeds is a lively contest in the US. Jayson Schayott holds the world record (according to Google) with 24 metres (78 feet 6 inches) at the 1997 De Leon Peach and Melon Festival.

WHAT TO LOOK FOR

Watermelons don't ripen any further once picked. They should feel heavy for their size, have a smooth round or oblong shape with a slightly dull rind that is free from bruises, cracks or dents. It should have a creamy yellow underside, and when tapped you should be able to hear a hollow sound, signalling its ripeness.

A cut piece of watermelon should have a good colour and be dense at the centre (watermelons can suffer from 'hollow heart'). Seedless melons are the most popular, but if buying with seeds, they should be black.

HOW TO STORE THEM

You can improve the eating quality of firm, uncut melons by leaving them in a cool, dry place for 2–4 days; the fruit won't become sweeter, but it will turn softer and juicier. Store cut pieces in the refrigerator, wrapped tightly in plastic wrap, and eat within 1–2 days. Ripe melons are also very fragrant, and the aroma of a cut melon can penetrate other foods.

Whole watermelons stored in a cool, dark place last longer (about 2 weeks) than if stored in the refrigerator.

WHAT'S IN THEM?

A slice of watermelon (about 160 g/5¾ oz) has about 160 kilojoules (38 calories), 0.5 g protein, no fat, 8 g carbs (all sugars), 1 g fibre, 140 mg potassium and although it has a high GI (78), the GL is low (6) as it is over 90% water.

WHAT ELSE?

Seedless melons can have a few mature black seeds or none at all. They are often covered in little coats where a seed did not mature, which are safe to eat.

HERO RECIPE

Melon, cucumber and red onion salad (page 203)

PARSNIP, YOGHURT AND DATE SALAD

Squishy dates and raw parsnip balance each other beautifully in this salad, which doesn't like to be kept waiting – it's definitely best served as soon as you've tossed it. Parsnips taste better as the weather gets colder, so winter is the perfect time to relish them unadorned.

PREPARATION TIME: 20 minutes | **SERVES:** 6

4 medium parsnips (about 600 g/
   1lb 5 oz)
10 soft pitted dates, roughly chopped
2 tablespoons roughly chopped mint
   leaves
150 g (5½ oz) natural yoghurt
1 tablespoon lemon juice
2 teaspoons runny honey
2 tablespoons olive oil
sea salt flakes and freshly ground
   pepper

Peel the parsnips and cut them in half lengthways. Remove any woody centres and discard. Coarsely grate the parsnips into a bowl.

Add the dates, mint, yoghurt, lemon juice, honey and oil to the bowl with the parsnips. Add salt and pepper to taste, and then gently toss all the ingredients together. Serve immediately.

TIP The fine-grained sweet flesh of tender young winter parsnips have the best texture for grating raw.

PORK MEATBALLS WITH FRESH GRAPES

Combining meat with grapes was common in Ancient times and is still popular in Middle Eastern cooking. The alchemy that occurs when combining juicy fresh and plump dried grapes with tiny sweet pork meatballs in a delicate sauce is a masterstroke. A fine dry sherry is a good swap for tea to plump the sultanas.

PREPARATION TIME: 25 minutes | **COOKING TIME:** 25 minutes | **SERVES:** 6

Put the pork, half the shallot, garlic and the hazelnuts in a bowl, and season with salt and pepper to taste. Wet your hand and clump the mixture together. Form the mixture into small balls about the size of a golf ball and then toss in flour to coat.

Put the sultanas in a small bowl and pour over the hot tea. Leave for 10 minutes to plump.

Heat the oil and butter in a sturdy pan, over medium heat, and fry the meatballs (in batches if necessary), moving them around the pan to colour evenly, for about 10 minutes or until cooked. Add the remaining shallot, cover the pan, reduce the heat to low, and cook gently until softened. Add the plumped sultanas with the tea, grapes (they can be halved if large) and stock. Simmer gently for 10 minutes with the lid off, or until the sauce reduces and thickens slightly.

If using, sprinkle with parsley just before serving.

600 g (1 lb 5 oz) minced (ground) pork
2 shallots, finely chopped
2 garlic cloves, crushed
3 tablespoons chopped hazelnuts
sea salt flakes and freshly ground pepper
plain (all-purpose) flour, for coating
100 g (3½ oz) sultanas (golden raisins)
150 ml (5 fl oz) freshly brewed hot black tea
2 tablespoons olive oil
3 teaspoons butter
1½ cups (270 g/9½ oz) seedless black grapes
200 ml (7 fl oz) chicken stock
2 tablespoons finely chopped parsley (optional)

TIPS Black grapes are particularly delicious in this recipe, but for a striking effect you may like to use a mixture of coloured grapes.

Other herbs to try include sage, thyme, marjoram and tarragon.

WILD RICE WITH FRESH GRAPES, WALNUTS AND FETA

Wild rice is technically not rice at all but a member of the grass family and native to North America. It holds its long shape when cooked, has a nutty texture and is a perfect foil here for the squirty grapes. Matchsticks of crunchy apple can be added with confidence.

PREPARATION TIME: 25 minutes | COOKING TIME: 45 minutes | SERVES: 6

1 cup (190 g/6¾ oz) wild rice

2 cups (500 ml/17 fl oz) vegetable stock

1 large orange

⅓ cup (80 ml/2½ fl oz) extra virgin olive oil

1 tablespoon red wine vinegar

sea salt flakes and freshly ground pepper

2 cups (360 g/12¾ oz) seedless grapes, preferably a mix of colours, halved if preferred

2 spring onions (green onions/scallions), sliced

½ cup (60 g/2¼ oz) diced celery

⅔ cup (95 g/3¼ oz) walnut pieces

⅓ cup (50 g/1¾ oz) crumbled feta

3 tablespoons roughly chopped curly-leaf parsley

3 tablespoons chopped mint leaves

Rinse the rice under cold running water, drain and put into a pot with the stock over medium heat. Bring to the boil and then reduce the heat to low and simmer, uncovered, for 45 minutes or until the rice is al dente – it should have a nutty bite to it when cooked. Drain the excess liquid from the pot, cover and allow the rice to stand for 10–15 minutes.

Cut the peel and white pith from the orange and cut the flesh into thin segments over a bowl to catch the juice. Whisk the juice together with the oil and vinegar, and add salt and pepper to taste.

Tip the rice into a large bowl and add the orange segments, grapes, spring onion, celery and walnuts. Pour over the dressing and toss. Scatter over the feta, parsley and mint before serving.

TIP For a stunning garnish sprinkle over pomegranate seeds before serving.

THAI RED DUCK CURRY WITH LYCHEES

Don't even consider making this amazing dish if you can't get your hands on fresh lychees. Tinned lychees are not a substitute. They are far too sweet, and during the process of canning their perfume-like flavour is lost and the texture changed considerably.

PREPARATION TIME: 15 minutes | **COOKING TIME:** 18 minutes | **SERVES:**6

Put the curry paste in a large pot over medium heat and fry for 3 minutes, or until fragrant. Add the coconut milk and simmer for 5 minutes. Pour in the stock, and add the duck, fish sauce and lime leaves. Stir lightly and then simmer for 5 minutes.

Add the lychees and tomatoes, and cook for 2–3 minutes to heat them through. Serve garnished with basil and chilli.

TIP Best-value cooked duck can be easily bought from a Chinese supermarket, or use pre-cooked vacuum-packed pieces.

⅓ cup (80 ml/2½ fl oz) Thai red curry paste

2 cups (500 ml/17 fl oz) coconut milk

1 cup (250 ml/9 fl oz) chicken stock

1.25 kg (2 lb 12 oz) roasted duck, boned and chopped

2 tablespoons fish sauce

3 kaffir lime leaves, torn

350 g (12 oz) lychees, peeled and deseeded

12 cherry tomatoes

1 handful basil leaves, torn

1 long red chilli, deseeded and thinly sliced

SALMON, LYCHEE AND SUGAR SNAP PEA SALAD

What is there not to like about the juicy, translucent flesh of lychees and their distinctive floral fragrance? Don't confine them to end-of-meal sweet treats: an after-thought they are not. As well as their good looks, they are perfect for rounding out a meal with many competing ingredients.

PREPARATION TIME: 30 minutes | COOKING TIME: 5 minutes | SERVES: 6

⅓ cup (80 ml/2½ fl oz) soy sauce

2 teaspoons caster (superfine) sugar

6 × 175 g (6 oz) skinless salmon fillets, cut into large chunks

2 tablespoons vegetable oil

375 g (13 oz) sugar snap peas

1 Lebanese (short) cucumber, thinly sliced

24 lychees, peeled, seeded and halved

1 handful coriander (cilantro) leaves

1 handful mint leaves

1 small red chilli, deseeded and finely chopped

½ cup (45 g/1½ oz) thinly sliced red onion

2 handfuls bean sprouts, trimmed

¼ cup (60 ml/2 fl oz) lime juice

2 teaspoons fish sauce

Whisk the soy sauce and sugar together in a bowl. Add the salmon and toss to coat. Cover and refrigerate for 10 minutes.

Heat the oil in a large sturdy pan over medium–high heat. Add the salmon in batches and cook for 2 minutes on each side, until golden. Set aside.

Bring a pot of lightly salted water to the boil. Add the sugar snap peas, reduce the heat and simmer for 20 seconds. Drain, refresh in iced water and drain well. Put the peas in a bowl with the cucumber, lychees, coriander, mint, chilli, onions, bean sprouts and salmon broken into chunks. Whisk together the lime juice and fish sauce, pour over the salad and gently toss. Serve immediately.

TIP Snow peas (mangetout), cut into thin strips, can replace sugar snap peas, and will need only 10 seconds in boiling water.

MANGO, FRESH COCONUT AND AVOCADO SALAD WITH THAI DRESSING

Thai flavours meld the tastes and textures of these tropical ingredients. The unripe avocado will demand a bit of work to grate, so do this in advance, put into a bowl, press plastic wrap on to the surface and then refrigerate. The dressing can be made a couple of days in advance and kept in the fridge.

PREPARATION TIME: 45 minutes | **SERVES:** 6

1 medium red capsicum (pepper)

1 cup (100 g/3½ oz) bean sprouts, trimmed

4 handfuls mixed Asian salad leaves (tatsoi, mizuna)

4 handfuls mixed coriander (cilantro), mint and Thai basil leaves

4 spring onions (green onions/ scallions), trimmed

1 firm–ripe mango, peeled and destoned

1 unripe avocado

2 cm (¾ in) piece ginger, peeled

⅓ cup (80 ml/2½ fl oz) lime juice

1 small red chilli, finely chopped

2 tablespoons fish sauce

sea salt flakes and freshly ground pepper

2 cups (160 g/5½ oz) finely grated fresh coconut

Cut the capsicum in half and remove the seeds and membrane. Cut the flesh into fine strips and put into a bowl with the bean sprouts, salad leaves and fresh herbs.

Finely slice the spring onions and dice the mango flesh. Peel the avocado (the flesh will be rock hard) with a vegetable peeler or small sharp bladed knife and then coarsely grate and put in the bowl with the spring onions and mango.

Finely grate the ginger into a small bowl, add the lime juice, chilli and fish sauce. Taste and add salt and pepper if needed. Pour over the ingredients in the bowl and gently toss. Serve topped with a generous spoonful of coconut.

TIPS This salad is delicious with prawns (shrimp), thinly sliced lamb backstrap, cooked chicken or roast pork fillet.

If you wish, replace the fresh coconut with 1 cup (65 g/2¼ oz) lightly toasted shredded coconut.

MANGO SALAD WITH FRESH COCONUT AND APPLE

To serve as a main meal this salad calls for seafood such as cooked prawns, grilled scallops, or torn chunks of cooked cold salmon or white-fleshed fish. Meat eaters could try thinly sliced strips of rare beef or pastrami.

PREPARATION TIME: 30 minutes | **SERVES:** 6

Peel the mangoes, slice the flesh from the stones in thin strips and put in a bowl. Cut the carrots into matchsticks and add to the mango. Without peeling the apples, cut them into quarters, core and slice into thin matchsticks. Halve the tomatoes and add to the bowl with the apples, lamb's lettuce and bean sprouts.

For the dressing, whisk together the honey, lime juice and olive oil. Stir in the cashews and season with salt and pepper to taste. Pour into the bowl and gently toss. Arrange the salad on serving plates and scatter over the coconut.

TIP If you wish, replace the fresh coconut with ⅔ cup (50 g/1¾ oz) lightly toasted shredded coconut.

2 firm, almost ripe mangoes
2 medium carrots, scraped
2 granny smith apples
12 cherry tomatoes
4 handfuls lamb's lettuce (corn salad)
 or baby watercress
2 handfuls bean sprouts, trimmed
½ cup (40 g/1½ oz) coarsely grated
 fresh coconut

HONEY AND LIME DRESSING
2 teaspoons honey
juice of 2 plump limes
¼ cup (60 ml/2 fl oz) olive oil
½ cup (60 g/2¼ oz) roasted cashews,
 coarsely crushed
sea salt flakes
1 teaspoon cracked black pepper,
 or to taste

CHARRED SPICED FISH WITH CHOPPED PAPAYA SALSA

Cajun chef Paul Prudhomme popularised blackening at his restaurant K-Paul's Louisiana Kitchen by dipping fish in milk before coating with dried spices. The fierce high heat scorches the outer surface of the fish while keeping the flesh moist. This recipe is a gentler approach that does not demand cooking outdoors. What's more, the soothing coolness of papaya tempers the spice.

PREPARATION TIME: 20 minutes | **COOKING TIME:** 8 minutes | **SERVES:** 4

Make the salsa before cooking the fish by combining all the ingredients in a bowl. Stir and set aside.

Pat the fish fillets dry with paper towel. Stir together the thyme, oregano, pepper, paprika, garlic, oil and lemon juice in a small bowl to form a paste.

Make a couple of knife slash marks on the skin side of the fish and, using your fingers, smear the paste all over the fish and into the cuts.

Heat a non-stick sturdy pan over high heat and, when very hot, carefully place the fish in the pan, skin side down. Cook for 3 minutes to 'blacken' the fish (it will be very smoky), turn the heat down, then carefully turn the fish over to cook for a further 3 minutes. Serve the fish topped with the chopped papaya salsa.

TIP If you want a peppery kick to the salsa, add a few of the papaya seeds.

CHOPPED PAPAYA SALSA

½ small firm papaya, peeled, deseeded and diced
½ yellow capsicum (pepper), deseeded and diced
½ red capsicum (pepper), deseeded and diced
1 small Lebanese (short) cucumber, deseeded and diced
1 handful coriander (cilantro) leaves, chopped
1 small red or green chilli, finely chopped
juice of 1 lime

4 × 200 g (7 oz) white fish fillets, skin on
½ teaspoon dried thyme
½ teaspoon dried oregano
½ teaspoon freshly ground pepper
1 tablespoon sweet smoked paprika
2 garlic cloves, crushed
2 tablespoons olive oil
juice of 1 lemon

SHREDDED CHILLI GINGER CHICKEN AND PAPAYA SALAD

Pork or lamb would also work very well in this ying–yang combination of hot, sweet, spicy ingredients. And don't shy away from using the green peppercorns. They are the unripe berries of black pepper and have a mild and fresh flavour. By comparison, papaya seeds are quite pungent and, if liked, toss some into this salad to give a kick of heat.

PREPARATION TIME: 25 minutes | COOKING TIME: 35 minutes | SERVES: 6

⅔ cup (170 ml/5½ fl oz) vegetable oil
1 teaspoon crushed red chilli
3 tablespoons finely grated ginger
3 garlic cloves, crushed
zested strips from 1 orange
1 tablespoon sesame oil
2 teaspoons Chinese five-spice
⅓ cup (80 ml/2½ fl oz) lemon juice
6 skinless chicken marylands (thigh with drumstick attached) (about 1.3 kg/3 lb)
1 large shallot, finely chopped
1 tablespoon drained green peppercorns
sea salt flakes and freshly ground pepper
1 large papaya (about 1 kg/2 lb 4 oz), peeled, deseeded and cut into wedges
375 g (13 oz) mixed peppery salad greens (watercress, rocket (arugula) or mizuna)
1 handful mint leaves, torn
1 handful Thai or sweet basil leaves, torn

Put half the vegetable oil, chilli, one-third of the ginger, garlic, orange zest, sesame oil, Chinese five-spice and one-third of the lemon juice in a large bowl and mix well.

Wipe the chicken with kitchen paper and put into the bowl. Turn to coat, then cover with plastic wrap and refrigerate for at least 4 hours.

In a small bowl, whisk the remaining oil, lemon juice and ginger, with the shallot and peppercorns, adding salt and pepper to taste.

Preheat the oven to 180°C/350°F (fan 160°C/315°F). Line a baking tray with baking paper.

Drain the chicken pieces, retaining the marinade, and arrange them on the prepared oven tray. Roast for 40–45 minutes, turning frequently, until golden and cooked through. To check, insert a fine skewer into the thickest part of the chicken and if the juices run clear it's cooked. Remove the chicken to a platter and allow to cool.

When the chicken has cooled, pull it apart into large pieces and put in a large bowl with any of the cooking juices. Pour in half the dressing, toss well and refrigerate for 20 minutes. Gently fold the papaya through the chicken. Put the salad greens in another bowl with the mint, basil and remaining marinade. Toss gently and arrange with the chicken and papaya salad on a large platter or serving plates.

MELON, CUCUMBER AND RED ONION SALAD

Here is a refreshing salad that makes the most of melons in summertime. The watermelon really sings in this recipe. You can use one with or without seeds – we love the contrast of jet-black seeds against rosy pink flesh. It's best served a little warmer than fridge cold.

PREPARATION TIME: 20 minutes | SERVES: 6

Carefully cut away the rind and white part of the watermelon, and the rind and pale outer hard flesh of the honeydew melon. Cut the slices into shard-like pieces and put in a large shallow dish. The pieces can be any shape so long as the melon is thinly sliced.

Cut the onion in half and slice it as thinly as possible and then add to the dish with the melon.

Peel the cucumber if the skin is tough. Slice as thinly as possible and add to the dish. Toss everything lightly together and leave at room temperature for about 1 hour to allow the melon juices to form, which make up the dressing. The salad can be refrigerated at this stage and then brought to room temperature about 30 minutes before serving. Serve sprinkled with the mint.

- 6 × 1 cm/½ in thick slices watermelon
- 6 × 1 cm/½ in thick slices honeydew melon
- 1 medium red onion
- 1 medium Lebanese (short) cucumber
- 2 tablespoons coarsely chopped mint leaves

TIP Instead of mint, snipped micro radish sprouts give this salad a slight tang. Crumbled aged pecorino or parmesan and a splash of olive oil and lemon juice also make a nice variation.

APPLE SPONGE PUDDING

Some recipes lead you to the taste of home. This is one of them. Nothing difficult or fancy here, just fragrant apple nestling under soft sponge. Serve with thick, pure cream.

PREPARATION TIME: 20 minutes | **COOKING TIME:** 40 minutes | **SERVES:** 6

5 large apples
⅓ cup (80 ml/2½ fl oz) water
1 teaspoon grated lemon zest
4 whole cloves
2 eggs
½ teaspoon vanilla extract
¼ cup (55 g/2 oz) caster (superfine) sugar
½ cup (75 g/2¾ oz) self-raising flour, sifted

Preheat the oven to 180°C/350°F (fan 160°C/315°F).

Peel, core and thickly slice the apples, then put them in a pot with the water, lemon zest and cloves. Bring to the boil over medium heat, then reduce the heat to low and gently simmer, covered, for about 5 minutes, or until the apples are just fork-tender. Tip them into a 6 cup (1.5 litre/52 fl oz) ovenproof dish and cover with foil to keep hot.

Whisk the eggs and vanilla in an electric mixer until pale and foamy. Gradually add the sugar, beating until it is dissolved and the mixture becomes thick and creamy. Using a metal spoon, fold in the sifted flour quickly and lightly, and then spoon the mixture over the hot apples. (It's important for the apples to be hot because this will help the sponge start to cook immediately, making it lighter when cooked.) Bake for 30–35 minutes, or until golden brown.

TIP The sweetness of the stewed apple base relies on the variety of apples used. For a slightly tart, tangy taste, choose granny smith and for a sweet and aromatic flavour, royal gala apples work well.

APPLE ROSE TART

Possibly it was American author Rose Levy Beranbaum who first came up with the ingenious concept of using thin apple slices to produce a full-blown rose when cooked. Instead of one large rose tart you could make smaller versions using muffin tins. Either way, this is as pretty as a picture and has an addictive apple taste.

PREPARATION TIME: 30 minutes | **COOKING TIME:** 35 minutes | **SERVES:** 8

To make the pastry, put the almond meal, rice flour, arrowroot, salt and cold butter in a food processor and pulse-blend until the mixture forms small lumps. Add the egg and pulse-blend again, until the dough just clumps. Form the dough into a ball, flatten into a disk, cover with plastic wrap and refrigerate for 30 minutes. Roll the pastry out using rice flour or arrowroot to prevent sticking (or roll between sheets of baking paper) and line a 22 cm (8½ in) loose-based flan (tart) tin. Trim the edges and refrigerate for 20 minutes.

While the pastry chills, cut the apples into quarters, core and slice them as thinly as possible so that you can bend them slightly without breaking the slice. Put the apple slices in a large bowl, add the lemon juice, sugar and cinnamon and very gently toss.

Preheat the oven to 210°C/410°F (fan 190°C/410°F).

Starting from the outside of the pastry case, arrange the apple slices curved unpeeled side up, around the pastry in circles and working into the centre with each slice overlapping the last one. The circles should look like tightly packed petals of a rose with very little space between them because the apples will shrink a little when cooked.

Bake the tart for about 25 minutes, or until the apples are cooked and the pastry crisp and golden.

Heat the jam in a small saucepan until syrupy then brush over the top of the apples. Continue cooking the tart for a further 10 minutes, or until the glaze is bubbling. Cool before serving.

PASTRY
1 cup (100 g/3½ fl oz) fine almond meal
½ cup (80 g/2¾ oz) rice flour
½ cup (65 g/2¼ oz) arrowroot
½ teaspoon sea salt flakes
125 g (4½ oz) very cold butter, diced
1 egg, whisked

6 medium apples, unpeeled
2 tablespoons lemon juice
⅓ cup (75 g/2¾ oz) caster (superfine) sugar
1 teaspoon ground cinnamon
4 tablespoons apricot, raspberry, plum or cherry jam, to glaze

BANANA AND PEANUT ICE CREAM

One of the easiest and most amazing ice cream recipes ever. Frozen ripe bananas are blitzed until creamy. For this, a powerful blender produces a better result than a food processor. The bananas will go through various transformations: crumbly, gooey, looking like oatmeal and finally the consistency of soft-serve ice cream.

PREPARATION TIME: 15 minutes | SERVES: 6

Put the banana in a blender and blitz until smooth and creamy. (Because the bananas are frozen solid this is a noisy process.) When the mixture is smooth, add the peanut butter, honey, yoghurt and peanuts, then pulse-blend. Pour the mixture into a freezer-proof container, cover with the lid and freeze. This will keep for up to 2 months.

TIP If you like, replace the chopped roasted peanuts with ½ cup (80 g/2¾ oz) blueberries.

4 large ripe bananas, peeled, cut into chunks and frozen
¼ cup (70 g/2½ oz) crunchy peanut butter
¼ cup (60 ml/2 fl oz) runny honey
⅔ cup (190 g/6½ oz) natural yoghurt
⅓ cup (50 g/1¾ oz) chopped roasted peanuts

KIWI, BLUEBERRY AND AVOCADO GREEN TEA POPSICLES

Avocado provides colour and delivers a rich creamy texture to these popsicles without tasting of avocado. For a twist, replace the green tea with matcha (powdered green tea) blended with coconut milk.

PREPARATION TIME: 25 minutes | **COOKING TIME:** 5 minutes | **SERVES:** 6

200 g (7 oz) blueberries
1 teaspoon caster (superfine) sugar
3 large kiwi fruit
1 small very ripe avocado
1 tablespoon honey
1½ cups (375 ml/13 fl oz) brewed
   green tea, cooled

Depending on their size, have ready at least 6 large popsicle moulds and sticks.

Put the blueberries and sugar in a small pot over medium heat. Gently shake the berries, just until their skins burst and they start to release juice. Remove the pot from the heat and tip the berries, along with the juices, into a bowl to cool.

Peel the kiwi fruit, chop roughly and put in the bowl of a food processor. Halve the avocado, remove the stone and add the scooped soft flesh to the kiwi fruit. Add the honey and cold green tea, and blend to a smooth purée.

Put an equal amount of blueberries with their juice in each popsicle mould and fill with the kiwi and avocado mixture. Leave a little gap – about 1 cm (½ in) – at the top, as the liquid will expand when it's frozen. Depending on the size of the moulds, add more green tea if necessary to fill. Gently stir with a long skewer, pop in the sticks and freeze.

To remove the moulds, dip them briefly in warm water and then serve the popsicles.

QUINOA BLUEBERRY PANCAKES WITH SQUISHY FRUIT YOGHURT

This is a splendid way of using any left-over quinoa. When its added to buttermilk pancake batter, the result is a thick, moist pancake that's hefty but not heavy.

PREPARATION TIME: 20 minutes | **COOKING TIME:** 5 minutes | **MAKES:** 16

1 cup (185 g/6½ oz) cooked quinoa
1½ cups (210 g/7½ oz) wholemeal flour
2 teaspoons baking powder
2 eggs
1 cup (250 ml/9 fl oz) buttermilk
1 tablespoon honey
1 teaspoon vanilla extract
1 cup (150 g/5½ oz) blueberries
2 teaspoons softened butter, for frying

FRUIT YOGHURT
1 cup (180 g/6½ oz) sliced strawberries
1 cup (260 g/9 oz) natural yoghurt
1 large passionfruit, scooped pulp

Put the quinoa, flour and baking powder in a large bowl and lightly mix together.

In another bowl, whisk the eggs, buttermilk, honey and vanilla together until the mixture is smooth. Pour the wet mixture into the flour mixture and whisk until just combined. Tip in the blueberries and stir gently. Do not overbeat: a few lumps are fine. The mixture should be the consistency of softly whipped cream. If not, add more buttermilk or flour.

Lightly smear the bottom of a large non-stick frying pan with a small amount of the butter and melt over medium heat. When the butter appears to foam, drop in tablespoonfuls of the batter, allowing room for spreading. Cook for about 2 minutes, or until tiny bubbles appear on the surface, and then flip and cook for about 2 minutes or until golden brown on the other side. Wipe the pan clean with paper towel and repeat with more butter, until all the batter has been used.

Put the strawberries in a bowl and mash until squishy, then fold in the yoghurt and passionfruit pulp. Serve the pancakes warm, with a dollop of fruity yoghurt on top.

TIP For fluffier pancakes, separate the eggs and beat the yolks with the buttermilk. Whisk the whites to soft peaks before folding into the batter.

SOUSED BERRIES WITH MINT AND WHIPPED RICOTTA

This recipe is all about the quality of the balsamic vinegar. Don't forfeit taste by using a cheap 'balsamic' – there's no such thing. Imitation balsamic is basically wine vinegar with colouring added, and bears no resemblance to the noble balsamic carefully aged to dark brown, syrupy perfection. Check the label for the words 'grape must', 'aged grape must', 'Mosto d'Uva' or 'DOC', and you'll know it's good.

PREPARATION TIME: 25 minutes | **SERVES:** 6

Lightly swirl the berries in cold water, drain well and pat dry. Hull the strawberries and then cut them in half or, if very large, into quarters. Put in a bowl with the other berries. Pour over the balsamic vinegar and add the mint. Gently toss and then cover and refrigerate if you are not serving them within the hour.

Whisk the ricotta, milk and orange zest together in an electric mixer until smooth and fluffy. Serve the berries with their juice and a big dollop of fluffy ricotta.

> **TIP** Be sure to prepare the berries just before using them or they will become soggy and lose their flavour.

about 500 g (1 lb 2 oz) mixed berries (strawberries, blackberries, blueberries)
¼ cup (60 ml/2 fl oz) aged balsamic vinegar
3 tablespoons finely shredded mint leaves
1½ cups (345 g/12 oz) ricotta
¼ cup (60 ml/2 fl oz) milk
2 teaspoons finely grated orange zest

STRAWBERRY, RHUBARB AND APPLE OAT CRUMBLE

Rhubarb stalks can vary in colour from green to a perky bright red, and we often, wrongly, assume that the red stalks are 'ripe' and sweeter. Colour and sweetness are not related, and some green varieties produce very sweet stems. Smaller stalks will be tender, while thicker stalks tend to become stringy. When choosing, stalks the size of a finger are a good measure.

PREPARATION TIME: 25 minutes | **COOKING TIME:** 30 minutes | **SERVES:** 6

Preheat the oven to 180°C/350°F (fan 160°C/315°F).

Put the rhubarb, apples, strawberries, honey and half the cinnamon in a bowl. Toss well and spoon into a deep ovenproof dish.

In a bowl, combine the oats, butter, brown sugar, nuts and remaining cinnamon, and rub together with your fingers until the mixture is lumpy and crumbly. Spread on top of the fruit and bake for about 30 minutes, or until the fruit is soft and bubbling up at the edges, and the top is golden and crunchy.

TIP Thinly sliced ripe pear or blackberries would be a lovely addition to the fruit mixture.

5 rhubarb stalks, trimmed and chopped

3 small cooking apples, cored and coarsely grated

200 g (7 oz) small strawberries, hulled

2 tablespoons runny honey

2 teaspoons ground cinnamon

1 cup (90 g/3¼ oz) rolled (porridge) oats

50 g (1¾ oz) butter

½ cup (100 g/3½ oz) lightly packed soft brown sugar

⅔ cup (100 g/3½ oz) coarsely chopped raw nuts (almonds, hazelnuts, walnuts, pecans)

GRAPEFRUIT, ORANGE AND APEROL GRANITA

It's hard to beat a refreshingly crunchy granita in a heatwave. For this granita, elbow grease is needed: there are no shortcuts. Only regular beating with a fork about every half-hour during the freezing process will produce 'free-running', not clumpy, large, flavoured ice crystals.

PREPARATION TIME: 15 minutes, plus freezing | **COOKING TIME:** 10 minutes | **SERVES:** 6

2 cups (500 ml/17 fl oz) freshly squeezed red grapefruit juice
1 cup (250 ml/9 fl oz) freshly squeezed orange juice
½ cup (110 g/3¼ oz) caster (superfine) sugar
thinly sliced peel of 1 orange
½ cup (125 ml/4 fl oz) Aperol
½ vanilla bean, split lengthways and seeds scraped (optional)

Put the grapefruit and orange juice, sugar and orange peel in a pan, over medium heat, and stir until the sugar dissolves. Remove the pan from the heat, and stir in the Aperol and vanilla seeds if using. Allow to cool.

Remove the orange peel and pour the mixture into a freezer-proof container. Cover with plastic wrap and freeze. When the mixture starts to freeze about 1 cm (½ in) around the edges, stir with a fork, breaking up any icy chunks. Do this several times – about every 30 minutes or so – until the mixture becomes slushy and frozen. This granita is delicious on its own, or spooned over fresh oysters or fresh fruit desserts.

TIP Aperol is an Italian bitters related to Campari, but has only half the alcohol and is lighter in colour, with a more delicate flavour than Campari. To replace the Aperol, use the juice of tangelos or Seville oranges.

LEMON PASSIONFRUIT PUDDING

When the world looks grey, make this pudding. Feather-light sponge sits atop a sunny sauce flecked with black passionfruit seeds. Don't strain out the seeds: they give a slight crunch to the texture. The addition of lemon zest gently dulls the intensely aromatic passionfruit. Don't let the pudding sit for long before serving (not that you'll be able to resist).

PREPARATION TIME: 20 minutes | **COOKING TIME:** 50 minutes | **SERVES:** 6

Preheat the oven to 180°C/350°F (fan 160°C/315°F). Lightly grease an 8 cup (2 litre/68 fl oz) ovenproof dish with butter.

Beat the egg yolks and half of the sugar with an electric mixer until thick and creamy. Stir in the butter, milk, sifted flour, lemon zest and juice. Cut the passionfruit in half and scoop the seeds and pulp into the bowl.

In a separate bowl, whisk the egg whites to soft peaks and then gradually add the remaining sugar, beating until the mixture is stiff and glossy. Lightly fold the egg whites into the passionfruit mixture and then pour the mixture into the prepared dish.

Place the dish in a large, deep roasting pan and fill with enough hot water to come halfway up the sides of the dish. Bake for 45 minutes, then turn the oven off and leave the pudding in the oven for an extra 5 minutes to finish cooking in the residual heat.

TIP Baking in a water bath prevents the egg-rich sauce curdling, insulating it from the direct heat of the oven.

3 eggs, separated
1 cup (220 g/7¾ oz) caster (superfine) sugar
30 g (1 oz) butter, melted
1 cup (250 ml/9 fl oz) milk
½ cup (75 g/2¾ fl oz) self-raising flour
grated zest and juice of 1 large lemon
5 large, plump passionfruit

ALMOND-CRUSTED FLOURLESS 'BOILED' CITRUS CAKE – TWO WAYS

Sometimes a choice is a delicious dilemma. The longer method of gently simmering the citrus fills the kitchen with beautiful aromas or there's the super-quick microwave shortcut. The almond crust is not essential.

PREPARATION TIME: 20 minutes | **COOKING TIME:** 50 minutes | **SERVES:** 10

4 large mandarins or 2 large oranges
6 eggs
1 cup (220 g/7¾ oz) caster (superfine) sugar
1 teaspoon baking powder
2½ cups (250 g/9 oz) almond meal
½ cup (50 g/1¾ oz) flaked almonds (optional)

TIP The cake has a stubborn habit of sinking slightly in the centre as it cools, but this is nothing to worry about. It's the taste – the wanton appeal – that matters.

Preheat the oven to 180°C/350°F (fan 160°C/315°F). Grease 22 cm (8¾ in) spring-form cake pan with butter and line with two layers of baking paper.

Boiling method: Wash the citrus and put them in a pot with water to cover. Bring to the boil, reduce the heat and gently simmer for 2 hours. Remove from the heat and cool for a few minutes, then roughly chop, removing any large seeds. Put the skin and flesh in a food processor, blitz to a fine purée and then cool.

Microwave method: Wash the fruit and, using a fine skewer, pierce all over. Place in a microwave-proof bowl with cold water to about 5 mm (¼ in) of the bowl. Cover and microwave on high (1000 watts, 100 per cent power) for 4 minutes or until the fruit is pulpy. Chop and purée as above.

Whisk the eggs in an electric mixer until thick, pale and creamy. Gradually add the sugar and baking powder. Continue to whisk until the mixture has the consistency of lightly whipped cream. Using a large metal spoon, gently fold in the almond meal (break up any lumps first) and citrus purée, until well combined.

Pour the mixture into the prepared pan and bake for about 10 minutes, then scatter with the almonds. Continue to bake for a further 40–45 minutes, until a skewer inserted into the middle of the cake comes out with a few fine sticky crumbs. If the almonds are browning too much, cover the cake with foil. Cool in the pan on a wire rack for 15 minutes before carefully removing to cool completely.

PLUMPED WALNUT PRUNES WITH ORANGE IN SPICED PORT

Prunes are a unique ingredient – don't be put off by their wrinkly appearance. This disguises their real goodness: an intense winey sweetness, squidgy succulence and chewy darkness. Downright indulgence. They're the basic ingredient for an international roster of classic dishes. In this recipe, steeped in port, they become plump and luscious.

PREPARATION TIME: 20 minutes | **COOKING TIME:** 3 minutes | **SERVES:** 6

18 walnut halves
18 large pitted prunes
½ cup (125 ml/4 fl oz) freshly
    squeezed orange juice
1⅔ cups (420 ml/14 fl oz) port wine
    (rich ruby or tawny port)
2 strips orange zest
1 cinnamon stick
2 whole star anise
1 cup (260 g/9 oz) vanilla bean
    yoghurt
seeds from 1 pomegranate

Push a walnut half into each prune through the opening where the stone was removed. Place filled prunes in a heatproof bowl.

Put the orange juice, port, orange zest strips, cinnamon stick and star anise in a pot and bring to the boil over medium heat. Reduce the heat to low and gently simmer for 3 minutes, covered, then pour over the prunes. Cover the bowl with plastic wrap and leave at room temperature to cool. If not using immediately, refrigerate where they will keep for 2 weeks, giving you an instant dessert.

Serve with a dollop of yoghurt sprinkled with pomegranate seeds.

TIP Although most of the alcohol from the port will evaporate when simmered, you can just use orange juice if you prefer.

KIWI, BANANA, ORANGE AND GRAPE CRUSH

Here you can use either the green-fleshed kiwi fruit or the sweeter, more aromatic golden kiwi fruit. For a change, use the deep red juice from blood oranges to give a sweeter flavour with a distinct hint of raspberry and a more intense aroma than your average orange.

PREPARATION TIME: 15 minutes | **SERVES:** 4

Roughly chop the kiwi fruit and banana. Remove the tiny stems from the grapes and put the grapes into a blender with the kiwi fruit, banana, yoghurt, orange juice and honey. Blend to the consistency you prefer. A chunky texture can be used as a dessert and a smooth consistency is lovely as a topping for desserts such as poached pears.

TIP Although most people prefer to peel kiwi fruit, the fuzzy skin on organic fruit is perfectly edible and produces an interesting taste. Wash thoroughly before eating

4 large kiwi fruit, peeled
1 medium banana, peeled
1 cup (180 g/6 oz) sweet seedless green grapes
1 cup (260 g/9 oz) natural yoghurt
1 cup (250 ml/9 fl oz) freshly squeezed orange juice
1 tablespoon runny honey

BAKED PEACHES BOMBE ALASKA

Don't be tempted to peel the skins off the peaches before you roast them, as it helps them keep their shape. Choose a yellow peach if you want a subtle tangy taste and a slightly more robust flavour and a white peach for a more delicate flavour. A white-fleshed peach cooks in less time than a yellow peach.

PREPARATION TIME: 15 minutes | **COOKING TIME:** 20 minutes | **SERVES:** 6

Preheat the oven to 200°C/400°F (fan 180°C/350°F). Line a baking tray with baking paper.

Wash the peaches, halve and remove the stones. Fill the hollow with some of the date syrup and place on the baking tray. Roast for 15 minutes, or until the fruit just softens.

Remove from the oven and place on a wire rack or tray.

Blend together the ricotta, raspberries with their juices and almonds. Spoon an equal amount of the mixture into the centre of each peach.

Using an electric mixer, whisk the egg whites until frothy. Gradually add the sugar, 1 tablespoon at a time, beating until the sugar dissolves and the mixture is thick and glossy. Spoon the meringue into a dome shape over each peach to completely enclose the filling. Bake for about 8 minutes, or until the meringue just starts to brown. Remove from the oven and serve immediately.

TIP If date syrup is not available, try honey.

3 large ripe peaches
1 tablespoon date syrup
½ cup (115 g/4 oz) ricotta
⅓ cup (40 g/1½ oz) raspberries, crushed
2 tablespoons finely chopped toasted almonds
2 egg whites
½ cup (110 g/3¾ oz) caster (superfine) sugar

NO-BAKE POACHED PEAR FLAN WITH LIME CREAM

Sometimes a traditional pastry crust just doesn't do justice to a spectacular filling. This is one of those times. This no-need-to-cook food processor pastry is chock full of flavour, and is refrigerated so it can be prepared the day before. So too can the 'creamy' cheese filling. Each pear variety has its own personality in texture and flavour. Choose a mild and sweet variety with subtle, fragrant citrus notes – bartlett pear comes to mind.

PREPARATION TIME: 30 minutes | **COOKING TIME:** 15 minutes | **SERVES:** 8

1 cup (65 g/2¼ oz) shredded coconut
100 g (3½ oz) hazelnuts or almonds
12 pitted soft dates, chopped
1 teaspoon finely grated ginger, plus
    2 cm (¾ in) piece ginger, peeled
1 teaspoon ground cinnamon
4 medium pears
½ cup (110 g/3¾ oz) caster (superfine)
    sugar
2 whole star anise
1 small lime, thinly sliced
2 cups (500 ml/17 fl oz) soda water
    (club soda)

LIME CREAM
¾ cup (200 g/7 oz) ricotta
½ cup (100 g/3½ oz) reduced-fat
    cream cheese
½ cup (130 g/4½ oz) natural yoghurt
1 teaspoon finely grated lime zest
2 tablespoons warmed honey

Line a 23 cm (9 in) flan (tart) pan with baking paper with overhanging sides to make it easy to lift the flan out.

Put the coconut in a food processor and blitz until fine. Add the hazelnuts, dates, finely grated ginger and cinnamon and pulse to a fine-crumb texture. Don't worry if it is a bit more coarse than fine. Tip the mixture into a bowl and, using your hands, clump it together and press it evenly into the base and sides of the prepared tin. Refrigerate for about 20 minutes, until firm.

Peel the pears, cut into thick wedges and remove the core (leave the stalk on for decoration if you like).

Put the sugar, peeled ginger, star anise, lime and soda water in a large pan. Stir over medium heat until the sugar dissolves, then reduce the heat to low and drop in the pears. Cover the pan and gently simmer for about 10 minutes, or until the pears are just tender. Remove the pan from the heat and leave the pears to cool in the liquor. Lift the pears out with a slotted spoon and drain well.

Whisk together the ricotta, cream cheese, yoghurt, lime zest and 1½ tablespoons of the honey until smooth and creamy. Spoon the mixture into the flan and arrange the pears on top. Brush the pears with the remaining honey.

WINTER FRUIT POACHED IN MULLED WINE TOPPED WITH GRANITA

This recipe is simple to prepare, nothing can go wrong, and making it ahead of time only adds to the colour and flavour. Boldly flavoured, beurre bosc pears have an almost smoky sweetness and are a favourite for poaching as they retain their shape when cooked.

PREPARATION TIME: 15 minutes | **COOKING TIME:** 25 minutes | **SERVES:** 6

Put the wine, water, sugar, cinnamon sticks, black peppercorns, bay leaves, cardamom pods, cloves, and lemon and orange peel in a deep pan over high heat and bring to the boil.

Reduce to a gentle simmer, add the quinces, if using, and poach them for about 25 minutes. Add the apples and pears, and simmer for about 10 minutes or until just tender. Leave the fruit to cool to room temperature before adding the prunes and, if using, the blackberries.

Strain one-third of the liquid, pour into a freezer-proof container (preferably with a lid or covered in plastic wrap) and freeze. Cover and refrigerate the remaining liquid and fruit.

To serve, roughly scrape the frozen cooking liquor with a fork to create large icy flakes. Arrange the fruit, spices and cooking juices in a large dish or divide between bowls. Just before serving, spoon some of the spiced wine granita on top of the fruit.

2 cups (500 ml/17 fl oz) red wine

1½ cups (375 ml/13 fl oz) water

2 tablespoons caster (superfine) sugar

3 cinnamon sticks

2 black peppercorns

2 bay leaves

3 cardamom pods, cracked

2 whole cloves

2 thin strips each of lemon and orange peel

2 medium quinces, peeled, cored and thickly sliced (optional)

2 large apples, peeled, cored and quartered

3 medium firm ripe pears, peeled, cored and halved

6 pitted prunes

1 handful frozen blackberries (optional)

CARPACCIO OF PINEAPPLE WITH CHILLI SYRUP

Here, family and friends will expect an innocent dessert of finely sliced pineapple in sweet syrup. But life is never what it seems, and the sudden hit of chilli heat, tempered by cooling mint, pungent ginger and soothing lemongrass are the rewards of such innocence.

PREPARATION TIME: 25 minutes | COOKING TIME: 12 minutes | SERVES: 6

2 cups (500 ml/17 fl oz) water
1 cup (220 g/8 oz) caster (superfine) sugar
1 lemongrass stalk, finely chopped, sliced
2 cm (¾ in) piece ginger, sliced
2 small red chillies, deseeded and cut into very thin strips
1 medium sweet ripe pineapple
1 small handful small mint leaves

Put the water, sugar, lemongrass and ginger in a pan and bring to the boil, stirring to dissolve the sugar. Simmer for about 10 minutes or until the mixture is slightly syrupy. Add the chillies, remove the pan from the heat and set aside to cool.

Peel the pineapple, taking care to remove all the eyes. Using a strong serrated knife, slice the pineapple into very thin slices and then arrange them, overlapping, in a circle on serving plates.

Drizzle the syrup over the pineapple and sprinkle with finely shredded mint leaves.

TIP Make sure you use a sweet pineapple – remember, pineapples do not become sweeter, only older once picked.

OVEN-ROASTED PLUMS WITH COUSCOUS CRUMBLE

The slow gentle cooking of plums in the oven not only develops the juices and flavours perfectly, the fruit keeps its shape. Properly prepared couscous is light and fluffy, not gummy or gritty. During cooking, this crunchy couscous crumble is stained a deep red garnet by the plum juices.

PREPARATION TIME: 20 minutes I **COOKING TIME:** 30 minutes I **SERVES:** 6–8

Preheat the oven to 180°C/350°F (fan 160°C/315°F).

Scatter the plums in an ovenproof dish and splash with ¼ cup (60 ml/2 fl oz) of the water. Cover the dish and bake for about 15 minutes.

While the plums are cooking, prepare the couscous. In a pot, bring the remaining 3 cups (750 ml/25½ fl oz) of water just to boiling point. Pour in the couscous, cover and take the pot off the heat to steam for 10–15 minutes. Fluff with a fork. Stir through the pecans, brown sugar, coconut and cinnamon.

Pile generous amounts of the crumble mixture over the top of the plums and dot with the butter. Bake, uncovered, for about 12 minutes, or until the crumble is golden and the mixture bubbling.

12 large ripe sweet plums, halved and stones removed
3¼ cups (810 ml/28 fl oz) water
2 cups (380 g/13½ oz) whole wheat couscous
½ cup (60 g/2¼ oz) chopped pecans
2 tablespoons soft brown sugar
1 cup (65 g/2¼ oz) shredded coconut
1 teaspoon ground cinnamon
2 tablespoons softened butter

TIP Don't confuse couscous with pasta. Couscous is made of crushed durum wheat semolina – not the ground type used for pasta. Couscous should never be boiled (ignore package instructions if it says to boil) just rehydrated and steamed.

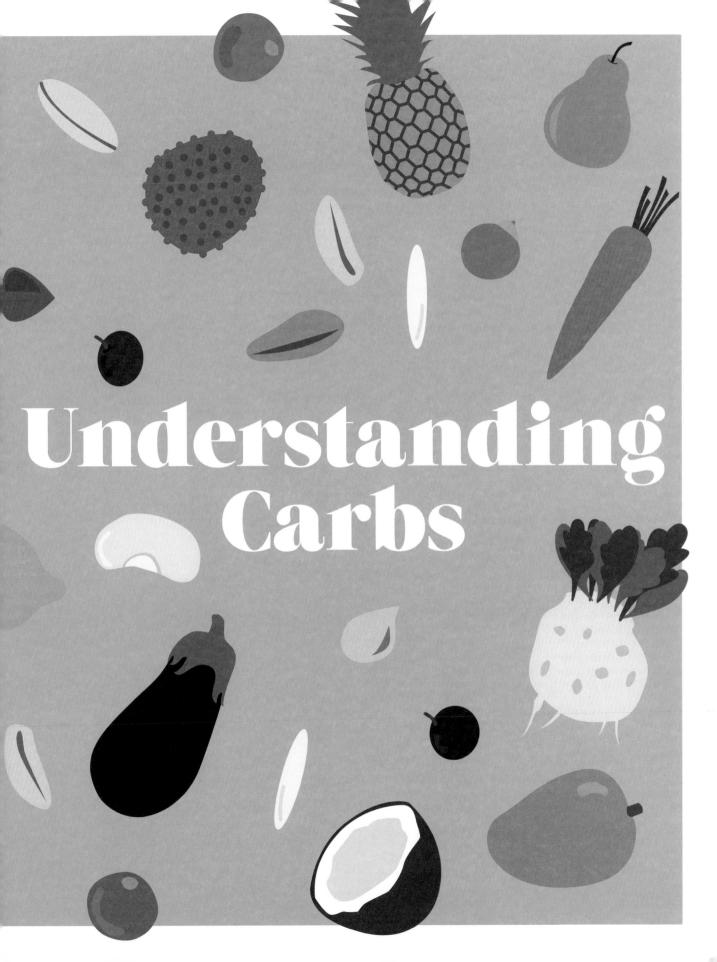

Understanding Carbs

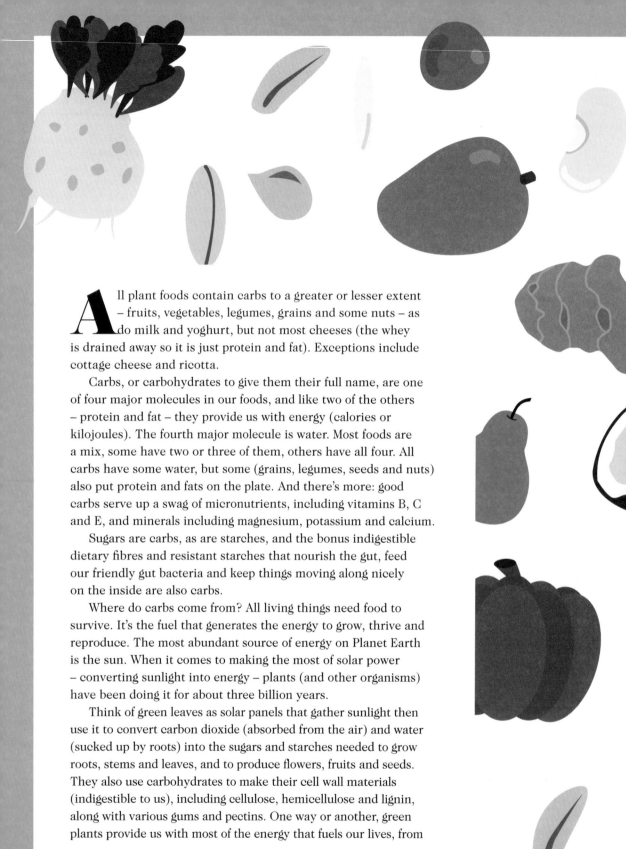

All plant foods contain carbs to a greater or lesser extent – fruits, vegetables, legumes, grains and some nuts – as do milk and yoghurt, but not most cheeses (the whey is drained away so it is just protein and fat). Exceptions include cottage cheese and ricotta.

Carbs, or carbohydrates to give them their full name, are one of four major molecules in our foods, and like two of the others – protein and fat – they provide us with energy (calories or kilojoules). The fourth major molecule is water. Most foods are a mix, some have two or three of them, others have all four. All carbs have some water, but some (grains, legumes, seeds and nuts) also put protein and fats on the plate. And there's more: good carbs serve up a swag of micronutrients, including vitamins B, C and E, and minerals including magnesium, potassium and calcium.

Sugars are carbs, as are starches, and the bonus indigestible dietary fibres and resistant starches that nourish the gut, feed our friendly gut bacteria and keep things moving along nicely on the inside are also carbs.

Where do carbs come from? All living things need food to survive. It's the fuel that generates the energy to grow, thrive and reproduce. The most abundant source of energy on Planet Earth is the sun. When it comes to making the most of solar power – converting sunlight into energy – plants (and other organisms) have been doing it for about three billion years.

Think of green leaves as solar panels that gather sunlight then use it to convert carbon dioxide (absorbed from the air) and water (sucked up by roots) into the sugars and starches needed to grow roots, stems and leaves, and to produce flowers, fruits and seeds. They also use carbohydrates to make their cell wall materials (indigestible to us), including cellulose, hemicellulose and lignin, along with various gums and pectins. One way or another, green plants provide us with most of the energy that fuels our lives, from the fossil fuels formed millions of years ago to the foods we grow in our gardens and on our farms. And there's more: there's the oxygen they release into the atmosphere so we can all breathe easy.

HOW PLANTS FUEL OUR LIVES

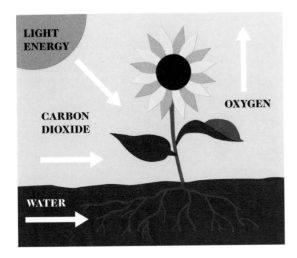

So how do we use a plant's energy? When we eat fruit or tubers, our bodies convert their sugars and starches into the glucose that provides energy to power our body, our brain, our blood cells, our reproductive organs and our muscles during vigorous exercise day in and day out.

WHAT CARBS DO

Good carbs are multi-talented molecules that play a number of key roles in our body. First and foremost, our brains and nervous system, red blood cells, kidneys and our exercising muscles much prefer to use them as their energy source. But they also give our cells structure, are part of our genes (the sugar ribose is part of our DNA) and play a part in the function of some proteins. And on top of all this they give us great enjoyment with the taste, flavour, aroma, texture and colour they bring to our meals with family and friends.

Carbohydrates are made up of carbon, hydrogen and oxygen, so you can see where the name comes from. For example, the chemical formula for glucose is $C_6H_{12}O_6$, which stands for six carbon atoms and six water molecules (H_2O = one water molecule; six water molecules = $H_2O \times 6$). In this book we've chosen to refer to them as carbs most of the time.

There are many kinds of carbohydrates. The four most common in our foods and drinks are sugars, oligosaccharides, starches and dietary fibres. Here's a summary of what they are and what they do.

SUGARS

Sugars are the simplest form of carbohydrate. Again, there are many kinds. The six main sugars in our foods are either monosaccharides or disaccharides (*saccharum* is Latin for 'sugar') and they all end in 'ose'.

Monosaccharides are single-sugar molecules (*mono* is Latin for one). The three most common ones in our foods are (in alphabetical order):

- *fructose*, which is found in fruits, honey, and agave and maple sap. It makes up around half of the carbs in a typical piece of fruit and is commonly called fruit sugar. It is about 50 per cent sweeter than glucose.
- *galactose*, which is found in milk, yoghurt and whey and is 20 per cent less sweet than glucose.
- *glucose*, which is found in fruits, grains, vegetables, and honey. Here's what a glucose molecule looks like.

Disaccharides are two single-sugar molecules joined together (*di* is Latin for two). The three most common ones in our foods are (in alphabetical order):

- *lactose*, glucose plus galactose, which is found in milk. All mammal milk contains lactose, but human mother's milk, which is part of a baby's very special fuel mix, is the richest by far. Lactose is also added to foods during processing.

- *maltose*, glucose plus glucose, which is found in grains such as barley and in malt and malted foods and beverages. It is commonly added to foods as an ingredient.

- *sucrose*, glucose plus fructose, which occurs naturally in fruit, sugar cane (a grass) and sugar beets, the sap of maple and birch trees. It is the most common form of sugar added to foods and drinks in most parts of the world, with the exception of the United States, where high-fructose corn syrup is used because it's cheaper for historical and political reasons we won't go into here. Here's what a sucrose molecule looks like:

OLIGOSACCHARIDES

Chains of 3–9 glucose molecules joined together are called *oligosaccharides*, which literally means 'a few sugars' (*oligo* is Latin for 'a few'). They are only slightly sweet. The main ones found in foods or increasingly used in food processing are as follows:

- fructo-oligosaccharides (FOS), which are short chains of fructose molecules found naturally in fruits and vegetables such as asparagus, bananas, chicory root,

ADDED AND FREE SUGARS

The World Health Organization (WHO) recommends that we consume no more than 10 per cent of our energy from what it calls free sugars. This may reduce our risk of developing tooth decay, and also help us limit our intake of excess calories. The sugars WHO is talking about are added sugars from table sugar, honey, syrups (glucose syrups such as rice syrup), fruit juices and fruit juice concentrates. What does 10 per cent free sugars look like? For the average adult consuming 2070 calories (8,700 kilojoules) a day, it's about 13 level teaspoons or 54 grams of free sugars.

garlic, Jerusalem artichokes, leeks, legumes, onions and wheat; and in wholegrain foods, especially rye. They are actually a form of dietary fibre and they play a role as prebiotics, the non-digestible components of plant foods that promote good gut health by feeding the friendly bacteria (probiotics) in the large intestine (bowel). Inulin is one you will increasingly see on food labels as manufacturers add it to products to boost fibre content and reduce regular added sugars. While it may be good for digestive health for some, it can be digestively challenging for those with irritable bowel syndrome.

- *maltodextrins* (*modified food starches*), which are mostly man-made carbs manufactured by the partial hydrolysis (using water to break down large molecular chains) of starch (from corn, potato, rice, wheat or tapioca) and they may or may not be gluten free depending on the starch source. They are widely used by the food industry as moderately sweet or even flavourless food additives to provide bulk and texture in processed foods. Food manufacturers are increasingly replacing added regular sugars in processed foods with maltodextrins (plus a non-nutritive sweetener if sweetness is required) responding to consumer (and governmental) demand for no added sugars. But they're not better for our health. They contribute to tooth decay, provide empty calories and raise our blood glucose levels more rapidly than regular sugar. (The GI of table sugar or sucrose is 65; maltodextrin's GI is estimated to be 75.) Here's what a maltodextrin molecule looks like:

STARCHES

Starches are part of the large group of *polysaccharides* (many sugars) – long chains of glucose molecules. They are found naturally in a wide range of foods including grains, legumes, potatoes and other starchy vegetables, nuts and seeds. Milled to make a flour or meal, we use them in our cooking to make breads and sauces. There are two kinds: amylose and amylopectin.

- *Amylose* is a straight chain of glucose molecules that tend to line up in rows like a string of beads and form tight, compact clumps that are harder for our bodies to gelatinise (see box, page 236) and digest.

- *Amylopectin* is a string of glucose molecules with lots of bushy-looking branching points, such as you see in some types of seaweed or a tree. Amylopectin molecules are larger and more open, and the starch tends to be easier for our bodies to gelatinise and digest.

WHAT IS DEXTROSE?

Dextrose is just another term for glucose. It comes from 'dextrorotatory glucose', because a solution of glucose in water rotates the plane of polarised light to the right (*dextro* is Latin for 'right'). If you see dextrose in an ingredients list of processed foods and drinks, it probably means that the added glucose was produced from cornstarch. Without going into the chemistry of how they do that here, the process is similar to the way our body converts starches to glucose during digestion. Levulose is another term for fructose and means 'left turning' (*laevus* is Latin for 'left'), because a solution of fructose in water rotates the plane of polarised light to the left.

WHAT IS GELATINISATION?

Have you ever tried to eat raw rice or dried beans or raw potato? Not a good experience. That's because the starch in these foods is stored in hard, compact 'granules' that make it virtually impossible for our starch-digesting enzymes to attack and digest. And that's why we cook them. It makes the difference called 'gelatinisation', that is, it softens them up.

Let's take rice. The absorption method tells us to throw 1 cup of rice into the pot with 1½ cups of water and bring to the boil. Reduce the heat and simmer, covered, for 20 minutes or until the water has been absorbed. Remove from the heat, keep covered and set aside for 5 minutes.

So what happens in the cooking pot? The starch granules absorb the water, swell up and some burst, freeing thousands of starch molecules. We now have fluffy rice and a food we have no difficulty tucking into and digesting, because our highly specialised starch-digesting enzymes have a lot more accessible surface area to attack.

DIETARY FIBRE

This is what we refer to as the 'BTU' (bowel tune-up) carb. Most dietary fibres are large molecules with many different mono-saccharides that come mostly (but not exclusively) from plants and provide much of the bulk in our stools. When we eat fibre-rich foods like prunes, the fibres are not broken down and metabolised during digestion; instead, they go through our stomach and small intestine into our large intestine, where hordes of good bacteria waiting for a feed greet them enthusiastically. There are numerous ways to group dietary fibres; the most common one is whether or not they're soluble in water.

- **Water-soluble fibres** (usually just called soluble fibre) include gums such as agar, fructo-oligosaccharides such as inulin, mucilages such as psyllium, and pectins. They are found in fruits, vegetables, legumes and some grains (oats and barley). They may help reduce blood cholesterol levels and keep blood glucose levels on a more even keel, but how successful this will be will depend in part on the degree of food processing and how much you eat.
- **Water-insoluble fibres** (usually just called insoluble fibre or roughage) include cellulose, hemicellulose and lignins. They are mostly found in vegetables, wheat and other whole grains, nuts and seeds. They primarily help us move our bowels (laxation is the technical term), and in this way they can help reduce the risk of constipation.

HOW WE DIGEST, METABOLISE AND ABSORB CARBS

Most of the carbs in the foods we eat are digested in the stomach and small intestine, absorbed into the bloodstream and, one way or another, converted into glucose. For most carbs, the process is relatively simple.

As we have explained, starches and maltodextrins are simply chains of glucose joined together by chemical bonds. During digestion, small proteins called amylases in our saliva and intestinal digestive juices (secreted by the pancreas) snip the bonds so we wind up with pure glucose in the small intestine, which is then absorbed into the bloodstream.

WHAT IS GLYCOGEN?

Glycogen is a kind of starch that our bodies make and store as backup in the liver and muscles (we can store 1500–1900 calories/6000–8000 kilojoules worth). It comes from the carbs we consume and provides energy we can draw on when our carb stores run low with fasting or intense exercise. When carb stores run low, our bodies convert the glycogen back into glucose to power our muscles and brains.

Specific enzymes in our small intestine – lactase, maltase and sucrase – break the disaccharides lactose, maltose and sucrose down into their constituent monosaccharide molecules (glucose, fructose and galactose), which are then absorbed into the bloodstream.

The glucose molecules can be absorbed directly into the cells of most of the body's tissues and organs, where they usually end up as pyruvate and adenosine triphosphate (ATP), which is our body's main energy currency. Normally, pyruvate is also converted to ATP, producing more energy. The galactose and fructose molecules, however, need to go to the liver for further processing.

In the liver, fructose is rapidly removed from the bloodstream, phosphate is added via a catalysing enzyme, and the resulting phosphorylated fructose enters what is known as the glycolytic pathway, where through a series of chemical reactions, it usually ends up as pyruvate and ATP. Similarly, galactose is extracted from the blood and converted to glucose in the liver, and then converted to pyruvate and ATP, just like glucose.

This is when the blood glucose story begins. When the glucose molecules enter the bloodstream, our blood glucose (sometimes called blood sugar) levels (BGLs) rise. This is the signal for the pancreas to release the hormone insulin, which tells most of the body's organs and tissues to get to work and absorb the glucose from the blood to fuel our brain, cells, tissues and muscles. Insulin also stops our liver from releasing glucose from its glycogen stores.

WHY OUR BLOOD GLUCOSE LEVELS MATTER

Our body converts the sugars and starches to glucose at very different rates. Think of it as the highs and lows of carb digestion. And this is where the glycemic index (GI) can help us make better food choices. The GI is particularly useful for people who need to manage their BGLs. It is

WHAT IS RESISTANT STARCH?

Many scientists categorise resistant starch as another form of dietary fibre these days because of what it does. It's actually starch that resists digestion and absorption in the small intestine and zips through to the large intestine largely intact to be fermented into short-chain fatty acids, like acetate, propionate and butyrate by those good gut bacteria we have down there. Current research suggests it may well be as important as fibre in helping reduce the risk of colorectal cancer, so it has a lot of fans.

It's found naturally in unprocessed cereals and wholegrains, firm (unripe) bananas, beans and lentils. But you can create it in your own kitchen when you make potato, rice or pasta salad – starchy foods that you cook and then cool.

just a dietary tool providing a numerical ranking (from 1 to 100) that gives us an idea as to how quickly our bodies will digest particular carb foods and how fast and high our BGL is then likely to rise. Think of it as a 'carbo speedo'.

- High GI: 70 and over
- Medium or moderate GI: 56–69
- Low GI: 55 and under

Why does it matter how high our BGL goes? As with blood pressure, there's a healthy range and a risky range. Having BGLs in the normal range over the day is good for our body because it also will lower our day-long insulin levels. Having high BGLs from eating too many high-GI foods can put pressure on our health, because it means our pancreas has to work extra hard producing more insulin to move the glucose into the cells, where it provides energy for the body and brain. It's never a good idea to overwork or overstress body parts. They can wear out or stop functioning properly. We can't easily replace our pancreas.

DOES FIBRE LOWER THE GI?

Not necessarily. It depends on amounts, size and processing.
- Soluble fibre may lower the GI of some foods, but they need to contain appreciable amounts, and the size of the fibre molecules needs to be large enough to have an effect.
- Insoluble fibre can help slow the rate of carbohydrate digestion or absorption if it is largely intact. However, highly processed added fibres usually do not have the same effect.

There are many benefits to switching to low GI good carbs that will trickle the glucose into the bloodstream. They can help us cut cravings and feel fuller for longer, stay in shape better by minimising body fat and maximising muscle mass, and decrease the risk of some chronic conditions, such as type 2 diabetes and heart disease. Throughout this book we provide the GI values of the good carbs we like to cook with and serve to family and friends.

Research around the world over the past 35 plus years shows that switching to eating mainly low GI carbs throughout the day that will trickle glucose into our bloodstream lowers our day-long BGLs and insulin levels helping us:

- manage our appetite because we will feel fuller for longer
- minimise our body fat
- maximise our muscle mass
- decrease our risk of type 2 diabetes and heart disease.

How is the glycemic index of a food measured? A small group (10 or more) of healthy people follow an internationally standardised procedure. Each person is typically given a 50 gram portion of available carbohydrate (sugars, maltodextrins and starches, but not dietary fibre), then their blood glucose levels are measured every 15–30 minutes for the next 2 hours. This process is followed for both a standard food (glucose or white bread) and a test food, on two separate days. The BGLs from both days are then plotted on a graph, the dots are joined to create a blood glucose curve, and the area under the blood glucose curve is calculated using computer software. The result for the test food is divided by the result for pure glucose to derive the glycemic index value, which is simply a percentage.

Speed of digestion is only one part of the story. Quantity counts. How high our blood glucose actually rises and how long it remains high after we eat a meal containing carbs depends on both the amount of carbs in a food or drink and its GI. Some fruits, like melons for example, have a high GI but not many carbs as they are mostly water, so their glycemic impact will be negligible unless you massively overdo it.

Researchers from Harvard University and the University of Toronto came up with a term to describe this 'speed–quantity' combo: glycemic load (GL). It is calculated by multiplying the GI of a food by the available carbohydrate content (carbohydrates minus fibre) in the serving (expressed in grams), divided by 100 (because GI is a percentage). (GL = GI/100 × available carbs per serving.)

For example, a typical medium-size apple has a GI of 38 and contains 15 grams of available carbohydrate. Its GL therefore is $38 \times 15 \div 100 = 6$. If you are hungry and the apples are particularly crispy, juicy and delicious, and you eat two, the overall GL of this snack is 12.

What does this all mean for our health and wellbeing? One unit of GL is equivalent to 1 gram of pure glucose. So the higher the GL of a food or meal, the more insulin your pancreas needs to produce to drive the glucose into your cells. When we are young, our pancreas can produce enough insulin to cover the requirements of high GL foods and meals, but as we get older, it may no longer be able to cope with higher insulin requirements. This is when type 2 diabetes and other lifestyle-related diseases can start to develop.

IT'S NOT JUST CARBS THAT AFFECT OUR BLOOD GLUCOSE

Carbs have the most profound effect on our BGLs. But protein and fat may also increase our BGLs due respectively to increased glucose output from the liver and acute insulin resistance. They also affect insulin responses, and the effect in some scenarios is comparable to that of carbs.

Insulin is an anabolic hormone – it stimulates glucose and amino acid (building blocks of proteins) uptake by our body's cells, and stimulates glycogen and fat synthesis within them. Perhaps unsurprisingly, many recent weight-reduction diets home in on insulin for its weight-promoting effects, and as carbohydrate is one of the most potent stimulators of insulin secretion, it has been singled out as the primary cause of weight gain in the modern era.

Carbs in foods and drinks are potent stimulators of insulin release, but they only explain around half (47 per cent) of the variation in our blood insulin levels. Foods high in protein and fat also increase our insulin requirements. Research to date shows that whey protein is the most potent insulin stimulator, followed by fish, beef, egg and chicken.

Fats may lower insulin requirements when we first consume them because they delay the rate at which foods are emptied from the stomach into the small intestine and absorbed into the blood. However, an increasing body of evidence suggests that they raise insulin requirements 3–5 hours after a meal, most likely due to increased insulin resistance.

So when you read the latest diet book singling out carbs as the dietary villain behind the global obesity and diabetes epidemics, advising you to quit them and replace them with protein and fats, remember that all three calorific macronutrients have an effect on our BGLs and blood insulin levels. As always, beware of the unintended consequences of fad diets in general, and the one-nutrient-at-a-time approach in particular.

PUTTING IT ALL ON THE PLATE

We burn a mix of three key fuels that we get from the foods we eat. Dietitians and nutritionists call these fuels 'macronutrients' because our bodies need lots of them. They provide us with energy (kilojoules or calories) and, in wholesome foods, they also come with vitamins and minerals.

- Carbohydrates (carbs) from fruit, vegetables, legumes, grains, some nuts and milk give us much more than energy, they provide us with the fibre, vitamins, minerals and the phytonutrients we need.
- Fats from nuts, seeds, oils, avocados, fish, meat, dairy foods and coconuts provide us with the fatty acids that are part of our cell membranes, and help us absorb the fat-soluble vitamins A, D, E and K.
- Proteins from dairy foods, eggs, fish and other seafood, red meat, chicken and other poultry, legumes, nuts, seeds and grains are the body builders. They maintain our body tissues and, when wholesome, help us meet our needs for certain vitamins (especially B vitamins) and minerals (especially iron, zinc and calcium from dairy foods).

While alcohol does not meet all of the requirements to be a true macronutrient (e.g. growth and development) it is found in relatively large amounts in many beverages enjoyed by humans for many thousands of years, and is a source of energy that can be utilised by our bodies.

It's often said that we run on fuel just as a car runs on petrol. The running part is right. But there are significant differences. Fuel

CALORIE COUNTDOWN

- 1 gram of carbohydrate (sugars and starches) contains 4 calories or 16.5 kilojoules
- 1 gram of protein contains 4 calories or 17 kilojoules
- 1 gram of fat contains 9 calories or 37 kilojoules
- 1 gram of alcohol contains 7 calories or 29 kilojoules

storage is one. Cars have a set storage capacity: when the tank is full, it's full. The excess runs over the rim and is wasted. We, on the other hand, seem to have unlimited capacity for storage, even if we constantly overfill the 'tank'. We don't waste the excess, we store it as fat. This would have been a handy feature in days of yore, as it would have provided a reserve of energy to call on in a poor season or when the hunters had a run of bad luck. But hunger isn't an issue for most people in the developed world these days. Dealing with excess is our biggest challenge.

Our fuel mix changes at different stages of our lives, too. A growing baby has different needs from a toddler, teenager, sedentary adult, very active adult, an elderly person, or someone with a chronic condition such as diabetes.

BABY'S VERY SPECIAL FUEL

For the first 6 months of life, Mother's milk provides the perfect mix of nutrients (carbs, fat, protein, vitamins and minerals) – and water – for our babies to grow and thrive. Mother Nature made it sweet, so it is very appealing to babies. They don't like sour.

The sweetness comes from a special sugar called lactose found only in milk. Our human milk has the highest concentration of lactose of any mammal, almost double that of cow's milk, coming in at some 7 grams of lactose per 100 millilitres (3½ fluid ounces), or little over ⅓ cup. Why so much? One reason is probably to satisfy our fast-growing, energy-hungry, glucose-demanding brain. Scans show that a baby's brain reaches more than half adult size in the first 90 days of a baby's life.

Mother's milk also contains special carbs called oligosaccharides (see page 234), but think of them as prebiotics, foods that friendly bacteria in the large intestine chomp on to thrive. It's thought that the special oligosaccharides in human milk may be one of the reasons why breastfed babies tend to have less gastrointestinal disease than bottle-fed babies.

WE CAN PICK OUR MIX

After infancy, we have considerable flexibility in our fuel mix options because we are omnivores. Our diet is not limited to 'one size fits all' because we evolved to be adaptable. That's what made us successful in populating the planet and thriving in very different parts of the world.

While our fuel mix needs to include all three of the macronutrients, there are no strict rules about how much of each our bodies need, despite what some diet books proclaim.

You only have to look around the world to see that there are very different dietary patterns with very different fuel mixes associated with good health and long life. Traditional Mediterranean and Japanese diets, which are both linked with a long and healthy life, couldn't be more different. The Mediterranean diet is relatively high in fats and tends to be rather moderate in carbs. The Japanese diet, like most Asian diets, is high in carbs and low in fats. What they have in

MOTHER'S MILK FUEL MIX FOR BABIES
Per 100ml (3½ fl oz)

ENERGY

Kilojoules	280
Calories	67

MACRONUTRIENTS

Carbohydrate (mostly lactose)	7.0 g
Fat	4.2 g
Protein	1.3 g

MICRONUTRIENTS

Calcium	35 mg
Sodium	15 mg
Phosphorus	15 mg
Iron	76 mg
Vitamin A	60 mg
Vitamin C	3.8 mg
Vitamin D	0.01µg

common and what seems to matter most is that they are based on good, wholesome foods and ingredients – mostly plants.

In what author and researcher Dan Buettner called 'Blue Zones', the story is the same. In these communities he reports that people don't follow diets, cut out foods or go to the gym but are 10 times more likely than the rest of us to be living a healthy, active life until they are 100. How? They eat food, not too much, mostly plants; are active every day; get plenty of sleep; are not stressed out; and have strong social connections. He found that their diets are as noteworthy for their diversity as for what they share. In Loma Linda, California, they are vegans. In Costa Rica, their diet includes eggs, dairy and meat. In Ikaria, Greece, and Sardinia, Italy, they practise variations on the theme of the Mediterranean diet. In Okinawa, Japan, a traditional plant-based, rice-centric diet produces the same outstanding results.

On the home front, our tastes and our family background play a large part in what we eat and like to eat. In the end, the overall quality and quantity of the foods we consume is what really matters. That means building healthy eating habits and being a good role model for the next generation, who are watching us more carefully than we know.

Day to day and over the short term, we know that low-GI carbs are best for our blood glucose levels and sustained energy, and dietary fibre may help lower blood cholesterol levels and keep us regular. The evidence is stacking up showing much longer term benefits. Long-term observational studies including the Blue Zones studies provide compelling evidence that dietary patterns rich in low-GI carbs and dietary fibre reduce the risk of weight gain, type 2 diabetes, coronary heart disease and certain kinds of cancer, such as colorectal cancer.

And that's why we wrote a book about cooking with good carbs. We wanted to share the news about the long-term health benefits of making them a part of your day and to give you some delicious ways to do so.

We also wanted to cut through the confusion and help you enjoy good food and good health, with good information to make good decisions about the foods you prepare and enjoy with family and friends. There's no need to mortgage the house and rush out and stock up on celebrity superfoods such as teff, maca, sprouted grains and pepitas or even fill your fridge with pricy salmon and blueberries. Good wholesome foods you can afford and your family will enjoy will do the trick. After all, full tummies and clean plates is what it's all about. That means shopping for:

- lean protein – dairy foods, eggs, fish and other seafood, red meat, poultry and legumes. These are the body builders. They maintain our body tissues and help us meet our needs for certain vitamins (especially B vitamins) and minerals (especially iron, zinc and calcium from dairy foods if you eat them).
- good fats – nuts, seeds, oils, avocados and coconuts. These provide us with the fatty acids that are part of our cell membranes and help us absorb the fat-soluble vitamins A, D, E and K.
- good carbs – fruit, starchy vegetables, legumes (beans, peas and lentils), seeds, grains and milk or yoghurt that give us much more than energy. They provide us with the fibre, vitamins, minerals and phytonutrients we need.

WHAT ABOUT THE MICROBIOME?

Our microbiome is a collection of around 40 trillion bacteria (mostly), fungi and viruses that live both on the surface of our body and inside our gastrointestinal tract (from the mouth to the large intestine).

A typical adult's microbiome weighs around 1 kilogram, equivalent to some of our essential organs. Believe it or not, there are about 10 times more bacteria in our microbiome than there are cells in our body, or put another way, 90 per cent of the cells in our bodies are microbial and only the remaining 10 per cent are human!

The composition of our microbiome is not static. It changes throughout the course of our lives, in sickness and health, and can be manipulated with antibiotics and transplants – and by the foods we eat – in a way our genes cannot. Manipulating our microbiome may hold the answers to the treatment of conditions that may not seem to have anything to do with bacteria, such as obesity and type 2 diabetes. For example, preliminary research in humans is showing that the proportion of these microorganisms is different between overweight and slim people. However, it is not yet known whether it is the differences in the types of bacteria that cause people to gain weight or whether the differences are the result of people being overweight. Put simply, are they the cause or the effect? At this stage we just don't know.

Just as you can cultivate healthy soil for your garden, there is growing evidence that you can help cultivate a healthier microbiome too.

Eating live varieties of healthy bacteria can help to improve the balance of bacteria in your gut. For years the yoghurt industry has been extolling the virtues of yoghurt and fermented milk with claims that it contains *Lactobacillus acidophilus*, *Lactobacillus casei* or bifidobacteria. These varieties are generally beneficial to health, but not all probiotics live up to their claims. To make sure the bacteria gets through to your bowels alive (after going through the harsh stomach environment), buy fresh products well within their use-by date. The number of live bacteria decreases rapidly as the product ages – particularly if it has not been stored correctly. Even half an hour in the boot of your car on a hot day is enough to kill off most useful bacteria. You can also increase the amount and quality of prebiotics in the foods and beverages you consume.

Most beneficial bacteria thrive on a healthy diet of dietary fibres and resistant starch – and these only come from the good carbs we enjoy in our meals.

RECIPE NUTRITIONAL ANALYSIS

VEGETABLES

Energy	Energy	Protein	Fat	Saturates	Carbohydrate	Sugars	Starches	Fibre	Sodium	Potassium
Shredded beetroot, carrot and nashi slaw with cumin and lime dressing (page 32)										
890 kJ	210 Cal	3 g	16 g	2 g	12 g	11.5 g	0.5 g	5 g	65 mg	345 mg
Beetroot with orange-sherry dressing and soft herbs (page 35)										
695 kJ	165 Cal	6 g	3 g	0 g	24 g	24 g	0 g	9 g	160 mg	835 mg
Fermented beetroot, carrot and cauliflower (page 36)										
430 kJ	100 Cal	5 g	0.5 g	0 g	15 g	15 g	0 g	9.5 g	3065 mg	920 mg
Eggs coddled in a spicy capsicum and tomato sauce (page 38)										
1180 kJ	280 Cal	12 g	19 g	5.5 g	14 g	6 g	8 g	4 g	350 mg	415 mg
Roasted ratatouille with hummus (page 40)										
605 kJ	145 Cal	3 g	11 g	1.5 g	8 g	3 g	5 g	4 g	70 mg	170 mg
Carrot and red lentil soup with lemon (page 41)										
1360 kJ	325 Cal	15.5 g	11 g	2 g	36 g	6 g	30 g	7 g	1045 mg	730 mg
Potato and silverbeet with a carrot, nut and oat crust (page 42)										
1365 kJ	325 Cal	10 g	17 g	3.5 g	30 g	4 g	26 g	7 g	280 mg	1025 mg
Cauliflower and leek soup (page 43)										
775 kJ	185 Cal	7 g	11 g	4 g	13 g	6 g	7 g	4 g	740 mg	795 mg
The original roasted whole cauliflower (page 45)										
430 kJ	100 Cal	2 g	9 g	1 g	2 g	2 g	0 g	2 g	395 mg	325 mg
Celeriac slaw with capers, walnuts and lemon (page 46)										
900 kJ	215 Cal	3 g	20 g	2 g	5 g	5 g	0 g	4 g	105 mg	285 mg
Roasted celeriac and carrots with mirin and apple juice glaze (page 49)										
615 kJ	145 Cal	1 g	6 g	1 g	15.5 g	14 g	1.5 g	4 g	60 mg	340 mg
Eggplant with chopped green capsicum and pomegranate sauce (page 50)										
1225 kJ	295 Cal	2 g	29 g	4 g	6 g	6 g	0 g	3.5 g	30 mg	250 mg
Salad of red leaves with fennel and Jerusalem artichokes (page 53)										
780 kJ	185 Cal	4 g	11.5 g	1.5 g	14 g	6 g	8 g	5.5 g	165 mg	825 mg
Trio of onions and herb salad with ricotta on toasted grain bread (page 54)										
880 kJ	210 Cal	7 g	13 g	3 g	15 g	3 g	12 g	4 g	220 mg	210 mg
Chicken stock (page 55)										
Nutritional information not able to be calculated										
Lemon chicken with golden onions and green olives (page 56)										
2460 kJ	580 Cal	50 g	37 g	8 g	13 g	11 g	2 g	2.5 g	480 mg	1095 mg

Energy	Energy	Protein	Fat	Saturates	Carbohydrate	Sugars	Starches	Fibre	Sodium	Potassium
Lamb shanks with winter vegetables and parsley-mint gremolata (page 58)										
1790 kJ	425 Cal	34 g	23 g	8 g	17 g	6 g	11 g	7 g	850 mg	1265 mg
Parsnip, celeriac and potato mini bakes (page 59)										
535 kJ	130 Cal	2 g	9 g	4 g	7 g	3 g	4 g	3 g	90 mg	360 mg
Simple fish stew with potatoes (page 60)										
1840 kJ	440 Cal	72 g	8 g	2 g	16 g	4 g	12 g	4 g	520 mg	1850 mg
Potato patties with yoghurt and green herb sauce (page 61)										
840 kJ	200 Cal	7.5 g	16 g	5 g	7 g	2 g	5 g	1 g	245 mg	315 mg
Potato salad with green beans, peas and buttermilk-herb dressing (page 63)										
845 kJ	200 Cal	8 g	4 g	2 g	30 g	5 g	25 g	5.5 g	80 mg	1075 mg
Potato and pea curry (page 64)										
725 kJ	175 Cal	5.5 g	7.5 g	1.5 g	19 g	6 g	13 g	4 g	210 mg	565 mg
Trio of pumpkin roasted with chestnuts and hot mint sauce (page 65)										
945 kJ	225 Cal	3.5 g	10 g	1.5 g	28 g	20 g	8 g	6 g	30 mg	445 mg
Roasted pumpkin soup with harissa (page 66)										
985 kJ	235 Cal	6 g	15 g	2.5 g	17 g	12 g	5 g	5 g	690 mg	905 mg
Chopped salad of sweetcorn, soya beans and quinoa with lemon-basil dressing (page 68)										
1110 kJ	265 Cal	14 g	6.5 g	1 g	32 g	5 g	27 g	9 g	465 mg	570 mg
Chicken and corn soup with toasted tortilla and avocado (page 69)										
1540 kJ	370 Cal	26 g	19 g	4 g	21 g	4 g	17 g	7 g	1030 mg	695 mg
Roasted corn with chilli and lime peanut butter (page 71)										
1500 kJ	360 Cal	14 g	19 g	3 g	28 g	9 g	19 g	12 g	155 mg	785 mg
Pan-roasted sweet potato and beetroot with grapefruit glaze (page 72)										
970 kJ	230 Cal	4.5 g	13 g	1.5	22 g	16 g	8 g	6 g	60 mg	560 mg
Sweet potato, quinoa, spinach and red lentil burgers with tahini-mint yoghurt (page 74)										
500 kJ	120 Cal	5 g	2 g	0.5 g	18 g	6 g	12 g	4 g	35 mg	375 mg
Fresh tomato sauce for pasta (page 75)										
635 kJ	150 Cal	2.5 g	12 g	2 g	6 g	5 g	1 g	3 g	45 mg	480 mg
Tomato and fig salad with burrata and date-mint dressing (page 77)										
1035 kJ	245 Cal	6 g	15 g	5 g	21 g	20 g	1 g	4 g	145 mg	485 mg
Green tomatoes with a chopped olive and herb sauce (page 78)										
875 kJ	210 Cal	5 g	16 g	2 g	9 g	9 g	0 g	4 g	210 mg	505 mg
Salmon curry with lychees and tomatoes (page 81)										
1550 kJ	370 Cal	33 g	22 g	4.5 g	8 g	7 g	1 g	2.5 g	645 mg	650 mg

LEGUMES

	Energy	Energy	Protein	Fat	Saturates	Carbohydrate	Sugars	Starches	Fibre	Sodium	Potassium
Glazed ginger soya beans (page 94)	395 kJ	95 Cal	4 g	2 g	0.5 g	13 g	8 g	5 g	3.5 g	1220 mg	190 mg
Tuna, egg and seasonal vegetables with basil-lemon dressing (page 96)	1525 kJ	365 Cal	23 g	24 g	4 g	13 g	4 g	9 g	3 g	450 mg	790 mg
Roasted snapper fillets with fennel and citrus on white bean purée (page 97)	2260 kJ	540 Cal	43 g	24 g	7 g	23 g	9 g	14 g	12 g	680 mg	1400 mg
Salmon, white bean and dill fishcakes (page 98)	1585 kJ	380 Cal	25 g	13 g	2 g	34 g	2 g	32 g	12 g	240 mg	1300 mg
Baked red kidney and butter bean ragout (page 100)	1975 kJ	470 Cal	15 g	30 g	4 g	28 g	4 g	24 g	14 g	85 mg	1260 mg
Lamb and broad bean stew with silverbeet (page 101)	2825 kJ	675 Cal	43 g	52.5 g	18.5 g	5.5 g	3 g	2.5 g	8 g	500 mg	1100 mg
Spiced chickpea and broad bean soup (page 103)	705 kJ	170 Cal	9 g	6 g	1 g	15 g	4 g	11 g	8 g	900 mg	430 mg
Fresh green herb hummus (page 104)	940 kJ	225 Cal	6.5 g	17 g	2 g	9 g	1 g	8 g	5 g	205 mg	195 mg
Smoked paprika potato and chickpea salad (page 107)	1825 kJ	435 Cal	14.5 g	19.5 g	3.5 g	46 g	9 g	37 g	8 g	225 mg	1500 mg
Sumac-roasted chicken with chickpeas, barley and fruit stuffing (page 108)	2620 kJ	625 Cal	47 g	43 g	12 g	12 g	3 g	9 g	3 g	475 mg	740 mg
Spiced lentils with roasted vegetables (page 109)	2035 kJ	485 Cal	18 g	25 g	3 g	40 g	20 g	20 g	16.5 g	380 mg	1390 mg
Baked fish with lentils, tomatoes and olives (page 111)	515 kJ	125 Cal	7 g	5 g	1 g	12 g	3 g	9 g	2 g	280 mg	195 mg
Dal with curry spices (page 112)	1595 kJ	380 Cal	14 g	21 g	2.5 g	30 g	5 g	25 g	10 g	425 mg	645 mg
Sweet spiced lamb with avocado pea crush (page 115)	1840 kJ	440 Cal	37 g	29 g	8 g	5 g	2 g	3 g	5 g	135 mg	900 mg
Spiced beef with onions and yellow split peas (page 116)	1895 kJ	450 Cal	48 g	16 g	3.5 g	24.5 g	9 g	15.5 g	8 g	300 mg	1350 mg
Omelette with garden peas, feta and mint (page 119)	2350 kJ	560 Cal	28 g	47 g	21 g	6 g	2 g	4 g	4 g	740 mg	310 mg

Energy	Energy	Protein	Fat	Saturates	Carbohydrate	Sugars	Starches	Fibre	Sodium	Potassium
Hot and sour mushroom and barley soup with broccolini (page 132)										
990 kJ	235 Cal	6 g	13.5 g	2 g	20 g	2 g	18 g	6 g	685 mg	395 mg
Lamb shanks with barley, garden peas and mint (page 135)										
1665 kJ	400 Cal	27 g	13.5 g	5 g	37.5 g	4 g	33.5 g	8.5 g	560 mg	630 mg
Crispy cauliflower with buckwheat and pine nuts (page 136)										
1505 kJ	360 Cal	6 g	27 g	3.5 g	21 g	5.5 g	15.5 g	5.5 g	255 mg	505 mg
Buckwheat pikelets *per pikelet* (page 139)										
210 kJ	51 Cal	2.5 g	2.5 g	1 g	5 g	1 g	4 g	0.5 g	30 mg	50 mg
Chilli-ginger peanut butter soba noodles with silken tofu (page 140)										
985 kJ	235 Cal	8.5 g	20 g	3 g	5 g	3 g	2 g	3 g	900 mg	265 mg
Mixed mushroom buttermilk soup with rolled oats and peas (page 141)										
710 kJ	170 Cal	7.5 g	8.5 g	5 g	14 g	6 g	8 g	3 g	775 mg	455 mg
Garlicky mushrooms with onions and thyme on oat mash (page 142)										
1225 kJ	290 Cal	10 g	16 g	4 g	25 g	3 g	22 g	5.5 g	100 mg	525 mg
Mixed grains salad with marinated zucchini (page 145)										
1590 kJ	380 Cal	5 g	31 g	4 g	18 g	5.5 g	12.5 g	5 g	150 mg	410 mg
Quinoa 'risotto' with pumpkin, carrots and hazelnuts (page 146)										
2085 kJ	500 Cal	15.5 g	28.5 g	4 g	40.5 g	12.5 g	28 g	9.5 g	425 mg	905 mg
Fish soup with Thai flavours and rice noodles (page 147)										
1010 kJ	240 Cal	24 g	14.5 g	3 g	3 g	1.5 g	1.5 g	1 g	1645 mg	450 mg
Golden rice with peas and cashews (page 149)										
1295 kJ	310 Cal	8.5 g	16.5 g	3 g	29 g	3.5 g	25.5 g	5.5 g	435 mg	285 mg
Brown rice risotto with peas and prawns (page 150)										
1160 kJ	2780 Cal	12 g	11.5 g	2 g	30 g	2.5 g	27.5 g	3 g	585 mg	275 mg
Wild rice pilaf with mushrooms and almonds (page 153)										
1045 kJ	250 Cal	8.5 g	13 g	2.5 g	21.5 g	2 g	19.5 g	4 g	370 mg	390 mg
Burghul and red lentil soup with sizzling mint and chilli (page 154)										
1290 kJ	310 Cal	9 g	16 g	5 g	29 g	4 g	25 g	6 g	540 mg	500 mg
Spaghetti with green tomatoes and fresh herbs (page 155)										
2180 kJ	520 Cal	15.5 g	24 g	5 g	60 g	7.5 g	52.5 g	5.5 g	100 mg	515 mg
Ribbon pasta with broad beans and pancetta (page 156)										
1920 kJ	460 Cal	17 g	16 g	3.5 g	58 g	0.5 g	57.5 g	6 g	415 mg	290 mg
Fregola and blood orange salad with fennel (page 159)										
1050 kJ	250 Cal	6 g	10 g	1.5 g	33 g	8.5 g	24.5 g	4.5 g	165 mg	315 mg

GRAINS *continued*

	Energy	Energy	Protein	Fat	Saturates	Carbohydrate	Sugars	Starches	Fibre	Sodium	Potassium
Jerusalem artichokes with farro, spinach and oyster mushrooms (page 160)	675 kJ	160 Cal	6 g	10 g	1.5 g	10 g	3.5 g	6.5 g	4 g	35 mg	700 mg
Farro with roasted winter vegetables, prunes and walnuts (page 161)	1650 kJ	395 Cal	12 g	33 g	4 g	10 g	10 g	0 g	5 g	50 mg	710 mg
Farro and green lentils with cherry tomatoes and marinated feta (page 162)	1490 kJ	355 Cal	15 g	24 g	5 g	17.5 g	3 g	14.5 g	6 g	220 mg	605 mg
Lamb, feta and burghul meatballs (page 165)	1650 kJ	395 Cal	26 g	21 g	7 g	23.5 g	5 g	18.5 g	6 g	295 mg	610 mg
Roasted beetroot purée and burghul with mixed fresh herbs (page 166)	2025 kJ	485 Cal	5 g	39 g	5 g	26 g	6 g	20 g	6 g	110 mg	375 mg

FRUIT

	Energy	Energy	Protein	Fat	Saturates	Carbohydrate	Sugars	Starches	Fibre	Sodium	Potassium
Parsnip, yoghurt and date salad (page 188)	710 kJ	170 Cal	3 g	7 g	1.5 g	21 g	16 g	5 g	4.5 g	65 mg	545 mg
Pork meatballs with fresh grapes (page 191)	1605 kJ	385 Cal	22 g	21 g	6 g	26 g	21.5 g	4.5 g	3 g	200 mg	635 mg
Wild rice with fresh grapes, walnuts and feta (page 192)	1380 kJ	330 Cal	10 g	26 g	4 g	14 g	13.5 g	0.5 g	5 g	350 mg	445 mg
Thai red duck curry with lychees (page 193)	2595 kJ	620 Cal	52 g	38.5 g	21 g	16 g	13 g	3 g	3 g	1630 mg	835 mg
Salmon, lychee and sugar snap pea salad (page 194)	2035 kJ	485 Cal	40 g	31 g	6 g	11 g	11 g	0 g	3 g	1150 mg	815 mg
Mango, fresh coconut and avocado salad with Thai dressing (page 196)	830 kJ	200 Cal	5 g	14 g	8 g	11 g	10.5 g	0.5 g	6 g	670 mg	530 mg
Mango salad with fresh coconut and apple (page 197)	1135 kJ	270 Cal	4 g	16 g	4 g	25 g	22.5 g	2.5 g	6 g	50 mg	525 mg
Charred spiced fish with chopped papaya salsa (page 199)	1285 kJ	305 Cal	41 g	13 g	2 g	4 g	3.5 g	0.5 g	3 g	175 mg	990 mg
Shredded chilli ginger chicken and papaya salad (page 200)	2680 kJ	640 Cal	43 g	45 g	8.5 g	14 g	13 g	1 g	7 g	265 mg	1280 mg
Melon, cucumber and red onion salad (page 203)	235 kJ	55 Cal	2 g	0.5 g	0 g	10 g	10 g	0 g	2.5 g	40 mg	290 mg
Apple sponge pudding (page 204)	820 kJ	195 Cal	4 g	2 g	0.5 g	40 g	29 g	11 g	4 g	110 mg	220 mg

Energy	Energy	Protein	Fat	Saturates	Carbohydrate	Sugars	Starches	Fibre	Sodium	Potassium
Apple rose tart (page 205)										
1560 kJ	375 Cal	4.5 g	20.5 g	9 g	42 g	33 g	9 g	4 g	265 mg	245 mg
Banana and peanut ice cream (page 207)										
1125 kJ	270 Cal	8 g	11 g	2 g	34 g	30 g	2 g	3.5 g	50 mg	470 mg
Kiwi, blueberry and avocado green tea popsicles (page 208)										
385 kJ	90 Cal	1 g	4 g	1 g	12 g	12 g	0 g	2.5 g	5 mg	215 mg
Quinoa blueberry pancakes with squishy fruit yoghurt (page 210)										
470 kJ	110 Cal	4.5 g	2.5 g	1 g	16.5 g	6 g	10.5 g	2 g	70 mg	220 mg
Soused berries with mint and whipped ricotta (page 211)										
725 kJ	175 Cal	7.5 g	10 g	5 g	12 g	12 g	0 g	2 g	120 mg	320 mg
Strawberry, rhubarb and apple oat crumble (page 213)										
1480 kJ	355 Cal	6 g	18 g	5.5 g	42 g	32 g	10 g	6 g	70 mg	430 mg
Grapefruit, orange and aperol granita (page 214)										
505 kJ	120 Cal	1 g	0 g	0 g	23 g	23 g	0 g	0.5 g	5 mg	210 mg
Lemon passionfruit pudding (page 217)										
1250 kJ	300 Cal	6.5 g	8 g	4.5 g	49 g	40 g	9 g	3 g	175 mg	155 mg
Almond-crusted flourless 'boiled' citrus cake – two ways (page 218)										
1375 kJ	330 Cal	10 g	20 g	2 g	27 g	27 g	0 g	3 g	75 mg	330 mg
Plumped walnut prunes with orange in spiced port (page 220)										
1185 kJ	285 Cal	5 g	6 g	1 g	29 g	28 g	1 g	6 g	40 mg	485 mg
Kiwi, banana, orange and grape crush (page 221)										
865 kJ	205 Cal	5 g	2.5 g	1.5 g	39 g	38 g	1 g	3.5 g	50 mg	640 mg
Baked peaches bombe Alaska (page 223)										
740 kJ	175 Cal	5 g	4 g	1.5 g	30 g	30 g	0 g	2 g	65 mg	300 mg
No-bake poached pear flan with lime cream (page 224)										
1315 kJ	315 Cal	8 g	13 g	5 g	40 g	37 g	3 g	4.5 g	120 mg	350 mg
Winter fruit poached in mulled wine topped with granita (page 227)										
1180 kJ	280 Cal	2 g	1 g	0 g	45 g	40 g	5 g	17 g	35 mg	615 mg
Carpaccio of pineapple with chilli syrup (page 228)										
735 kJ	175 Cal	1 g	0 g	0 g	43 g	43 g	0 g	2 g	5 mg	165 mg
Oven-roasted plums with couscous crumble (page 229)										
1535 kJ	365 Cal	8 g	15 g	8 g	45 g	11 g	34 g	7 g	45 mg	350 mg

INDEX

Published in 2017 by Murdoch Books, an imprint of Allen & Unwin

Murdoch Books Australia
83 Alexander Street
Crows Nest NSW 2065
Phone: +61 (0) 2 8425 0100
Fax: +61 (0) 2 9906 2218
murdochbooks.com.au
info@murdochbooks.com.au

Murdoch Books UK
Ormond House
26–27 Boswell Street
London WC1N 3JZ
Phone: +44 (0) 20 8785 5995
murdochbooks.co.uk
info@murdochbooks.co.uk

For Corporate Orders & Custom Publishing, contact our Business
Development Team at salesenquiries@murdochbooks.com.au.

Publisher: Corinne Roberts
Designer and Illustrator: Hugh Ford
Editorial Manager: Emma Hutchinson
Project Editor: Kate Wanwimolruk
Photographer: Alan Benson
Stylist: Vanessa Austin
Home Economist: Ross Dobson
Production Manager: Rachel Walsh

A cataloguing-in-publication entry is available from the catalogue of
the National Library of Australia at nla.gov.au.

ISBN 978 1 74336 816 9 Australia
ISBN 978 1 74336 817 6 UK

A catalogue record for this book is available from the British Library.

Colour reproduction by Splitting Image Colour Studio Pty Ltd,
Clayton, Victoria
Printed by 1010 Printing International Limited, China

IMPORTANT: Those who might
be at risk from the effects of
salmonella poisoning (the
elderly, pregnant women, young
children and those suffering
from immune deficiency
diseases) should consult their
doctor with any concerns about
eating raw eggs.

MEASURES GUIDE: We have
used 20 ml (4 teaspoon)
tablespoon measures. If you
are using a 15 ml (3 teaspoon)
tablespoon add an extra
teaspoon of the ingredient for
each tablespoon specified.

*We think the illustrations
are fabulous. Hugh claims
this is because he beavered
away all night long, night
after long night. However, with
all that creative energy, we
suspect he was secretly tucking
into the recipes in the book.*